Turn of the Century

Canada 100 Years Ago

James E. McKenzie

Detselig Enterprises Ltd.

Calgary, Alberta, Canada

Turn of the Century

© 1999 James E. McKenzie

Canadian Cataloguing in Publication Data

McKenzie, James E.

Turn of the century

Includes bibliographic references and index.

ISBN 1-55059-181-9

Canada – History – 1867-1914. I. Title.

FC540.M34 1999   971.05'6   C99-910181-1

Detselig Enterprises Ltd.
210-1220 Kensington Rd. N.W.
Calgary, Alberta T2N 3P5
Canada
Telephone: (403) 283-0900
Fax: (403) 283-6947
E-mail: temeron@telusplanet.net
www.temerondetselig.com

Detselig Enterprises Ltd. appreciates the financial support for our 1999 publishing program, received from Canadian Heritage and other sources.

All rights reserved. No part of this book may be reproduced in any form or by any means without permission in writing from the publisher.

Printed in Canada

ISBN 1-55059-181-9

SAN 115-0324

Cover design by Dean Macdonald

Dedication

*To my kids,
Andrew, Craig, Catherine,
Stanley and James McKenzie,
inheritors of the 21st century*

Cover Photo: Arrival of the Governor General, the Earl of Minto, in Dawson, Yukon Territory, August 14, 1900. Courtesy Glenbow Archives, NA. 912-3

Table of Contents

Introduction — vii

Chapter 1: How We Welcomed the 20th Century — 11

The 20th century has only 99 years — 11
Jail doors flew open on New Year's Eve — 15
Farewell to a wonderful century — 17
How much has changed in Canada during this century? — 22
'The Grandest Sovereign put aside her earthly crown' — 27

Chapter 2: How We Loved Our Mother Britain — 31

Canada was tied to Britain's apron strings — 31
Canadians flocked to Britain's war in South Africa — 35
Citizen-soldiers resented army's Colonel Blimp mentality — 39
Was the future King George V slightly tipsy? — 41
Children were taught to love both their countries — 45
Canadian homes for English orphans — 48
George Washington never won a battle — 50

Chapter 3: How the West Was Done — 53

Regina was a busy but muddy little place — 53
Life, death and trivia – it was all in *The Leader* — 56
How a Yankee outsmarted Canadian sharpies — 59
From political hack to great journalist — 62
Flamboyant former MP took his own life — 64
Axe murderer hanged for killing parents, 3 children — 68
The deadly side of train travel — 69
Canada's 'Titanic' struck an iceberg — 72

Chapter 4: How About Those Easterners? — 75

She was the Indian princess of poetry — 75
Connor and Watson, Canadian myth-makers — 77
Annie conquered Niagara Falls in a barrel — 80
Canada strutted its stuff in Paris — 82
Ontario farmers were sure to succeed — 84
Original Parliament Buildings lost in fire — 86
Hull and Ottawa engulfed by a massive fire — 89
Terrorists tried to blow up the Welland Canal — 92
Three dots heard around the world — 95
Canadians loved their electric trolleys — 98

Chapter 5: How Different They Were — 101

'Oh, what a good preacher is sickness' — 101

The assimilator's solution to the Indian problem — 103

Indians had a reputation for good behavior — 107

Vicious discrimination against Chinese — 109

Women pulling plows caused a misunderstanding — 112

French-Canadians were frequently put down — 115

Party newspapers loved their politicians — 118

Chapter 6: How it Was for Women — 123

Young woman's diary reveals her inner-most thoughts — 123

Under the law, kids belonged to the father — 129

Children died in alarming numbers — 131

Marriage was meant to last a lifetime — 134

Anti-booze women were on the march — 136

Illegal birth control was commonly practised — 141

Rules or not, she was the boss — 143

Chapter 7: How Everyday Life Was Lived — 145

Improve your sex life with an electric belt — 145

No social safety net to protect the poor — 150

Gramophone told funny stories and delivered prayers — 153

Canadians have been hockey fans for a long time — 155

Much was expected of students and teachers — 158

Catalogue was the early equivalent of a shopping mall — 161

Ho, ho, ho! Santa slid down the chimney a century ago — 164

Did you hear the one about the man who dropped 50 feet? — 167

Horses played a big role in the old days — 169

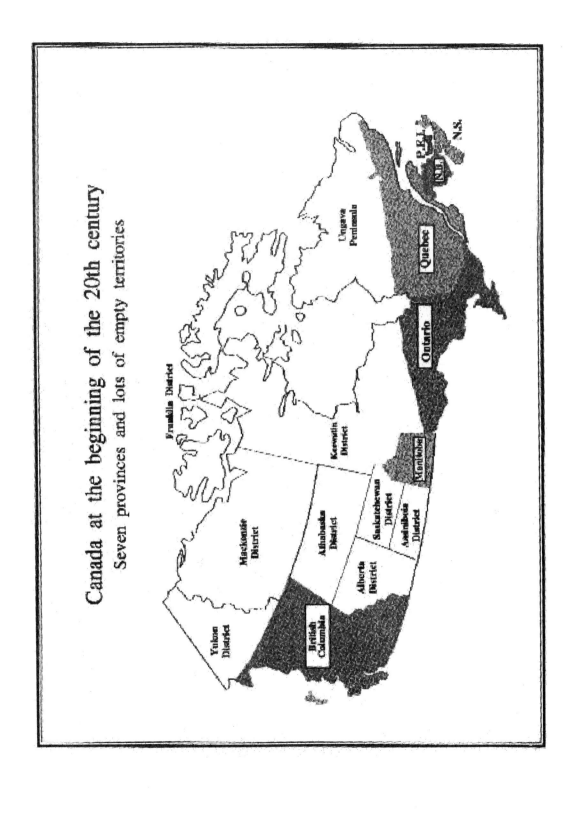

Introduction

People are talking a lot these days about all the amazing things which have happened over the past 100 years. Like old-timers about to pass from this life into the next, we want to recall and evaluate our time in the 20th century before we say goodbye. It's happening all over the world as the countdown continues toward the new century and the new millennium.

In Canada, we recall many significant people and events of the 20th century: our prime ministers, our sports heroes, the years we were at war, the day we finally got our own flag, the night Quebec almost voted for independence and so forth. A century is a long time. There's a lot of ground to cover.

But one particularly timely and important part of this country's 20th-century history remains only dimly recalled. The earliest part of our era, the time when the 19th century ended and transformed itself into the 20th century, has received little attention from chroniclers and historians. Little has been said about what was going on during those first days and months which marked the start of the era. The reason for this in part is that there's nobody left to speak for those times.

You can find all kinds of people to recall most parts of the 20th century, veterans of the Second and First World Wars, for example, and people who remember such things as the coming of television and radio, the first airline passenger services and even the advent of the automobile. But the further back you go, the tougher it is to find survivors. When you try going back 100 years, to the horse and buggy era, you find that it's just out of reach, in terms of human life. The folks who lived then are all dead now, or so old that they are incapable of recalling or telling us about it.

There's no shortage of information about the turn of the century in other parts of the world. If you look at all the major century-in-retrospective books, you find they start with discussions about the United States, Great Britain, and other places at the beginning of the century, but Canada is barely mentioned. Even Australia gets bigger play than we do, because that country became a new entity on the first day of the new century when several smaller colonies combined, while we had already had our Confederation, decades earlier. As the new century opened, we Canadians were just chugging along in our own unspectacular fashion, slowly emerging from British colony to independent nation.

Canadian history books generally give the very first part of the century short shrift. The events of those special first days are lumped together with longer time periods. For instance, we get books about the Laurier era, which ran from 1896 to 1911. Such books usually make no effort to stop at the point where the new century began, or to even mention what happened on that memorable New Year's Eve when the 19th century died and the 20th century was born.

This book is an attempt to freeze the clock, and to dwell on those very early days and months, when the 20th century was new. In a way, this book is meant to be a benchmark, a place to start when we talk about all the changes which have taken place in Canada during the 20th century. If we are going to appreciate where we've been and what we have become in the present century, we need to know what things were like at the beginning of the century.

I got interested in this specific time period a couple of years ago, when my son Craig and I were talking about the elaborate New Year's Eve parties being planned to mark the end of the 20th century. We wondered what kinds of celebrations were held at the end of the 19th century, and I decided to look it up. Although I found several history books devoted to that general time period, there was nothing specific about year-end bashes, and very little about ordinary life in general.

The pages of the many Canadian history books I consulted were full of politics and economics. There was plenty of information about the nation's constitutional dilemmas (yes, the politicians were flogging that tired old horse away back then), and there was all kinds of talk about our trade relations with the Americans (yes, free trade and jealousy of the States were hot topics back then), but none of the books told me what I wanted to know. I was interested in finding out about parties, but not the political kind. I was interested in finding out about a landmark occasion, but not the one on which the British commissioners (yawn) reached a decision on where the Canadian-Alaskan boundary should be located.

I realized that if I wanted to find out whether they sang "Auld Lang Syne" on the New Year's Eve back then, Canada's ample stock of earnest, scholarly and dull-as-dishwater history books weren't going to be much help. Canadian historians, by and large, have been a tedious lot, more concerned with generalities than specifics, more interested in preparing neat provincial overviews than in looking at the untidy lives of ordinary Canadians.

Recent suggestions by some scholars that we should get back to basics by teaching Canadian history as a series of dates, economic advances, constitutional developments and so forth don't carry much weight with me. As far as I can see, we never stopped following that snore-monger approach. That's why most Canadians take little interest in their own country's history. It's not that our history is dull; it's that most of our historians are pedantic plodders, and the way they teach Canadian history is lacking in the human touch.

I found that if I wanted to know what real life and real people were like back then, I would have to forget the history books and look elsewhere. Being a journalist, I naturally turned to old newspapers, and glory be, I found exactly what I was after. From the information-filled pages of the press of the day, I learned that Canadians didn't go nearly as wild at the end of the 19th century as they will at the end of the 20th, on Dec. 31, 1999.

But what was really interesting was that Canadians didn't celebrate Dec. 31,

1899, as a special occasion, because that wasn't the last New Year's Eve of the 19th century. The end-of-the-century party wasn't held until a year later, on Dec. 31, 1900. You'll find out why in the first chapter of this book. You'll also discover what the folks back then did to mark the great occasion. It makes an interesting comparison to all the current hoopla, and shows how much, and yet how little, Canadians have changed when it comes to partying over the past 100 years.

My trip to the library to look at those old newspaper pages turned out to be the first of many such visits. I quickly got hooked on the old papers, which now exist in microfilm form. As you roll the reel along from page to page, you come across many details showing what life was like in Canada during that time. You see reports of social events, ads for the latest products, stories about the day-to-day triumphs and tragedies in the community, and how major happenings in the world were perceived by ordinary Canadians.

I found, for instance, that less than a month after the new century began, the death of an 81-year-old woman in Great Britain had a profound impact on people in this country. Queen Victoria was a dowdy old widow who, despite the fact that she had never set foot in Canada, was our head of state. Her death marked the end of the old era and the start of the new one, neatly coinciding with the first days of the new century, and it unleashed a torrent of grief that reminded me of the way we reacted late this century to the death of another British royal, Princess Diana.

I also learned that the Queen's successor, King Edward VII, had been in a position remarkably similar to the one Prince Charles currently finds himself in. Edward, like Charles, had been Prince of Wales for a very long time, and was well into middle age by the time he assumed the throne. I also found that Edward, like Charles, passed his idle days enjoying extra-marital sex, and that he was so notorious for his womanizing that the radical press dubbed him Edward the Caresser.

The old newspapers, along with magazines like *Saturday Night* and *The Canadian Magazine,* provided a cornucopia of details of life in Canada at the start of the 20th century. It was like going back in time and living there, keeping up with the news much as we do today, by monitoring the news media. But the newspapers and magazines were the only media available back then, radio, television and the Internet all being products of the 20th century. Still, the press was a more than adequate source.

There was an overwhelming amount of information available. The magazines were full of human-interest features, and were a lot like magazines are today. But the newspapers were much different than they are today. Our current versions skim over the facts, and are written for busy people with little time to do much more than glance at the headlines. Newspapers at the turn of the century were filled with much more information, because they were the only source of the news, and because people had the time to sit down and read for a spell to discover what was happening in the communities and in the world.

I soon concluded that I had enough material to write a dozen books, and that

I'd have to decide what to include and what to leave out. I decided to concentrate on what I found to be most significant and interesting, and to make arbitrary but necessary decisions as to what to pursue and what to let pass by. The microfilmed papers and magazines slid past my eyes as I worked the hand cranks on those awkward but efficient viewing machines found in most libraries.

One event quickly stood out, in part because it made a personal connection with me. I recalled that when I was a kid back in the 1950s, old men who used to march in Remembrance Day parades were said to be veterans of the Boer War. Frankly, I didn't know much about that war until I started this project. I learned that Canada was smack in the middle of a war in South Africa when the 20th century began. We were helping the British assert their imperial authority over a rag-tag group of white South Africans known as the Boers.

From a late-20th-century perspective, I found it was a tacky war which totally missed the point that the blacks of South Africa were an oppressed majority. But in the press of the day, the war was presented as a great and noble adventure, enthusiastically supported by English-Canadians, but seen very differently by French-Canadians, who felt that fighting and dying for the Union Jack was not Canada's real destiny. Obviously, the split in this country between English and French goes away back, and the Boer War was the dividing point at the start of the century, just as the Quebec independence movement is today.

I discovered that in this, as in many ways, things today in Canada aren't much different than they were a hundred years ago. I found, for instance, that at the start of the century, Canadians took a great interest in the Stanley Cup, just as they do today. I found that there were lots of poor people in this country, just as there are today, but they couldn't go down to the welfare office and get a handout, as they can now. But they managed to get by anyway.

And I discovered that while couples didn't have easy access to birth control devices, as they do today, they managed to figure out what to do anyway to limit the size of their families. I even learned that early-century Canadians had their own version of Viagra, the modern sex stimulant drug for men. It wasn't a pill. I was an "electric belt," which you strapped on to give yourself a charge. On that uplifting note, I'll end this introduction and invite you to read and enjoy this book of bits and pieces from the far end of the 20th century.

Chapter 1
How We Welcomed the 20th Century

The 20th century has only 99 years

At the stroke of midnight on Dec. 31, 1999, we'll all bid farewell to the 20th century – all, that is, except a few hard-liners who will mutter in their champagne that it's happening a year too early. These spoil-sports insist that the 20th century doesn't end until Dec. 31, 2000, but few people will pay much attention to them.

The news media, big business, bars and restaurants, and Canadians in general have come to the conclusion that when we leave 1999, we leave an old era, and that era can be described as either the 20th century or the 2nd millennium. Whatever you want to call it, it will be finished come Dec. 31, 1999, and all eyes will be looking ahead.

But oh, what fools we be! We're cheating our beloved 20th century out of its final year. An examination of the past reveals that the 20th century didn't start in 1900. It began on Jan. 1, 1901, so only 99 years will have elapsed when we celebrate the start of the 21st century on Jan. 1, 2000.

Yet while it may be reasonable to wait, we won't. Billions of dollars stand to be made out of the start of the new century and the new millennium. Have you tried to book a hotel room for Dec. 31, 1999? Have you seen the prices they're charging for dinner on that Friday evening? Have you seen all that new millennium junk they're trying to unload as quickly as possible? Those who stand to profit won't let history stand in their way, and besides, the public is eager to get going as well, especially advanced-middle-agers like me, who might not make it to Dec. 31, 2000, and so are happy to see the new century arrive a year early.

Young or old, we're an impatient lot, we late-20th century creatures. We're always in a rush to get somewhere interesting, and the 21st century promises to be very interesting indeed. So on New Year's Eve in 1999, practically everyone will be celebrating the big event.

But are we just rushing things, or is there a case to be made for bringing in the new century a year ahead of time? I think there is, and a very logical case it is. It's logical to think that the years beginning with the same number are the years that make up a century. So logically our century should begin in 1900 and end in 1999. That's a lot neater than having our century consist of 99 years which start with 1901, and one final year, 2000.

My argument may be logical, but it didn't wash with people a century ago. To them, the first day of 1900 was just another New Year's Day. It was that way in Canada, the United States, Great Britain and throughout most of the rest of the than they do today. Scholars and pundits of the day approached the subject with a logic which made sense to them. They maintained that the modern era started in the year 1 A.D., and that the 1st century ran from that year to the end of year 100, the 2nd century ran until the end of the year 200, and so forth right on up until the 19th century, which ended at the close of the year 1900.

Thanks to modern scholarship, we can see now that this was a simple-minded approach, for a couple of reasons. For one thing, why did the first century start with the year 1? Why didn't it begin with the year 0? Or was there no year 0? Did we magically jump from the end of 1 B.C. to the start of 1 A.D.?

And for another thing, scholars now know that time wasn't kept in the way we now keep it until several centuries after the death of Christ. In those early days of the modern era, people didn't go around saying they lived in the 1st century or the 2nd century or whatever. Early modern-era dates and the concept of centuries were imposed retroactively by historians on those long-ago times.

In fact, many scholars now believe that Christ was born in the year we now call 4 B.C., or four years before the advent of the modern era. If they're right, then the 21st century and the third millennium are

A TWENTIETH-CENTURY TOAST.

Hail! New-born Cycle! Hail!
A royal greeting waits thee here!
May peace and happiness be thine,
May all your years be filled with cheer!

Manitoba Free Press, Jan. 1, 1901

world. Germany was an exception. The Kaiser ordered his army's guns to fire as a salute to the new century on Jan. 1, 1900. But then, he was so ornery that he went on, 14 years later, to start World War I.

Why did the 20th century start for most people in 1901, rather than 1900? Because 1901 was the "right" year, according to the authorities of the time, and the early 20th century was a time when people paid much more attention to authorities already well under way, since they would have started in 1996. Or would that have been 1997, or perhaps even 1995? It's confusing, isn't it, and anyway the whole idea is absurd, don't you think?

But the debate shows that the concepts of time in general, and centuries in particular, have a rubber-like quality. Time and its measurement are inventions of man, not natural phenomena, and as such they can be manipulated by man to suit the circumstances. And man, oh man, we're all ready for a big end-of-the-century party, the sooner the better, so let's get on with it.

But no matter what anybody says, you still find people insisting that we should hold off for the extra year. Some of them are what might be charitably described as "scholars" and "calendar pedants." They get quite testy about it, but others take a more reasonable approach. One of these sensible people is Trevor Quinn of Regina. In an article published in his local daily newspaper, *The Leader-Post*, Quinn acknowledged that "a great deal of planning, effort and money have already been invested in events scheduled, inappropriately, for midnight, Dec. 31, 1999."

Quinn suggested that rather than tossing a wet blanket on all the party plans, we should start a year-long celebration to give thanks for the many wonderful things we have – music and museums and families and friends and all the rest of it. We would start giving thanks on Dec. 31, 1999, and celebrate the goodness of life all through the year 2000, in preparation for what Quinn calls "the proper arrival" of the new century and the new millennium on Jan. 1, 2001. Great idea, Trevor!

It's interesting to note that the debate over when the new century should start is of considerable vintage. It stretches back at least 200 years. If you look at old newspapers and magazines from the late 18th and 19th centuries, you find heated debates over what was then known as the "century dispute."

In 1799, an American magazine called the *Porcupine* insisted that "we are now in the last year of the century, and whoever denies this has no more brains than an oyster." But a New England newspaper, the *Connecticut Courrant*, took the opposite position, insisting that 1800 was the last year of the century, and accusing anyone who thought differently of being an idiot. A venerable English institution took the same stand. In a commentary published near the end of 1799, *The Times* of London thundered:

> *"We have uniformly rejected all the letters and declined all discussion upon the question of when the present century ends, as one of the most absurd that can engage the public attention, and we are astonished to find it has been the subject of so much dispute, since it appears to be perfectly plain.*
>
> *"The present century will not terminate till January 1, 1801, unless it can be made out that 99 equals 100. Eighteen centuries are 1800 years. Then how can 18 centuries be completed till the year 1800 has expired? Every century begins with one, and the next century will begin on January 1, 1801. It is a silly, childish discussion and only exposes the want of brains of those who maintain a contrary opinion."*

The debate re-ignited at the end of the 19th century. A Toronto newspaper, *The Globe*, published a letter from a Presbyterian clergyman named John Kay who argued in favor of ending the century at the end of 1899. Kay explained his position by suggesting that the years in the century be treated in the same way that money is counted out.

Suppose somebody is paying a debt of $100, Kay said. The person would lay out a dollar bill, then say "one." He would lay out a second bill and say "two." He would keep doing this until all 100 bills were laid out. The full $100 debt would be paid when the 100th dollar bill was laid out, but the last number that he would have called out at that point would have been "ninety-nine." By the time the man said "one hundred," the debt would have already been eliminated. And so, Kay reasoned, the 19th century should end on the last day of the year 1899.

This intriguing argument drew many replies from people, most of whom insisted that Kay was wrong. One letter to the newspaper from a man named J. C. Gibson said that each number should be called out first, and then the dollar bill should be put on the table, not the other way around. So "one hundred" should be called first, and then the 100th dollar bill should be put down. In the same way, Gibson said, the year 1900 must be completed before the 19th century has ended. "Mr. Kay should not let his dollars go bang like that," Gibson suggested with a dig at the Presbyterian clergyman's Scottish heritage. "He should hang on to his first dollar and make it represent a whole year, parting with it Scots-like by degrees."

The question of where, rather than when, the new century begins is less contentious. A magazine article written in 1900 tells readers that the first light of day in the new century will fall on Antipodes Island, a small chunk of land jutting out of the South Pacific. An article written in 1998 tells modern readers the same thing.

The original story ran in *Pearson's Magazine* in December 1900. The article pointed out that Antipodes Island would see the new century's first light because the island is close to the International Date Line, an imaginary line of longitude connecting the North and South Poles. The line is where one day changes into the next. And it is along this line, Pearson's explained, that the new century would begin "at the sixth stroke of midnight," as Dec. 31, 1900, became Jan. 1, 1901. The first dawn of the new century would also occur along this line, the article noted. But because of the tilt of the earth's axis, the dawn would not come to all places along the line at the same moment. "The first sun of the 20th century will rise on the places along or near the date line in the order of their position, from the south upward," the article explained.

Since the most southerly point of land along the line is Antipodes Island, "this tiny spot of earth will first see the 20th century dawn. A few minutes later Bounty Island will see it. Then it will sweep along the northeast coast of North Island, New Zealand, then over Vanua Levu, in the Figi Islands. Next it will shine on the scattered coral islets of the Ellice group." The article concluded with a summary of the progress the dawn will make on the first day of the new century as the sun moves east around the globe.

"In six hours and 25 minutes it will gild the temples and palaces of Calcutta . . . . In 12 hours and 25 minutes it will have crossed Montmartre and touched the base of the Eiffel Tower in Paris . . . . In 17 hours and 20 minutes it will be flowing round the feet of the Statue of Liberty . . . . In three hours more it will have reached the Golden Gate. Thence it will cross a stretch of ocean unbroken by rock or islet back to the dawn line, and so will be accomplished the evening and morning of the first day of the 20th century."

Today, you can find the same story in many newspapers and magazines. But the twist on the story is usually a little different. For instance, a piece by Reuters News Agency which ran in *The Globe and Mail* in 1998 told readers that Pitt Island, east of New Zealand and about 1000 kilometres northeast of Antipodes Islands, will be the first inhabited place to greet the new millennium. The Reuters article said the sun will rise on the island just seconds before 4 a.m. on Jan. 1, 2000.

But the *Globe* article, like its predecessor 98 years earlier, acknowledged that Antipodes Island is still the place where the new century's dawn will first rise. "Anyone wishing to beat Pitt Islanders to the millennium should venture southwest to the uninhabited Antipodes Islands, where dawn will break five minutes earlier," the article advised. In keeping with the more commercial nature of modern society, the Reuters article didn't go on with the details about the geographical progress of the sun. Rather, it said that a number of quick-buck artists on South Pacific islands were planning millennium tours, promising well-heeled visitors they will be the first to see in the year 2000.

The article also reflected the more cynical nature of the modern era. It said schemes had been proposed by various South Pacific islands to introduce daylight saving time, or to shift the date line, in a bid to make the day begin an hour earlier. Such late-20th-century skullduggery would not be successful, the article predicted. It quoted scientists as saying: "The arbitrary and unilateral moving of time zones or the International Date Line does not give rise to any level of credibility in the international navigation community. Any claim on the first millennium sunrise from a place geographically quite removed from the traditional date line lacks sense, as any country in the world could do the same."

Jail doors flew open on New Year's Eve

Bangs, bongs, bells and whistles marked the start of the 20th century in Canada at midnight on Jan. 1, 1901. From coast to coast, Canadians greeted the new century with enthusiasm, confident that the coming years would bring the nation the sustained growth and lasting prosperity that had eluded them since Confederation.

In Quebec, the nation's oldest city, a 99-gun salute was fired from the Citadel. The first 49 rounds were a requiem for the old century, while the last 50 marked the birth of the new one. Why not a 100-gun salute, or better still, a 200-gun salute? Because 99 guns was the "biggest salute that could be authorized on an occasion of this kind," a newspaper report explained. "A 100-gun salute is fired only on such occasions as the proclamation of independence or the coronation of a Sovereign."

New Year's Eve was a solemn occasion for religious people across Canada. According to one account from the province of Quebec, "divine service was held at midnight, followed by Holy Communion in most of the Anglican churches and by midnight mass in the Roman Catholic ones."

In Montreal, the ringing of the fire bells on New Year's Eve was a tradition, but in 1900 there was a problem. The custom was to "spell out" the year in numbers. In 1899, the bells had been rung in a 1-8-9-9 pattern. But there was no symbol for zero, and therefore no way to ring out 1900. Someone suggested that 10 bells be used to indicate 0, but the problem was solved with a simpler expedient. The firemen simply rang 12 bells to indicate that midnight had arrived.

In Toronto, the New Year was to be rung in for the first time by Big Ben, the huge bell atop the new city hall. A crowd of 5000 awaited the event in the chilly night. The building, illuminated with electric lights, was darkened at 11:57. A hush came over the crowd. At 12 sharp, the lights flashed on and the quarter hours were struck, but Big Ben's giant clockwork hammer was not working, so the 240-pound clapper had to be operated by three men using a pulley arrangement.

Twelve booming strokes rang out from the heavy-toned giant, then 20 more to salute the new century. The sound of whistles, sirens, firecrackers, trumpets, screams, shouts and songs filled the air. The assembled Torontonians broke into "Auld Lang Syne". The Grenadiers played "The Maple Leaf Forever", and the patriotic crowd followed with a rousing rendition of "Rule Britannia."

Here's how one poetic journalist summarized New Year's Eve in Toronto:

"As the night wore on, the flurry of snow ceased, the clouds gradually thinned, the air grew clear and sharp, the waxing moon, with a scant escort of stars, looked down, and a chill wind sprang up. So the New Year and the

Manitoba *Free Press*, Jan. 1, 1901

new century dawned with the cold light upon a whiteclad Toronto, whose clamor of bells and confused clamors of shouting and noise contrasted strangely with the quiet night and the solemnity of the moment."*

A party put on by one of Toronto's many fraternal lodges, the Brotherhood of Locomotive Firemen, featured a train headlight illuminating a giant "1900" sign at the front of the hall. At midnight, a sheet bearing the numbers "1901" covered the figures of the old century.

Meanwhile, at St. George's Hall, serious philosophical business was going on. Members of the Toronto Spiritualistic Association were told by Rev. Dr. Austin that the ideal woman of the 20th century would possess many virtues, including "fidelity, industry, strength, charity, wisdom and kindness of speech."

A giant bonfire was lit at Queenston, 10 miles north of Niagara Falls. The blaze was matched by a similar one across the Niagara River in Lewiston, N.Y., turning the event into a celebration of Canadian-U.S. friendship.

Hamilton welcomed the new year with wild enthusiasm. "At the midnight hour," reported the local newspaper, "there was the usual bedlam at the corner of King and James Streets, guns, rockets, bells and fireworks of various sorts making up the accompaniment to the wild ringing of church bells and bellowing of factory whistles.... Because it was a century occasion there was more noise than usual and more participators than is customary."

On New Year's Day in Ottawa, the governor general, Lord Minto, held a reception in his office in the East Block of the Parliament Buildings. All the leading citizens were there, including Sir Wilfrid Laurier, the prime minister, and Robert Borden, the new leader of the Opposition.

In Prince Albert, out in the North-West Territories, 50 prominent citizens enjoyed a feast which included oyster soup, whitefish, ham, goose, turkey, beef, cheese, salad, potatoes, corn, four kinds of pie, pudding, cake, nuts, tea and coffee. The local paper reported that "the look of contentment on the faces of the guests told the tale of thorough enjoyment."

But what was surely the most joyous party of the new century took place in Saint John, N.B, where Police Magistrate Ritchie ordered 25 inmates from the county jail into his courtroom on the afternoon of Dec. 31. He told them the new century would soon arrive, urged them to live better lives than they had lived in the old century, and announced they were all going to be set free. The lucky ones included two women who just a few days earlier had been sentenced to a year behind bars.

"Last night the grating doors on the cells swung wide open," a newspaper story dramatically reported. "Every bolt and bar was loosened, and the prisoners crossed the threshold from confinement into freedom, while the 19th century was passing into oblivion."

Farewell to a wonderful century

What were the most significant features of the 20th century? How about the atomic bomb, the rise and fall of communism, and the women's rights movement? Who were the most influential people of the century? Pope John, Mahatma Gandhi and Bill Gates? Mao Tse-tung, Marilyn Monroe and Diana, Princess of Wales? What were this century's most important inventions? The airplane, the birth control pill, the Internet.... you can fill in the rest.

Lists like these are being prepared in Canada and around the world as the 20th century draws to a close. We're a media-rich society, and the media love to create such lists. They're fun to read, and even more fun to take issue with. How could anybody in his right mind put Mao and Marilyn in the same category?

But such lists serve a serious purpose. We create them in an attempt to get a handle on history. We use them in a bid to make sense of the complex events which have taken place over the previous 100 years. We make lists to identify the handful of people who, of all the billions of men and women who lived during the past century, have played the most important roles in our recent history. When an event or a person appears on almost everyone's list, it's an indication that the event or person was truly significant for one reason or another, and will be remembered long into the future.... or at least until the end of the next decade.

Such exercises to separate the wheat from the chaff are nothing new. Our great-grandfathers engaged in similar pursuits 100 years ago, as the 20th century was about to start. Then, as now, there was disagreement over what events and which people should be put on the list, but since the 19th century was such a busy and fruitful block of time, there was no shortage of deserving candidates.

It's interesting to note that we remember bad guys best of all. Just as Adolph Hitler makes almost everybody's list of most-influential people in the 20th century, another military dictator from Europe – Napoleon Bonaparte – was widely chosen as the most historically significant individual of the 19th century. The French soldier, who rose from humble origins to become the emperor of his nation and the conqueror of much of Europe in the early 19th century, bore a striking resemblance to Hitler in terms of shaking up the world, although of the two, Napoleon was certainly much more admirable because he did a lot of good things as well as bad ones, while Hitler's accomplishments were all horribly negative.

As far as other influential people are concerned, the 19th century had a lot of them. It depends upon your perspective whether you include on your list those whose accomplishments were mainly political, scientific, literary or what have you. But most would agree that at least a few others belong on almost any list of the major figures of the century.

Abraham Lincoln is a popular choice. He was judged by many historians to have been the greatest president of the United States during the 19th century, and his claim to be on the list is even greater today, since he seems to have been better than any of the presidents the Americans elected in the 20th century as well. While Lincoln was only in office for a little more than one term, his leadership of the winning side in the American Civil War, and the fact that he freed the slaves, marked him for greatness not only during the 19th and 20th centuries, but very likely throughout the 21st century as well.

Karl Marx, the German philosopher and revolutionist, also belongs on the list of most-influential people of the 19th century. Marx wrote a book called *The Manifesto* in which he concluded that the capitalist class would be overthrown by a worldwide working-class revolution. *The Manifesto* influenced all subsequent communist literature, and revolutionary thought in general. Marx's theories sparked two of the 20th century's greatest events, the Russian and Chinese communist revolutions, and led to the establishment of the Soviet Union, Red China and the Cold War, which all played a huge role in 20th-century history.

Another influential 19th-century figure was Charles Darwin, the British scientist who laid the basis for the Theory of Evolution with his suggestion that all forms of life developed through the process of natural selection. Darwin influenced all of the life and earth sciences. He also undermined the authority of the Christian church, by suggesting that man was not specially created by God, as the Bible says he was. This fundamental attack on the church's doctrine played a big part in the secularization of society during the 20th century.

Dozens of others names showed up on various turn-of-the-century lists of people who played an important role during the 19th century. They included everybody from Alfred Nobel, the Swedish inventor, and Simon Bolivar, the South American revolutionary, to Mark Twain, the American humorist, and Charles Dickens, the English novelist. You can add to the list almost forever: Victor Emmanuel, the King of Italy; Feodor Dostoyevsky, the Russian writer; Richard Wagner, the German composer; Louis Pasteur, the French chemist; Henrik Ibsen, the Norwegian dramatist; and so on. It's interesting to note that with the exception of Victoria, the queen of Great Britain, and Florence Nightingale, the English nurse, virtually no women made the list.

It's also interesting that Canadian newspapers and magazines shied away from putting any of their fellow-countrymen on the list. The only possibility was Sir John A. Macdonald, Canada's first prime minister, but at the beginning of the new century he had been dead for only a decade. He was still closely associated with partisan politics and the Conservative party, so only those of the Tory persuasion would have been inclined to rank Macdonald among the great people of the century.

When it comes to listing the major events which took place during our own century, the fact that we had not one but two world wars is mentioned by virtually everyone. Wars also appeared on lists which were complied of the major events of the 19th century, but aside from the Napoleonic struggles and the American Civil War, none of the century's wars amounted to much in the overall scheme of things. The most significant ones were the Crimean War in Central Europe during the 1850s, the Franco-Prussian War of the early 1870s, the Spanish-American War of 1898 and the Boer War, which began in 1899 and was still going on when the century ended. But all in all, the 19th century was a generally peaceful period.

But the century had its share of disasters. These included an earthquake which killed 14 000 people in Italy in 1842, the Irish famine of 1846, the great Chicago fire of 1871 and a tidal wave which killed 2400 people in Japan in 1889.

There was lots of activity on the imperialistic front. It was during the 19th century that the British Empire expanded to include about a quarter of the world's people. Africa was colonized and exploited by Europeans during the 19th century, and it was during those years that the United States grew to become a world power. Explorers reached all but the most remote parts of the globe during the century, and major organizations such as the Red Cross and the YMCA were founded.

The century's most significant events in Canada were the development of democracy and responsible government, the political partnership forged by English- and French-speaking Canadians, Confederation in 1867 and the building of the transcontinental railway system in the 1870s and 1880s. The fact that we were not swallowed up by the United States enabled us to make ourselves into a strong and prosperous independent nation during the 20th century.

Other major world events during the 19th century included the emancipation of the Russian serfs, the liberation of Latin America from Spanish rule, the decline in Turkey's power, the rise of Japan, the building of the Suez Canal, the federation of Germany, and the great growth in literacy and popular education. There was also the rise of big business and the flourishing of the industrial revolution, with steam and electrical power being put to work by the forces of capitalism to vastly increase productivity or to exploit the masses, depending on your point of view. It was also during the 19th century that the wholesale exploitation of the earth's natural resources began, along with the worldwide pollution of the environment which plagues us so greatly today.

The first skyscrapers were built during the 19th century, and the Eiffel Tower was erected. The first steel mills were created, and the first cantilever bridges were built. Mass advertising and selling by mail were also introduced during those busy years. In science and medicine, there were many advances. These included the widespread use of immunization to fight disease, big advances in surgery and dentistry, the discovery of x-rays, the development of the atomic theory, and the realization that hygiene is important to health, and that germs cause diseases.

There was a significant increase in religious tolerance during the 19th century. As the Halifax *Herald* pointed out in an editorial on the last day of the old century:

> *"Very considerable bitterness was the rule during two-thirds or three-quarters of the century, but in more recent years bitterness has almost disappeared, as a result both of wiser heads and kinder hearts."*

Many of the lists of significant events of the 19th century focused not only on important happenings, key people and major changes to society, but also on improvements in everyday life. In fact, the 19th century was dubbed the Century of Progress, so great were the technological advances made during those years.

People at the start of the 20th century

knew that they were well off, compared to those who had lived before them. In fact, they felt they had reached a pinnacle in terms of comfort and lifestyle. Much of the progress had occurred during the past century. As the Windsor *Star* pointed out in an editorial published on the last day of the year 1900:

> *"The average mechanic of today in many respects is better circumstanced than the monarch of a century ago in the multitude of household conveniences comprising heating, water supply, lighting and plumbing, in modes of travel by rail and water, in modes of quick communication, including the telegraph, telephone and phonograph, in the sources of information, including the newspaper and the magazine, and in a thousand other ways."*

As the newspaper pointed out, even a king in 1801 could not do things which were commonplace for ordinary citizens a hundred years later. They could travel quickly and conveniently from Europe to North America, thanks to the modern steam-powered ship. They could learn of major news developments in remote parts of the world within a matter of minutes, thanks to the telegraph and undersea cables. And they could listen to the music of a symphony orchestra without leaving their own living rooms, thanks to electricity and the phonograph.

When you stop to think about it, the 19th century really was amazing . . . . perhaps even more amazing than the 20th century in terms of how much material and scientific progress was made over the previous 100 years. The 19th century claimed credit for all kinds of popular wonders which we take for granted today, along with their 20th-century extensions.

These included advances in transportation such as the steamboat, the railroad and even the bicycle. They included the development of ways to significantly increase the comfort of our homes, such as gas lighting, electric lighting, central heating, flush toilets and porcelain bathtubs. In the field of agriculture, improvements abounded. These included the steel plough and the reaping machine, which vastly increased the amount a farmer could grow and harvest.

Huge leaps were also made in people's ability to communicate with one another. These advances of the 19th century included the telegraph, the telephone, the transoceanic cable, photography, the phonograph, motion pictures, the linotype machine and the high-speed printing press.

And speaking of printing, a fit way to conclude this section is to reprint a few words which appeared in *The New York Times* at the end of the 19th century. Along with a lengthy review of the preceding century, the newspaper looked back to the very beginning of that century, and found the same kind of thinking was going on then that was going on at the start of the 20th century, and that no doubt will be going on at the start of the 21st.

"What thoughts were in people's minds a hundred years ago with regard to the change of the century?" *The Times* asked on Dec. 30, 1900. "An inspection of old books and periodicals gives us an answer to the question." The newspaper noted that both English and American publications at the end of the 18th century "were full of congratulations upon the achievements of their respective countries."

The Times quoted the *Gentleman's Magazine*, which bragged about the many accomplishments of the 18th century. "To prove that this century is unequalled by any of the preceding ones, especially in England," the magazine said, "we need but remark that it boasts a Newton, Locke, Johnson, a Handel, Wren, Chambers, Reynolds, Henway, Howard and many others." *The Times* also quoted a writer in the Baltimore *Gazette*, who reviewed the changes which had taken place during the 18th century, and concluded:

> *"If anyone is with us who lived at the beginning of the last century, it must certainly be an entertainment for him to see the different state of things of 1701 to that of the present time. It would, I imagine, be a much more desirable object to live till the year 1901, because a greater change in the affairs of the world seems to be promised."*

Those words, originally written almost 200 years ago, sound very much like many of the prophecies we read today that the 21st century will see even more and greater changes than we have experienced in the century just passed. It just goes to show that while many things change over the years, the idea that tomorrow will be even more amazing than yesterday is a recurring theme.

How much has changed in Canada during this century?

Here are some of the ways in which we are different than we were 100 years ago. Below this is a list of some of the ways in which we are the same as we were 100 years ago. As you read this book and gather other information from other sources, feel free to add to these lists. A test will be held on this material in history class next week.

- A century ago, there were no corporate taxes, no federal or provincial income tax, no GST or PST. The federal government raised 75 per cent of its money from excise taxes and duties on goods imported into Canada.

- Women couldn't vote in federal or provincial elections; under certain conditions they could vote in municipal elections, but they couldn't be the mayor or sit on council.

- You didn't need a driver's licence, but it didn't matter much; most Canadians had never even seen an automobile, let alone driven one.

- Our population was just 5.4 million, about one-sixth of what it is today.

- People believed that airplane flight was theoretically possible, but that it was a long way in the future.

- Medicare, welfare, RRSPs and government-run old-age pension programs didn't exist.

- The army was mainly volunteer, consisting of what was called the militia.

How We Welcomed the 20th Century 23

- Cocaine, opium and all other drugs were legal.
- Montreal was Canada's largest city; now it plays second fiddle to Toronto.
- The vast majority of Canadians were of European origin.
- There were only seven provinces; the remaining three became provinces in the 20th century. Saskatchewan and Alberta were part of the North-West Territories until 1905; Newfoundland was a separate British colony until 1949.
- Canada's final court of appeal was in Great Britain.
- Our soldiers were fighters, not peace-keepers; they were fighting a nasty war against the Boers in South Africa.
- From coast to coast, Canada had a grand total of just one female lawyer.
- The Canadian and U.S. dollars were of equal value.
- Engaging in homosexual sex was a serious crime.
- Abortions were illegal; so was selling any form of birth control device.
- Cities were full of horses, cows and chickens.
- Riding the train was the most common way of travelling across Canada.
- Most Canadians lived on farms.
- The mail order catalogue was a major means of selling goods, especially to people in rural areas.
- Refrigerators were kept cold with blocks of ice.
- Telegraph lines reached almost everywhere; telegrams and cables were the main means of quick long-distance communications, but long-distance phone service was developing rapidly.
- All cities and most towns had lively, competing newspapers; they didn't look like comic books, the way many of them do today.
- Indians, the handicapped and other victims of prejudice had no legal recourse when they were discriminated against; there were no human rights commissions.
- Kerosene lamps were the main source of light for farm homes.
- Outdoor toilets were common; toilet paper, far from being soft, white and fluffy, often consisted of the pages of an old catalogue.
- Most Canadians went to church; clergymen had a major say in the affairs of the community. They decided what was permitted and what was forbidden.
- Girls and young women who got pregnant used to get married to the fathers of their children; it was the right thing to do.
- Murderers were hanged.

- Electric street cars had signs informing riders that it was illegal to spit on the floor; in Toronto, the signs were widely ignored.
- A lot of babies died before their first birthday.
- Only a small percentage of students went on to university; total university enrolment across Canada was only about 6000. Many Canadian universities today have that many or more students on their own campuses.
- Cod were plentiful in the Atlantic fishery; the government didn't pay fishermen not to fish.
- The typical factory worker put in a 60-hour week.
- There was a lot of public sentiment in favor or making the sale and consumption of alcoholic beverages illegal. The idea of total prohibition made sense.
- Protestant religious studies and prayer were a key part of the elementary school curriculum.
- Prominent Canadians were knighted by the Queen, and thereafter used "Sir" in front of their first names; their wives were addressed as "Lady" followed by their last names – for example, Sir Wilfrid and Lady Laurier.
- The government closed down gambling halls, rather than running them and making enormous profits.
- Banks issued their own banknotes.
- Canada's currency system included $1, $2 and $4 bills.
- Big business was almost totally unregulated; the captains of industry could do pretty much whatever they wanted.
- Canada had no embassies and played no role on the international stage; its foreign affairs were handled by the British, who looked out for their own interests first, and Canadian interests second.
- Entry into Canada was almost unrestricted; people coming by ship were excluded only if they were criminals, suffering from disease or likely to become a charge on the public purse. An exception was made for Chinese. A $100 head tax was levied on Chinese immigrants to keep them out of Canada.
- You could get 160 acres of land in the West from the government just by paying a $10 registration fee. That worked out to less than seven cents an acre, but you had to settle on the land and farm it if you wanted to keep it.
- At the beach, women wore bulky, one-piece, over-the-shoulder and below-the-knee bathing suits; swimming men wore snug jerseys and tight-fitting, above-the-knee pants. They looked very silly.
- There were no day-care centres. Women stayed home and looked after their kids; if they had to work, relatives or friends cared for the children.

- There was no such thing as a Canadian citizen; Canadians were British subjects.

Here are some of the ways we are pretty much the same as we were at the beginning of the century:

- Roman Catholic bishops still insist that Canadian couples who use birth control devices are sinners; many parish priests have more sense.

- People still love to shoot snapshots of their kids and pets and send them to their friends.

- The St. Lawrence River and the Great Lakes are still the heart of our national waterway system.

- Ontario is still the biggest and richest province; people from the rest of Canada still hate Ontario's arrogance and are jealous of its success.

- The makers of products to take care of headaches, sleeplessness, bad breath and hundreds of other horrendous problems are still making exaggerated claims for their products. They still claim their snake-oil remedies are new and effective and better than their competitors' products. Canadians still fall for this nonsense and spend a fortune on this junk.

- Women still have justifiable complaints about not being treated equally by men. Males still hold almost all the nation's highest and best-paying positions.

- A French-Canadian Liberal from Quebec is in his second term as head of a majority government. It's a different man, but the description fits perfectly.

- Senators are still appointed, paid well and under-worked; they're still mainly old political hacks being rewarded by the government with a cushy job.

- French-Canadians still worry about being dominated by Canada's English-speaking majority, but now they've got the political clout to run circles around the anglos.

- Canadians continue to whine about everything the United States does or does not do; really stupid patriots insist that Canada is "much better" than the U.S.

- The U.S. is still a people magnet, drawing many of Canada's brightest and most-talented citizens. If the Yankees are so bad, why do so many of us want to live among them?

- The premiers are still demanding that Ottawa give the provinces more money.

- The big banks still do as they damn well please, but now they hire PR people to make themselves look good while they're sticking it to us.

- The British Queen is still Canada's legal head of state; an appointed governor general still fills in for our absentee sovereign, who generously pays us a visit every decade or so.

- Canada's birthday is still July 1; it is still a welcome summer day off work; and it is still celebrated with picnics, sporting events and other laid-back activities.
- Canadians still love to yak on the telephone.
- Civic officials are still saying that something must be done about rampant prostitution.
- Shakespeare is still a major part of the curriculum in high school English classes.
- Canadians are still free to travel around as they please, and they can live in any part of the country they wish to live in.
- Social reformers still complain that too many children are living in poverty. They're right, but the government still does nothing about this problem.
- The first Monday in September is still celebrated as Labor Day; most Canadians don't take the "labor" part too seriously, and enjoy goofing off on the last long-weekend of the summer.
- Smoking is still a popular, dirty and unhealthy habit.
- Hockey is still the nation's most popular sport.
- The government is still trying to attract well-heeled immigrants who will invest in Canada.
- "O Canada" is still played on patriotic occasions; although it's now our official national anthem, most Canadians still don't know the words, and those who do usually don't sing them.
- The Maple Leaf is still our national symbol; now it's the centre-piece of our national flag, which is rarely mistaken by foreigners for a beer label.
- Contact lenses are still available to correct vision problems; the glass semi-spheres of a century ago have been replaced by flexible plastic lenses.
- People in large cities still gather in large groups outdoors to celebrate New Year's Eve.
- Bicycles are still a popular form of exercise and entertainment.
- The federal police force still serves and protects the people in the North and the West; but now the former North-West Mounted Police are known as the RCMP.
- People convicted of the most serious crimes are still locked up in Kingston, Stony Mountain and other fortress-like federal penitentiaries; but now prisoners have lots of rights.
- Small retailers still complain that chain stores are ruining their businesses.
- The Maritimes are still economically depressed.

- Big companies with ties to the government still get government contracts and subsidies; supporters of the party in power still get government jobs.
- The Queen's Plate, run in May, is still Canada's top horse race.
- When the New York Stock Exchange sneezes, the Toronto Stock Exchange still catches a cold.
- We still take a day off in May to celebrate Queen Victoria's birthday; but now we just enjoy the day, giving little thought to the long-dead queen.

'The Grandest Sovereign put aside her earthly crown'

The death of Queen Victoria was the first big news event of the 20th century. The Queen's passing on Tuesday, Jan. 22, 1901, had a profound impact on Canadians, as did the death of another royal figure, Diana, Princess of Wales, 96 years later.

The loss of both members of the British royal family was greeted with a massive outpouring of public sadness – an indication that in this, as in many other ways, Canadians at the beginning and the end of the 20th century have a lot in common. We all remember the great display of public grief that accompanied the death of Diana in the summer of 1997. But when you look back on the much-older and more-greatly-revered Victoria in 1901, you find that it had an even greater impact on the Canadian people.

Diana was the tabloid princess who would never be Queen of England and had to content herself with being the Queen of the People's Hearts. Victoria was the real thing, the longest-reigning monarch in British history. You can't help wondering what the news reporting would have been like if round-the-clock live television coverage had been available when Victoria died. Certainly the newspapers and magazines gave the story huge play, and made no more effort to report it dispassionately than the modern media did when Diana was killed in a car crash.

Typical of the coverage on the day Victoria died was this headline which ran in the Toronto *Daily Star*: "Queen and Empress Passes Away to a Higher

The Globe, Jan. 23, 1901

Kingdom: The Grandest Sovereign the World Has Ever Known Lays Aside an Earthly Crown for One That Shall Never Tarnish."

Saturday Night magazine proclaimed that "in history, the dead Queen will be remembered as the greatest ruler of the greatest empire the world has ever seen .... Never before was there a Royal personage so closely identified for so long a period with the greatest progress of humanity." The magazine compared Victoria to another great queen, Elizabeth, who had ruled three centuries earlier and had also presided over an era of expansion and national glory. But the magazine noted that Victoria was even greater, for while the unmarried Elizabeth was notorious for her many sexual escapades, Victoria's faithfulness as a wife and mother put her at the pinnacle of national morality.

The Montreal *Gazette* said that "not for a thousand years has the English people had at its head one who so perfectly embodied the national ideals and aspirations." The Halifax *Chronicle* called the late Queen "the most wonderful woman that has ever lived." The Toronto *World* said she had "the most world-wide renown of any human being in recent times." Sir Wilfrid Laurier, Canada's prime minister, called her "a great ruler, whose manifold and exalted virtues have for three generations commanded the respect and admiration of the world." Archbishop Bruchesi of Montreal said the late Queen was "a perfect model for the whole world of those qualities and virtues that cause sovereigns to be beloved both of God and of man."

From all that, you can see that Victoria was more than a queen. Much like Diana, she was a cult figure. But while Diana was the embodiment of the glamor and narcissism which mark the modern age, Victoria stood for the solid virtues of dependability and continuity which were much more highly valued a century ago than they are today.

But she was even more than that. She was the embodiment of her nation. As her long reign progressed and as the empire expanded, Victoria became the focal point for all the self-congratulatory jingoism which marked the latter part of the 19th century. Victoria's reign coincided with Britain's greatest glory days. As the monarch, she became the personification of imperial splendor. When orators heaped praise on the woman Victoria, they were also talking about the empire, that collective entity which saw itself as the greatest political and social institution which had ever existed.

The high point of Victoria's reign was reached in 1897, just four years before her death, when the grandest celebration London had ever seen was held to mark the 60th anniversary of her ascension to the throne. In her last few years she kept herself in the public eye by inspecting troops and presenting medals during the Boer War.

Victoria was born on May 24, 1819. In Canada her birthday was annually celebrated – and still is – as a national holiday. She became Queen in 1837 at the age of just 18. At the time, the royal family was at a low point in terms of public esteem. The vibrant young Queen repopularized the monarchy, especially after she married a German prince named Albert and gave birth to nine children.

When Albert died in 1861 of typhoid fever, Victoria was shattered. She went into permanent mourning, wearing a dark silk dress and a white bonnet, and becoming known in private conversations as the Widow of Windsor. She was so devoted to her late husband that she had his clothes laid out on his bed each day, and fresh water put in his basin each morning.

Gradually emerging from seclusion, she became publicly active and visible until just a few weeks before her death. As it became clear that the end was near, the newspapers published daily bulletins from Osborne House, her home on the Isle of Wight in the English Channel, where she spent her last days. Her final hours were reported by a correspondent for *The Times* of London:

> *"All last night the Queen lay in her bedroom in the pavillion in a very restless state. It was locked, the only persons allowed within being the doctors, the dressers, and two maids, who were under the superintendence of Nurse Soal, from the sanatorium of the estate. The early morning bulletin, which spoke of diminished strength, showed that the end was drawing near, and in the meanwhile all the members of the Royal Family who were within reach were summoned.*
>
> *"All day long the Angel of Death has been hovering over Osborne House. One could almost hear the beating of his wings, but at half-past 6 those wings were folded, and the Queen was at rest. To those who knew her majesty best and most closely, as some of them have told me, the whole event seems incredible and unreal. To all of them the life of the Queen had seemed a part of the natural order of things, a thing as certain as the rising or the setting of the sun; and they are simply incapable of realizing what it means, and what feelings will be shared by almost all of those who were the Queen's subjects."*

Victoria was honored with a state funeral and an unprecedented 909-gun salute. She was a tough act to follow. Her eldest son, Albert Edward, who had waited for so long, finally succeeded her. The new monarch was well past his prime at the age of 59 when he became King Edward VII. The Canadian papers hailed the new king and made much of the fact

The Globe, Jan. 24, 1901. Edward and Alexandra.

that as a 20-year-old prince in 1860, he had visited Montreal and Toronto. He had not been back since, nor would he ever come to Canada during his reign.

When he was in his early 20s, his mother chose a princess from Denmark to be his wife. Edward and the tall and stately princess, who became known as Alexandra the Fair, were married in 1863. They settled in for the long wait until the time came for Edward to succeed his mother. As the long-time Prince of Wales, "Bertie," as his family called him, was given nothing of importance to do. He became an overweight, self-indulgent aristocrat who loved to party and gamble.

But when he became king the Canadian press said nothing about that, and instead turned him into a paragon of virtue and a worthy successor to the throne. The Charlottetown *Guardian* hailed him as "a most dutiful and loving son," while the Hamilton *Post* called him "a noble, practical and generous philanthropist."

The Toronto *Globe* came as close as any newspaper to being critical, damning him with faint praise by saying he had "more than ordinary capabilities." The paper also warned him indirectly not to adopt the imperial mannerisms of his mother by saying that Edward should prove to be "a wise, tactful, instructed constitutional monarch." The *Canadian Magazine* expressed a similar thought, predicting that "the new King as a constitutional sovereign will follow in the footsteps of the Queen, and while conserving the Royal prerogative to be consulted on all state matters, will not attempt to refuse the advice of his ministers or to run counter to the will of the nation as expressed in the houses of Parliament."

During his nine-year reign, Edward gave no cause for worry. He wasn't interested in turning back the clock to the era when British monarchs had real power. He was more interested in enjoying the prestige and pleasures that went with the job of being king. He brought a sense of joy to the monarchy which had been lacking under his beloved but dour mother. He gave the language a new adjective – Edwardian – which was synonymous with hedonism and elegant style. His extra-marital sexual appetites were so notorious that the less deferential press in England nicknamed him Edward the Caresser.

Chapter 2
How We Loved Our Mother Britain

Canada was tied to Britain's apron strings

Canada was far from being a grown-up country at the start of the 20th century. It was still a British colony, despite the fact that it was a third of a century old. Canada was like an aging but under-developed adolescent. We were slowly cutting the apron strings binding us to the mother country, but the process was achingly slow.

In 1901, Canadians still saluted the British flag, sang the British national anthem, and swore allegiance to the British monarch. A British general was in command of Canada's military forces, while a British committee made final decisions in Canadian court cases and British bureaucrats controlled Canada's foreign relations. A dispute with the U.S. over the Canada-Alaska boundary was settled in the Americans' favor when British diplomats sacrificed Canadian interests to foster Anglo-American relations.

While it controlled most of its own internal affairs in 1901, Canada did not achieved complete independence from Great Britain until several decades later. So it's not surprising that even today, Canada's sense of national identity remains weak. Having plodded in such an unspectacular fashion toward eventual political adulthood, Canada has no memorable or defining moments in its history to mark its coming of age, and no tradition of declaring its independence.

As the 20th century dawned, our relationship with Britain was like that of an aging child. We were unable and unwilling to remove ourselves from our domineering parent's authority. While strong enough to stand on our own, we chose to remain dependent on our mother, and to accept guidance and direction from above. The mother, for her part, wanted to hang on to her maturing but still-clinging child. Indeed, she wanted to draw her child into an even tighter relationship. So she subtly controlled and manipulated us, cleverly providing no occasion for us to stand up for ourselves and go our own way.

To retain her authority over Canada, Britain sent a variety of officials to the colony to be in charge in certain key areas. The most senior and important official was the governor general, who was the representative of the monarch and therefore the official head of the Canadian state. Today we choose our own governor general, who is usually a retired Canadian politician. But at the start of the century, the governor general was invariably from the mother country, and Canada had no say in the matter. The British simply picked the man to suit themselves, and the Canadians learned to live with him.

The governor general, who usually held office for about half a decade before being replaced by a clone-like successor, was generally a mid-level British aristocrat whose status skyrocketed once he was sworn into office. He went from being a lesser member of the elite in his own country to the pinnacle of society in Canada. No one ranked higher than the governor general, and no one was surrounded by more pomp and circumstance. The governor general lived in Rideau Hall, a magnificent residence in Ottawa. He wore fancy uniforms, had military escorts and was addressed as "Your Excellency." He was given all the respect due to the Crown, and when consultation was necessary, as it often was, it was the prime minister who came to the governor general's office, not the other way around.

Technically, the governor general could even dismiss the prime minister and his cabinet. But in practice, Canada was a parliamentary democracy like Great Britain, and the governor general was in a position similar to the British monarch. He reigned, but did not rule. He had the power to advise the government and the right to be consulted on important decisions, but he was supposed to stay out of politics. He had enormous prestige, but in fact he was just a surrogate. The British colonial office called the shots, and the governor general followed its direction.

Canada's governor general at the start of the 20th century was a British aristocrat named Gilbert John Elliot, who inherited an earldom and the title of Lord Minto. He was Canada's eighth governor general, and was typical of the string of Britishers who had held the post since the dominion was founded in 1867. He was personable if somewhat stodgy, not especially talented or bright, but a decent chap who had enjoyed a successful but unspectacular

Lord Minto. PAC

career in the British army before his retirement.

His only previous connection with Canada was in the mid-1880s, when he was a military aide in Ottawa and acted as chief of staff in the small British force which went to the North-West Territories to put down the Riel Rebellion. After his British army career, Minto settled into his hereditary seat in the House of Lords. He was in his early fifties, enjoying a life of genteel semi-retirement on his estate in the Scottish border district, when he received word that Queen Victoria had decided to appoint him governor general of Canada. That was in 1898. By the start of the new century, he was approaching the midpoint in his term.

Why was Minto, who had no political experience and knew nothing about the intricacies of Canadian politics, appointed to this exalted position? His British political masters selected him because he was a team player who could be relied upon to followA directions from London. He was part of the old boys' network, a graduate of Eton and Cambridge, a member of the horsy set on the fringes of the royal court. And most important of all, he held views similar to those of the British colonial secretary, Joseph Chamberlain, whose grandiose visions of a mighty British empire called for the colonies to play important supporting roles.

In Chamberlain's view, the colonies were useful to the mother country. They provided markets for British manufactured goods, homes for Britain's surplus population, and soldiers for the many frontier wars which Britain became involved in around the world as it sought to preserve and expand its empire. Minto's ideas on these matters were in harmony with Chamberlain's. This was most clearly demonstrated in 1900, when Minto tried to pressure the Canadian government into pledging Canadian military support for the British war effort against the Boers of South Africa, even before the outbreak of hostilities.

Minto urged Canada's prime minister, Sir Wilfrid Laurier, to make a public commitment to the British cause, and showed little understanding of the fact that some of Laurier's French-Canadian cabinet colleagues were strongly opposed. Minto also failed to appreciate that Canada had no vested interest in South Africa. The fact that Canadian leaders constantly vowed loyalty to the Crown and Great Britain made it easy for Minto to believe that Canada would follow Britain's wishes, but in fact the Boers were a huge ocean away from Canada, and posed no threat to either this country or the mother country.

The governor general did all he could to pull Canadian troops into the Boer War, going so far as to attend fight-for-the-flag events, thus coming close to crossing the line into active politics. When Laurier finally gave in to pressure from Ontario's jingoistic English-speaking voters and agreed to send volunteers to the Boer War, Minto was delighted. He praised the Canadian people for avoiding "the quibbles of colonial responsibility," in effect crowing over his victory. Laurier, ever the gentleman and dutiful British subject, did not publicly criticize Minto for interfering in political matters. He simply said he found Minto "very stiff."

But Minto's attitudes and actions were nothing compared to those of another official inflicted upon Canada by the British government. He was Edward Hutton, a major-general who was placed in charge of the Canadian militia. That job, like the governor general's position, was always given to someone from Great Britain, and never to a Canadian. The Canadian government accepted the argument that no Canadian was "experienced enough" to handle the job.

But in Hutton's case, Laurier and his colleagues did not welcome the military appointee, as they had welcomed the political appointee Minto. They gave Hutton the cold shoulder, sensing that he would put British interests ahead of Canadian interests, although Minto greeted Hutton like a long-lost brother. Hutton felt that his duty was to increase the efficiency of the Canadian militia and get it ready to fight Britain's battles, but the Liberals were not keen on moving in that direction.

This was a matter of policy and therefore a political decision. Hutton should have taken direction from the Minister of Militia, Frederick Borden. Instead, the arrogant Hutton plunged ahead with his schemes to reinvigorate the militia and foster a sense of British patriotism in Canada's citizen-soldiers. In this he largely succeeded, as can be seen from the big response which Canada gave when volunteers were sought to fight in South Africa, although he shouldn't get too much credit, because many English-Canadians were so eager to fight Britain's battles that they needed no one to urge them on.

Hutton's vigorous approach to his duties rubbed the Canadian government the wrong way, especially when he used Canadian newspapers and magazines to try and force the politicians to adopt his militaristic policies. He saw himself as a patriot, but in fact he was a newshound and a propagandist for the empire, fired with too much zeal. The government viewed him as a subordinate who was out of control, especially after he began promoting grandiose schemes for a huge standing army, ready to spring to the empire's defence around the globe.

In 1900, when details of his scheme to send Canadian troops to South Africa were published in a newspaper before the government had decided whether or not to send troops, Hutton's fate was sealed. The Canadian cabinet demanded that Hutton be recalled to Britain. His friend Minto hesitated before signing the order, but wisely did not defy the government and thereby create a constitutional crisis.

But in a British-orchestrated gesture enabling the arrogant Hutton to save face, he was permitted to resign, ostensibly so he could take a command in South Africa. So Canada got rid of a British appointee who foolishly pushed the colonials too far, and thus the nation took another baby step toward taking charge of its own affairs.

Dr. Borden, Minister of Militia. *The Canadian Magazine*, Aug. 1901

Canadians flocked to Britain's war in South Africa

At the turn of the century, when Canada got involved in its first overseas war, a young Niagara Peninsula man named John Winger couldn't wait to sign up. He volunteered for service in the first Canadian contingent sent to fight in the Boer War. It was billed as a noble cause, but many historians have come to see it as an unnecessary fight in a far-away land, undertaken primarily for the sake of British imperial glory.

But you'd never know it from the tumultuous send-off given to John Winger and his fellow soldiers, who were praised to the rooftops for embarking on a great patriotic crusade to preserve the honor of the British Empire. In the early 1900s, imperialism was at its peak, and a fellow like John Winger was seen as quite properly answering the call to duty.

Winger was one of more than 7000 Canadian volunteers who went to South Africa "to fight for the Queen." Their daily exploits in battle were reported in the newspapers, and their return to Canada was celebrated in countless parades and public ceremonies. The war was not particularly deadly. Battle and disease accounted in roughly equal numbers for the war's 244 Canadian deaths in the 32-month struggle. It seemed like a lot of casualties at the time, but it was small in comparison to the huge toll in human life extracted later in the century by the two world wars and the war in Korea.

But what it lacked in size, the Boer War made up for in enthusiasm. Historians would later conclude that while its purpose was far from noble, the war in South Africa was a landmark in Canada's emerging national consciousness. The Canadians fought together in units, rather than being split up among British regiments, so they became a great symbol of national pride. For decades after the fighting was over, Canadians recalled the heroism of their troops in South Africa at places with exotic-sounding names like Paardeberg, Bloemfontein, Mafeking and Leliefontein. The memory of the glory of such units as the Royal Canadian Regiment, the Mounted Rifles and Strathcona's Horse was honored on

Boer War soldier. SPA R-A 17636

Remembrance Days until the last Boer War veteran died, and their victories are celebrated in military messes to this very day.

The Canadians soldiers were praised for their resourcefulness, stamina and coolness under fire. They were remarkably good, in view of the fact that they were not professional soldiers and had little training. The first group, which included John Winger and about 1000 other Canadians, went into battle after just a month's instruction on board their ship *The Sardinian* (nicknamed "The Sardine") and two months of field training after their arrival in South Africa.

But they and the other Canadians who followed them fought bravely and well. Newspapers spared no detail to report the heroism of Canadians. There were stories about the four Canadians who held off 50 Boers in one engagement, and the three others who won the Victoria Cross for saving a gun from capture. Even the myths of the Canadians were recounted. One story told of a hearse which came loose in a storage area and was rolling down a hill. Members of the Canadian Mounted Rifles happened to be riding by. An officer ordered four men to stop the runaway. They did so, but later that day, when the same unit was on patrol, every man returned safely, except the four who had touched the hearse.

When the first troops came home at the end of 1900, they received a tumultuous welcome, particularly in Toronto, the centre of Canadian imperialistic sentiment. They were greeted as conquerors, although the struggle was far from over. The newspaper account of the triumphal return of John Winger to his home town conveys a sense of how popular the war was.

"Pandemonium reigned supreme when Bombardier John Winger returned to Port Colborne safe and sound on Thursday last, after being absent over a year in South Africa," reported *The People's Press*, a weekly newspaper. "The safe return of our noble soldier boy from the war was the grandest Christmas gift that could have been bestowed upon the community."

As the train bringing the young soldier home pulled into the station, "the explosion of torpedoes, firecrackers etc. must have reminded the hero of some of the scenes through which he had passed," the story continued. It went on to describe the community hall, which was packed with 700 citizens "anxious to see the man who helped whip the Boers. As our hero entered the hall, hundreds of people raised a shout of welcome and cheer after cheer, together with the noise of horns and other instruments."

The newspaper exuberantly reported that "it was a welcome which only a gallant soldier who had risked his life for his Queen and country could receive. No great orator, no great statesman, not even a member of the royal family could have won such a greeting from the people as did Bombardier Winger on Thursday night."

Yet for all the jingoism, the Boer War was a bitter battle between the mighty British Empire and a group of South Africans fighting for their homeland. The fact that the British had so much trouble with the Boers was a surprise to many people, who assumed that it was just going to be another easy frontier war of the kind that Britain had often fought in the 19th century. Years later, some people called it Britain's Vietnam, in the sense that a great power was humiliated by a much smaller one, as the Americans were by the North Vietnamese in the 1960s and 1970s. For all the British bragging about their great victory, the truth was that the mighty British Empire needed three years and 450 000 troops to defeat 40 000 Boer farmers.

But London was determined to control the recently discovered riches of gold of the Transvaal. That meant taking over territory from the Boers, who had established the Orange Free State and the South African Republic two decades earlier. The fighting broke out in October 1899. The Boers were well organized and had been armed by the Germans, who were emerging as rivals to the British for world power.

After the Boers racked up initial victories, the British sent reinforcements and committed themselves to waging a full-scale war. Imperialists such as the British colonial secretary, Joseph Chamberlain, said it was Canada's duty as part of the empire to help put down the Boers, and claimed that the fundamental issue of the war was the preservation of the rights of British subjects in South Africa.

The Canadian prime minister, Sir Wilfrid Laurier, didn't buy that argument. While he wanted to maintain Canada's close connection with Britain, he felt that Canada should be true to itself first, and it was obvious that Canada had no stake in this struggle, thousands of miles away on the African continent. Laurier also hoped to keep Canada out of the war because the vast majority of French-Canadians wanted no part of it. But English-Canadians were strongly in support of Britain's call for assistance to put down the Boers, so Laurier agreed to send the initial group of 1000 volunteers. That number increased sevenfold as young English-Canadians flocked to enlist.

The British gained the upper hand in army-versus-army warfare in 1900, but the stubborn Boers switched to guerrilla tactics, striking the British in lightning raids and then disappearing into the countryside. The British didn't know how to handle that. Eventually they set up small forts and linked them with barbed wire to prevent the Boers from having free movement through the countryside.

When that didn't bring the enemy to heel, the British burned farmhouses and crops. They took women and children from the farms to what they called "places of refuge" which were in fact concentration camps. Some 20 000 Boer civilians died in these camps, mainly of fever, measles and pneumonia. In an effort at reconciliation when the war ended in 1902, the senior British general, Lord Kitchener, welcomed the surviving Boers into the British Empire, while Canada welcomed its troops home as conquering heroes.

One of those who came back was a young officer named John Macrae, who at the time felt war was the highest achievement of mankind. A decade and a half later, Macrae served in the First World War. By that point he had come to recognize the futility of armed struggle to attain national ends. He wrote *In Flanders Fields*, one of Canada's greatest poems, which described the sadness rather than the glory of war.

In a revealing sidelight to the war, a Mohawk Indian named J. O. Brant-Sero who volunteered to fight for Canada was turned down because of his race. An avid supporter of the Empire, he travelled to South Africa at his own expense and tried to join the army there, but once again he was refused. So he signed on as a civilian worker, moving animals to the front and supervising black African workers.

But even in that capacity, Brant-Sero was made to feel unwanted. A British sentry who mistook him for a Boer arrested him, and he had to get his African workers to verify his identity. He went to London, where he wrote a letter to *The Times* complaining that he was "too genuine a Canadian" to be permitted to fight for his country.

At the outbreak of the war in October 1899, the tribal council on Brant-Sero's Six Nations reserve near Brantford in Southern Ontario offered to send 300 warriors to South Africa. Although most of them were members of the 37th Haldimand Rifles militia unit, "the offer was courteously declined by the Minister of Militia," Brant-Sero pointed out in his letter to *The Times*.

He recalled that the Six Nations Indians fought for the British in the American Revolution, and moved from New York State to their new home in Upper Canada (later Ontario) after the Americans won independence. "A history of Canada cannot be written impartially without recounting the warlike deeds of the Six Nations," Brant-Sero said in his letter. "We believe we have an interest in the Empire bought by the blood of our ancestors." The Six Nations Indians had farmed in their Canadian home for over a century, "and their progress is the pride of all true Canadians. . . . There is scarcely a calling, trade or profession in which these Indians are not represented. In social life, politics and literature, we occupy no small place."

Brant-Sero was not given an official explanation as to why he could not serve in the Boer War. The closest he got was a personal letter from a friend, a major in the Colonial Division, who told him that "the authorities refuse absolutely to enlist others than of European descent to do fighting in the war; therefore I do not think there is much use in your persisting in your endeavors to be enlisted. I am sure you deserve every credit for your patriotism, which, however, is nothing more than I should expect from one of our faithful allies and friends, the Six Nations Indians."

But the question remained: Why did the authorities want only people of European descent to fight in the Boer War? *The Times* provided the answer in an editorial on Jan. 2, 1901. It said that the "special circumstances of warfare in South Africa" were the reason why Brant-Sero and his fellow-Indians couldn't fight. "It was all-essential," *The Times* explained, "that no excuse should be given for the native populations of South Africa to try and exterminate the Boers, a task many of them would undertake with no small pleasure; and it had, therefore, been decided that we should not employ troops of other than what is called European descent."

The British feared that the sight of

non-white soldiers in British uniforms would give the South African blacks murderous ideas, and that the "kaffirs," who were far more numerous than the Boers, would wipe out the whites. The British wanted to defeat the Boers, but they didn't want to win the war, then face the prospect of having to deal with massive numbers of unruly kaffirs.

As *The Times* put it: "The South African war is a war between two white races, or two races of European descent, waged in the presence of an enormously preponderant population of a totally different character. In such a war it was thought better not to call in the aid of races who habitually furnish a whole army of defenders of the Empire."

The Times assured Canada's Indians and other non-whites throughout the empire that this particular case "does not constitute a precedent binding us in any degree to follow a similar course in any other emergency that may arise. That would be a fetter upon our power of Imperial defence which could not be tolerated for a moment." In short, the Indians of Canada and non-white colonials around the globe were told not to be discouraged. The British would be delighted to have them put their lives on the line elsewhere in the empire.

Citizen-soldiers resented army's Colonel Blimp mentality

Hordes of visitors pour into Niagara-on-the-Lake, Ont., each summer. The thriving community, once the capital of Upper Canada, is full of trendy boutiques and gourmet restaurants. But when Canadians went to Niagara-on-the-Lake during the summer a century ago, they didn't go to shop and relax. They went to fulfil their obligation as members of the Canadian military.

The Niagara-on-the-Lake common, a vast expanse of grassland and trees on the outskirts of town, was the site of an annual summer camp for the militia. Thousands of men spent 12 grueling days there each summer. Some were sincerely trying to learn how to defend their country, but many treated the camp as a lark. Absenteeism was high, discipline was hard to enforce, and more than the normal amount of soldiers' grumbling emerged from the trainees' tents.

Canada didn't have a regular army in those days. A volunteer militia was much cheaper than a standing army, and Canadian leaders realized there was no need for a large permanent force. The militia could be called out in an emergency, as it was in the rebellion of 1885, but its main role was to defend the nation against foreign attack, and that's where the problem lay. Canada didn't really need defending. It had been at peace with the United States since the end of the War of 1812-14, and the chances were remote that an attack would come from elsewhere, say Mexico or China.

If the threat came from Europe or Asia, many Canadians felt the nation's defence should be entrusted to the British, particularly since the commander of the militia was a British major-general. Royal Navy warships patrolled Canada's coasts from bases at Halifax and Esquimault, near

Victoria. In case of war, those ships could intercept the enemy, and British troops could be brought to Canada by the Royal Navy, just as they were taken to other parts of the empire when fighting was necessary.

But some politicians in Canada pushed for the establishment of a big domestic army. Senator L. G. Power wanted a law requiring all males between the ages of 16 and 60 to serve in the militia. He also favored importing enough rifles and artillery to equip 100 000 men. Powers felt these moves were necessary not only because Canada might be attacked, but because Canada might be called upon to send troops to other parts of the world to help fight Britain's wars. "This is a time of wars and rumours of wars," Powers maintained. "If England becomes involved in a war with France, Germany or Russia, we shall have to bear a share of the burden and the risk; but, in the case of war with the United States, Canada will be called upon to fight for her national existence."

Power spoke enthusiastically of the large armies maintained by South American countries like Brazil and Chile, saying that our comparatively small militia put us in the minor leagues when it came to armed strength. But few taxpayers were interested in spending millions of dollars so Canada could create a banana-republic-style army, and the government didn't have the slightest interest in importing trainloads of weapons so it could send armed troops to fight around the globe. The war in South Africa was more than enough, as far as the prime minister, Sir Wilfrid Laurier, was concerned.

Still, the militia was one of the largest organizations in Canada, and the officers who ran it were eager to see it grow. It had about 35 000 members, many of whom had close ties to the Conservative party. The Tories had more than their share of members who enjoyed playing soldier. They belonged to regiments in their home communities, taking part in parades and social activities throughout the year. That made being in the militia rather enjoyable, but then came the summer, and the requirement that the militia men go to training camps like the one in Niagara. This was where they were supposed to learn to be real soldiers. But they didn't learn much, and many of them didn't take it seriously.

The desertion rate was as high as 25 per cent. Hard-liners called for the jailing of a few deserters to set an example, while moderates suggested a graded pay scale to encourage men to complete their three-year commitment. Under that scheme, a private would earn 50 cents a day in his first year, 60 cents in his second and 75 cents in his third. But money was not the big problem. It was more a matter of morale. Militia members knew they were not learning useful military skills. Instead, they were being indoctrinated into the ways of the early 19th century British Army, which put the emphasis on drill and ceremony rather than on learning how to fight a modern war.

It was obvious to the lowliest private that the militia training program was out of date. The drills were based on the idea that soldiers would attack in line formation. The emphasis was on standing close together in orderly ranks and advancing slowly toward the enemy. That was how wars were fought in Europe in their great-grandfathers' era, but this was a poor way of dealing with an enemy which engaged in hit-and-run guerrilla tactics, as the Boers of South Africa did. Instead of practising parade ground manoeuvres, the recruits knew they should be learning such things as how to adapt to the terrain, take cover when fired upon and shoot straight. But their officers insisted on doing things the old-fashioned way.

A. T. Hunter, a member of the militia, wrote a scathing article for *The Canadian Magazine* in August 1901 describing the "elaborate piece of tomfoolery" which went on at the camp in Niagara-on-the-Lake. Hunter complained that the "absurd little rifle range" was inadequate, and that trainees didn't get to check their targets to see if they had hit anything. He said the typical trainee was supplied with "a toy bullet like that of a boy's pea-rifle, which bullet he is told to place on the bull's-eye by aiming at another spot. Such practice is extremely valuable because it teaches the green shot not to aim at what he wants to hit."

Hunter said the summer trainees didn't learn how to scout the enemy or set up guards to protect an outpost. Instead, they were taught "formal dressed-for-dinner guard mounting," which including learning how to salute officers. "The value of this ceremony is that it teaches a sentry not to pay any attention to the insignificant person who slides behind the sentry's back, but to carefully hold up and give the correct salutation to officers and armed parties who approach with the intention of being properly discovered by the sentry."

But the disgruntled citizen-soldier reserved his harshest remarks for the endless hours of foot drill that militia members endured. He pointed out that in battle, troops needed to know how to get down quickly to avoid being hit. The British had learned this in South Africa, but the Canada militia was still being taught how to stand erect, shoulder to shoulder, and march in tight formation "as did their ancestors at Waterloo.... After seven days it has become an instinct to the dazed recruit to look to a flank, to hold himself erect with his manly breast away out in front and his rear away out behind, to keep touch at half-arm interval with the man to his left or right."

Hunter wondered why the Canadians were being "carefully instructed in exactly the very things which for months every correspondent, critic and returned soldier has been denouncing as deadly imbecilities." He laid the blame on old-fashioned officers and instructors who were infatuated with teaching drill. Hunter concluded that this approach was potentially deadly. He urged the authorities to modernize the militia so the Canadians would learn "how to fight in the field and not how to march to their deaths." But change didn't come quickly. Many of the Canadians who died in the First World War 15 years later were sent overseas after being trained in the same archaic fashion.

Was the future King George V slightly tipsy?

Many people thought the heir to the British throne was drunk as he travelled across Canada in the fall of 1901. But the Duke of York and Cornwall was just suffering from the flu, according to a journalist who covered the nation's first royal tour. Hector Charlesworth, a reporter for *The Mail and Empire* who covered Canada's first royal tour, said watery eyes, a red nose and a raspy voice plagued the duke after His Royal Highness got soaked in a rainstorm.

But even if the duke had been as drunk as a skunk, the Canadian public would never have learned about it from Charlesworth and the other journalists who travelled with the duke and reported on his activities. They knew how the game was played. Never, ever, did the press say a bad thing about a member of the royal family in those days. It just wasn't done.

The ever-flattering Charlesworth was a pioneer in what turned out to be a 20th century journalistic industry in Canada – covering the steady parade of British royals who travelled across the nation, to the great delight of the Canadian public. The public worshipped the royals in those days. All good journalists knew this, and accordingly they couldn't say enough good things about royal visitors.

So it's not surprising that Charlesworth found the duke to be not only cold sober, but just a splendid chap all around. The reporter described the 36-year-old future king as "bronzed" in complexion, and said his beard had a "leonine tinge.... I have never seen coloration just like it in anyone else's – the precise tint of a lion's mane."

The fawning journalist detected "democratic sentiments" every time the duke departed from the tour's rigid program and took a moment to speak to an ordinary citizen. Charlesworth offered this flattering assessment of the great man and

The Duke of Cornwall and York. <u>The Globe</u>, Sept. 18, 1901.

his manner:

> "For a full month I saw him every day in all sorts of costumes, often several different ones in a single day; and though he looked well in the blue uniform of an admiral which he wore by choice for official ceremonies, the garb which really became him best was an ordinary grey sack suit, with the grey bowler hat he favored. This set off his trim, well-knit figure and gave him a jaunty bearing altogether attractive."

According to Charlesworth, the misconception that the duke was drunk stemmed from the fact that he caught the flu right after he arrived in Canada. He was in Quebec City, the first stop on the tour, on horseback taking a salute from troops on the Plains of Abraham, when a violent storm sprang up. Other members of the royal party ran for cover, but the heir to the throne stood firm. He got soaked and chilled, but when an aide rode out and slipped a military cloak around his shoulders, the duke impatiently threw it off.

"He was stubborn in his determination to endure all the rigours of the storm just as the marching soldiers were obliged to," according to the worshipful Charlesworth. "Royalty is always subject to mean slanders, and when I got back to Toronto I was amazed and indignant to learn that on all sides it was alleged that he had been partially intoxicated at Montreal and Ottawa and throughout his tour of the West. This I knew to be false."

The duke was on the final leg of an around-the-world tour which was undertaken to show the solidity of the British Empire. His ship, the *Ophir*, left England on Feb. 27, 1901, just a few weeks after the state funeral for Queen Victoria. The 482-foot vessel, which carried the duke and his wife, his official party and some 500 marines, sailors and crew members, was spanking new. It was a magnificent floating symbol of the strength and grandeur of the British Empire.

The royal party visited Gibraltar, Malta and Port Said before passing through the Suez Canal, then stopping in Aden and Ceylon. India was bypassed because a separate visit to that country was planned. So it was on to Singapore, Australia and New Zealand. Then the *Ophir* turned around and sailed across the Indian Ocean to Mauritius and South Africa before crossing the Atlantic and making its way to Canada.

The *Ophir*'s principal passenger was no stranger to the high seas. As a young man, the duke had embarked upon a career as an officer in the Royal Navy. At that time it did not appear that he someday would become king. He was the second son of Prince Albert Edward, Queen Victoria's successor, who became King Edward VII upon her death. When George's elder brother died suddenly in 1892, George was ordered to give up the pleasant life in the navy and prepare for sovereignty.

He was already the Duke of York, and when he inherited the Duchy of Cornwall upon the death of his brother, he acquired the double-barrelled title of Duke of York and Cornwall. His sense of duty was so great that he not only took over his late brother's role as heir-apparent, he also married his late brother's fiancée. She was Princess Mary of Teck, the daughter of a German nobleman and the grand-daughter of King George III. While Mary was still a girl, she was chosen by Queen Victoria to one day become queen herself.

Mary duly bore George two sons, who were left at home while she and the duke travelled around the world. Eventually both of those boys became king. The elder son, Edward Albert, succeeded his father in 1936, but abdicated later that year to marry an American divorcee, Wallis Warfield Simpson. The second son, Albert Frederick George, became King George VI after Edward abdicated. George reigned until his death in 1952, when he was succeeded by the present Queen, Elizabeth II.

According to Charlesworth, Mary was better looking in person than she appeared to be from her photographs. As he delicately put it. Mary was "a blooming young matron . . . . Her face was rather heavy in repose, but the loveliness of her fair complexion, the warm and almost dazzling blue of her eyes, and the elegance of her svelte figure, made her more interesting in a purely feminine sense than anyone, judging merely by old photographs, might believe. Her teeth were very beautiful also, and her smile was particularly gracious."

The *Ophir*, accompanied by four warships, arrived on Sept. 16 at the wharf in Quebec City. Government buildings were decorated with giant banners which said "Bienvenue." Lord Minto, the governor general, and the prime minister, Sir Wilfrid Laurier, had boarded the ship upstream, and so got off with the duke and duchess and basked in the cheers.

Some 3000 school children sang a newly popular patriotic song, "O Canada, Land of Our Ancestors," which subsequently became Canada's national anthem. S. N. Parent, premier of the province and mayor of Quebec City, expressed his loyalty to the British Crown. Despite the fact that the city's population was largely French, Parent spoke in English. He described French-Canadians as "a free, united and happy people, faithful and loyal, attached to their King and country, rejoicing in their connection with the British Empire and in those noble self-governing institutions which are the palladium of their liberties."

Then it was on to Montreal, where the royal party got a less enthusiastic welcome. Most French-Canadians were opposed to the Boer War, which was currently in progress in South Africa. They saw the British aggression there as an attack against members of a racial minority who, like themselves, were living under British rule. Mayor Raymond Prefontaine insultingly delivered his address in French. Although the duke spoke French, he remained calm and politely replied in English.

A CPR train, which was a palace on wheels, took the royals across the continent to the West Coast and back. The train had nine brand new cars and the latest in technical wonders and comforts. These included telephones and electric lights. There were also showers lined with grey waterproof cloth, the very latest in novelty and fashion.

The royal couple's car was the last one in the train, so they could enjoy an uninterrupted view from the rear platform. The car was panelled in walnut, with moldings and ornaments touched with blue and gold, decorations in the Louis XV style and a deep carpet in a quiet grey-green shade. The sofa, chairs and table were upholstered in blue velvet to match the draperies. The couple's night coach provided separate bedrooms panelled in silk, blue for the duke and pink for the duchess.

The stops across the nation consisted mainly of dull and repetitive ceremonies, with such a litany of speeches that the duke could have been forgiven if he took the occasional drink. But there were some interesting moments.

In Ottawa, the royals went down the rapids of Chaudière in rafts and dined with French-Canadian rivermen who gave an exhibition of dancing on revolving logs. An old lumberman told the royals he hoped they would have long lives, plenty of money and lots of babies. In Calgary, 2000 Indians assembled in full war paint and put on a fine show, but that night two of them got drunk and were arrested. Some of the English reporters covering the tour lectured their Canadian colleagues on the folly of treating distinguished Indian potentates in such an undignified manner.

On the way back east, the train stopped in Manitoba so the duke could go on a hunting trip. The duchess passed the time by going for a stroll, stopping to chat with field hands and plunging her arm deep into a bag of wheat as it was filling under a threshing machine's separator. As the star-struck Charlesworth told it, "she seemed to revel in the sensation of the fresh wheat pouring on her snowy skin."

In Niagara Falls, the duke and duchess insulted the Americans by refusing to cross the border to greet the governor of New York State, who had come from Albany with his daughters expecting to meet the royal party. The explanation given was that the royals were travelling around the world, but never leaving British territory, to demonstrate the vastness of the empire. But perhaps security had something to do with the decision. U.S. President William McKinley had been shot in nearby Buffalo just a couple of months earlier. Canadian authorities surrounded the duke with bodyguards during his trip, fearing an attempt on his life. They need not have worried. The royals received a warm welcome everywhere they went. In a speech soon after he returned to England, the duke summed up the trip this way:

"If I were asked to specify any particular impression derived from our journey, I should at once place before all others that of loyalty to the Crown and attachment to the old country by the colonists. It was indeed touching to hear the invariable references to `home' even from the lips of those who never had been, nor were ever likely to be, in these islands. In this loyalty lies the strength of a true and living membership in the great and glorious British Empire."

Children were taught to love both their countries

A hundred years ago, Canadians celebrated the same four major summer holidays that we celebrate today. Then, as now, the summer season started with the 24th of May and ended with Labor Day, and there were two holidays in between – Canada's birthday on July 1 and a Monday in August, which went under a variety of names from province to province, just as it does today.

But at the turn of the century there was a fifth special day for English-Canadians. It was known as Empire Day. It was celebrated on May 23, the day before Victoria Day. Empire Day was new, having been introduced just a couple of years earlier by the Ontario ministry of education. The idea was quickly picked up by schools in the other English-speaking provinces. The fact that the Boer War was under way made Empire Day even more special, since Canada was seen to be doing its duty by sending soldiers to fight for the British Empire in South Africa.

Empire Day was not just a day off classes. It was intended to give school children a healthy dose of imperial sentiment, and to impress upon them the importance of maintaining Canada's ties with Great Britain. It reflected the feelings of many English-Canadians, who wrapped themselves in the Union Jack and thought of themselves not as lowly colonials, but as members of the greatest empire the world had ever known. The celebration of Empire Day clearly showed what French-Canadians meant when they said they had just one country to which they owed allegiance, but English-Canadians had two.

On Empire Day, the youngsters were bombarded by speeches in which they were told that good citizenship consisted of loving both Canada and Great Britain. Empire Day in 1901 was marked by tributes to the late Queen, who had died just four months earlier, as well as expressions of loyalty to her son and successor, King Edward VII. The children were told that while devotion to an individual monarch was important, loyalty to the institution of the monarchy was even more vital. The meaning of "the Queen is dead, long live the King" was explained to the children.

Events during the morning of Empire Day included the singing of such patriotic songs as "Rule Britannia" and "The Maple Leaf Forever," readings from Rudyard Kipling's patriotic poems, and speeches praising the value of British institutions. The afternoon in most schools was devoted to parades and sports programs.

Empire Day celebrations lasted for 30 years before falling off during the Depression. The day was revived in the 1950s, with limited success. Efforts were made to revive it in the 1960s and 1970s by changing the name first to Empire and Citizenship Day, and then to Commonwealth and Citizenship Day, but there was little interest, and May 23 eventually became just another school day.

But Victoria Day has lived on, a century after the death of Queen Victoria, with fireworks still a key part of the occasion, although the once-inflexible date has been massaged. Today Victoria Day is celebrated on May 24 only if that date happens to fall on a Monday. Otherwise the holiday is advanced to the previous Monday, because a three-day weekend is deemed more important than sticking to the precise birth date of the long-dead monarch.

July 1 – Canada Day as our politicians have decreed that we should call it now – was known as Dominion Day at the start of the century. It had special significance in 1901, because it was the 34th anniversary of Confederation, and so it was celebrated as the third-of-a-century mark in the country's history. In speeches that day, comparisons were drawn between 1867 and 1901 to show the progress which had been made over the years. For example, it was pointed out that the nation's area had expanded sixfold since 1867, thanks largely to the acquisition of the North-West Territories, and that Canada's land mass was almost as large as Europe's, while its population was only as big as Belgium's.

In a Dominion Day editorial, *The Globe* said that Canada's position as a member of the British Empire was beyond question, but its relations with the United States could change. The newspaper noted that the Americans had been making friendly gestures of late, but Canada should not "display any eagerness to win that friendship." Rather, Canada should maintain an attitude of "good-humored independence" from its giant neighbor. Dominion Day in Toronto and across the nation was celebrated much as it is today, in a laid-back manner. Torontonians enjoyed the sound of bells ringing in the fire halls and schools for 15 minutes in the morning, followed by a parade, a regatta, sporting events, excursion trains and band concerts.

In Regina, the Sons of Scotland held their annual sports day at the Territorial Exhibition Grounds. The big event was a lacrosse match, with the locals losing 4-2 to Moose Jaw. Other events included high jumping, pole vaulting, hammer throwing and a tug of war between teams from the town and the North-West Mounted Police barracks. Both teams pulled "like grim death with every muscle and sinew straining to the utmost," *The Leader* reported, but the townies finally jerked the ribbon over the scratch mark and won the day.

In the evening, there was a concert in the Regina town hall, featuring a rendition of "My Heart's in the Highlands" by Mr. Angus, the new manager of the Bank of Montreal. Songs and recitations by many other performers took so long that the scheduled presentation of the sports prizes at the end of the evening had to be abandoned due to the lateness of the hour, *The Leader* reported, "much to the disappointment of some of the competitors, a few of whom were present solely for that object."

The holiday in August, now called a variety of things including Civic Holiday, Heritage Day, Simcoe Day and so forth, was also a vague holiday with an uncertain date at the start of the century. In most places it was celebrated on the first Monday in August, but in Manitoba it was held on Monday, Aug. 15, 1901, and was noteworthy because 2000 people climbed on a special train to Grand Forks, North Dakota. The Canadian visitors received a warm welcome from their American cousins, and no thought was given to the fogies back home who insisted that the Yankees were secretly plotting to take over Canada to fulfil their "manifest destiny."

U.S. and British flags fluttered everywhere in the light breeze under the cloudless sky in Grand Forks. The Canadian visitors were "welcomed by an outburst of enthusiasm and cordiality by the citizens of Grand Forks never before equaled in the history of Winnipeg excursions to American cities," the Manitoba *Free Press* reported. Following a big parade, members of secret societies, including Oddfellows, Workmen and Eagles, were taken to the lodges of their American brethren for lunch and drinks. Winnipeg's 90th Battalion militia unit drilled with members of the North Dakota National Guard, looking just as sharp as the Americans, but an international sports contest was a rout. The American hosts beat the Canadians in baseball 17-2.

Labor Day marked the end of the summer across Canada in 1901, just as it does today. There were parades to honor the working men and women of the country, especially in the cities where organized labor was strong. In Toronto, 83 000 people crammed into the Toronto Exhibition grounds. *The Globe* newspaper reported that the place "was pulsating with life," and concluded that "altogether, with the people, well dressed, prosperous looking, the exhibits showing what is best in art and manufacture, the visitor would have found at the Exposition yesterday an epitome of the best of Canadian life."

Canadian homes for English orphans

The telegram from the U.S. Immigration Service official was short and to the point: "Laura Cummings in custody. Come Monday and take her back." The 15-year-old Laura had been arrested in a brothel in Buffalo, N.Y., in April 1900. The curt message was sent to Barnardo's Homes, the child welfare agency in Toronto responsible for Laura's well-being. Alfred de Brissac Owen, the agency's director, dispatched a private detective to retrieve the troubled and troublesome teenager.

Barnardo's was a British organization which sent orphans and poor children from the slums of East London to live in Canada. Laura was one of the many boys and girls who had been dispatched across the Atlantic, but she was special because she had some sort of hold over Owen. In a note which came to light many years later, Laura promised Owen that "I will keep truly the secret of your coming out to Buffalo," an apparent reference to an illicit visit he made to the girl when she was in the States. The implication that they were engaged in sex was supported by the U.S. official who sent the telegram. He accused Owen of "immoral behavior," but was powerless to act because of the international border.

So nothing came of it, and Owen carried on as the Canadian head of the agency. Barnardo's was a huge organization. It operated several homes in England, and each year sent hundreds of children, from toddlers to adolescents, to Canada. The last group of Barnardo children came to Canada in the late 1930s.

Founded in the 1870s by a British philanthropist and physician named Thomas John Barnardo, the agency arranged for the youngsters to work as farm hands or domestic servants in Canada. The idea was to give them a better life than the one they had in England. At that time, poor families in Britain received no help from the government. They and their children were sent to workhouses, or the children were turned out into the streets to fend for themselves. They often ended up in prostitution or crime.

The theory was that a combination of fresh air and wholesome hard work in Canada would turn them into productive adults. But Laura Cummings and others like her were not happy about being uprooted from their homes, bad as they might have been. No thought was given to the children's rights. They were taken from their familiar environment and sent overseas against their will, or they were persuaded to go by officials who made glowing promises.

Life in Canada was rarely as good as they said it would be. Sometimes the children were beaten by their Canadian employers, and usually they were expected to work long hours for little or no money, but the children's most common complaints were the cold weather and loneliness.

But Barnardo called his operation a "rescue agency," and in powerful circles he was admired as a great Christian doing the Lord's work. At the turn of the century, about 1000 children a year were arriving by ship from Liverpool, where they were sent off to the accompaniment of bands, banners and hymns. Their possessions were carried in a single wooden box. Pinned to their coats were the names and addresses of the places in Canada where they were being sent. When they arrived in Halifax, they were loaded on trains known as Barnardo Specials and sent out across the nation.

Many of them went to the cities of Ontario, where wealthy people were always looking for cheap domestic servants. Others were sent to farms in the Northwest Territories, where labor was scarce and a strong child could be kept busy working from dawn to dusk. But Barnardo said that their life in Canada was much better than it had been in England. He called the children "street arabs" and "babes of London's moral slime." He conjured up images of vice and corruption in London's East End, and personally went out into the streets at night to gather up children sleeping in alleys and scrounging food from garbage containers.

Barnardo was good at raising money and winning support from prominent people in Britain and Canada. He played up stories of children who did well in Canada and painted pictures of firm but loving foster families raising youngsters to become useful adults. "Every boy rescued from the gutter is one dangerous man the less," he stated. "Each girl saved from a criminal course is a present to the next generation of a virtuous woman and a valuable servant."

But critics accused Barnardo of transporting England's social problems to Canada. They maintained that nobody but the cold-hearted English would allow their children to be taken from their homeland and sent overseas to whatever fate might be in store for them. There's no doubt that many of the Barnardo children had a less-than-ideal life when they came to Canada.

Laura Cummings, the girl who ended up in the Buffalo whorehouse, arrived in Toronto in 1897 as a wild and stage-struck girl of 12 with no intention of settling into a dull life in Canada. By the time she was 14, she had left her job as a servant girl and become an actress with a theatre company in Toronto. A Barnardo official stepped in, and Laura was placed in another home as a servant, but she ran away again and ended up hanging around concert halls and saloons in Buffalo before her arrest in the brothel. After being returned to Toronto, she was quickly shipped back to England.

The Canadian newspapers made much of cases in which Barnardo children got into trouble. The stories usually took the angle that "bad blood" was being brought into Canada, and that guttersnipes were taking up police and court time and costing the taxpayers money. There was little concern about the risks being taken in placing the children in unsupervised homes. While Canadians who applied to employ a Barnardo child had to provide information on their finances and religious beliefs, there was no examination of their personalities or their motives, and no screening to weed out unsuitable adults. Usually just one visit a year was made by a Barnardo official to the home, so the children were at the mercy of the people who employed them.

But Barnardo accented the positive, conjuring up visions of Canada as a wonderful land with "pure, healthy surroundings where vice, drunkenness and harsh treatment are unknown . . . . home, too, where family life and religious life are a blessed reality situated in a fair, garden-like country." He presented case studies to support this happy description. There was, for example, William Arthur Hughes, whose mother died when he was seven and whose father died a year later. His grandmother looked after William and four other children, but they were so poor they were starving. William was sent to Canada when he was 10. He thrived on a farm, growing up to become a strong young man skilled at working with machinery.

Barnardo claimed that only two per cent of the children who came to Canada got into trouble with the courts. Nothing at all was said about those who were abused in various ways, including sexually. Such things were usually not talked about at that time, and how the children made out was pretty much a matter of luck. The fortunate ones were treated by their employers as family members, while the unlucky ones were virtually slave laborers, or worse. It wasn't until 1925 that the Canadian government protected children by banning the entry into Canada of those under the age of 14 without their parents.

As for Laura Cummings, nothing was heard of her after she was returned to England. Owen, the agency director who apparently had sex with her, remained in his post until 1919, when he was accused of having sex with another Barnardo girl. He lost his job, but the case didn't go to court.

George Washington never won a battle

History, they say, is written by the winners. Not always. Consider the version of history put forward by J. Castell Hopkins in Canada's first encyclopedia, which was published over the course of the last years of the 19th century and the first years of the 20th. Hopkins, the editor of the five-volume encyclopedia, invited "a corps of eminent writers and specialists" to prepare articles on a variety of topics, but some things were so important that he handled them himself.

The American Revolution was one such topic, and reading what Hopkins has to say about it puts the event in a new perspective. Modern Canadians are bombarded by so much American propaganda that we seldom stop to think that there was a British point of view concerning the revolution. That's the view that Hopkins puts forward in his encyclopedia.

The way the Americans tell it, the colonists were oppressed by the British, who tried to impose unjust taxes on the colonists. Hopkins, in contrast, sees the colonists as ingrates and shirkers, unwilling to pay their share for all the wonderful things that Britain was doing for them.

"England had poured out blood and treasure like water for her colonies, and she naturally thought that they should make some return," Hopkins writes.

And what about that great American patriot, Patrick Henry, who bravely told the British to "give me liberty or give me death"? To Hopkins, Henry was a demagogue. Hopkins accuses him of helping to create not a new nation, but rather "a hopeless and permanent division of the (English) race." According to Hopkins, the American writer and political philosopher Tom Paine "stirred up all the bad blood and ignorant prejudices of a scattered people."

And what about King George III, vilified by the Americans as a tyrant? Hopkins paints him as a strong-willed ruler who simply "wanted to retain some control over his colonies." He even compares the king to the legendary U.S. President Abraham Lincoln. Both men simply wanted to preserve the unity of their nations, Hopkins maintains.

He claims that American General George Washington never won a battle, and that the Americans would have lost the war if it hadn't been for the help they got from France, Spain and Holland. Hopkins even makes the Declaration of Independence look bad, portraying it as "a distinct breach of faith on the part of the aggressive section of the colonies toward their friends and sympathizers in England."

The encyclopedia continues in this anti-American vein in a section on the United Empire Loyalists, who fled to Canada after the Americans won independence. This section of the encyclopedia, written by Col. George T. Denison, refutes the idea that the Loyalists were fools who were turned out of the United States after backing the wrong side in the revolution. Denison emphasized the many injuries inflicted upon these loyal British subjects by the rebellious Americans. The Loyalists were beaten up, robbed of their possessions and lands, and even had their women "insulted, pelted and abused," Denison explains.

He says Canada was lucky to get these fine people who fled north after the war. "We Canadians should thank God that our country was founded by so grand a type of men as the United Empire Loyalists," Denison says. "We are reaping the benefit of their honest character and lofty aims today." He describes the 30 000 Loyalists who fled to Canada as "people of culture and social distinction," and concludes that "Canada owes deep gratitude indeed to her southern kinsmen, who, from Maine to Georgia, picked out their choicest spirits and sent them forth to people her northern wilds."

These pro-British interpretations of history are the highlights of the encyclopedia, a 2700-page, five-volume epic which can still be found in some libraries, tucked away in the rare books section or sitting on some back shelf in the reference section. It's written in what seems today to be a stilted fashion, and it puts heavy emphasis on business and economics. You can find tons of information on mining, agriculture, forestry, the fisheries, insurance companies and the like, plus smaller amounts of material on the arts, literature, journalism, natural history, the militia and Canada's cities. The church receives a massive amount of coverage, with details of the history and theology of every religion in Canada, from the Anglicans and Roman Catholics to the African Methodists and Christadelphians.

In a preface written for the final volume, the chief justice of the Quebec Court of Queen's Bench, Sir Alexandre Lacoste, says that from the encyclopedia "we can obtain the most varied and comprehensive information in regard, practically, to every subject relating to Canada." But in fact there's almost nothing about the day-to-day lives of ordinary Canadians. You can't even find interesting pictures of people at work or at play. The photos are virtually all formal portraits of turn-of-the-century big-wigs, giving a human face to government, the church and big business, but no feeling for what day-to-day life was like for the common folk.

Still, the encyclopedia was in keeping with its times. This was the era when the British class system prevailed in Canada. In the minds of people like J. Castell Hopkins, those who were rich, powerful and important were the only ones who counted. It was to be several decades into the 20th century before we adopted the concept that "everybody is somebody."

Chapter 3
How the West Was Done

Regina was a busy but a muddy little place

If someone had told Regina's 2249 citizens in 1901 that their community's population would swell to 180 000 by the end of the century, they would have been pleased, but not surprised. The people of the Queen City have always had high hopes, and they've done well considering Regina's lack of natural advantages. There were no trees to provide lumber, fuel and shade, no hills to provide beauty and drainage, and no river to provide transportation or water.

Fertile soil was the town's only natural asset, but even that was not without a drawback. The soil turned into a gumbo-like muck when it got wet, creating a constant clamor from the citizens for the town council to build wooden sidewalks. You can get a sense of what it was like in Regina at the start of the century from this description by Bernard McEvoy, a writer who stopped by Regina on a trip from Toronto to the Pacific Coast:

> *"It straggles out from the railway on to the surrounding prairie, and its streets are the primeval black prairie soil, than which nothing is better for producing a thick, rich, tenacious mud . . . and should some of the seven inch-*

Women crossing a muddy street in Regina. SPA Williams Collection

es of rain, which is all the Territories are favoured with during the year, come during your visit, you would stand in danger of being covered in mud from head to heel."

Harry Graham, an aide to Lord Minto, the governor general, stopped in Regina on a cross-Canada trip and found the place terrible beyond belief.

"At Regina the country grows even more desolate and bare, and there is not even a shrub to refresh the weary plain-tired eye. The reason for the selection of this spot as the site of a town will always remain a mystery, as it would be impossible to find a more unloveable flat and unprofitable position. The mystery which surrounds the choice, by any sane white man, of this town for his earthly habitation is even more deeply shrouded and incomprehensible.

"There can be nothing to do here in the way of amusement except, perhaps, play billiards. It would be almost absurd to go out for a ride, as it is never possible to get out of sight of one's own front door. There is no privacy, because your neighbor, even though he be 10 miles off, can, from his window, observe you hanging out the clothes in your garden, or hoeing your turnips, and can almost see what you are having for dinner."

Why was Regina built in the middle of a flat and treeless plain on the bottom of a dried-up glacial lake, which accounted for its rich but sticky soil? The town owed its existence to the Canadian Pacific Railway, which less than two decades earlier had came rolling across the prairies from Winnipeg, 370 miles to the east. In August 1882, the train tracks met up with a tiny stream named Pile of Bones Creek. Six settlers set up a camp, and Regina was born.

More people came, if not in droves at least in decent numbers, and they built a nice little town during the remainder of the 19th century. By 1901 Regina had solidly established itself, but there had been no giant leaps forward, nor was there anything remotely resembling a boom.

Still, the first 19 years saw many interesting events and developments, including the trial and hanging of the infamous Louis Riel in 1885 and the establishment five years later of the Regina Electric Light and Power Company, which grew to the point where it could supply juice for street lights every night of the week, rather than just on Saturdays, as was the case when it started.

One of Regina's economic advantages was that it was the political capital of the Northwest Territories, so there were jobs for a good number of bureaucrats and officials. They ranged all the way from His Honor Amadee Emmanuel Forget, the lieutenant governor, and Col. Hugh Richardson, senior judge of the Supreme Court of the Northwest Territories, down to the four turnkeys who manned the town jail and the clerks who were kept busy pushing paper at the Dominion Land Office.

There were also quite a few cops around, since Regina was the headquarters of the North-West Mounted Police. Perhaps that accounted for the fact that there was little in the way of serious crime. At one meeting of the town council in 1901, considerable time was spent discussing the need for stricter enforcement of the bylaw which required bicyclists to dismount while riding on a sidewalk within 20 feet of a pedestrian. The usual fine for failing to do so was 25 cents.

The leadership of the town consisted of business and professional people who ran the municipal council and held the key positions on the various cultural, social and sports organizations. The only people who could vote in those days were men, spinsters and widows who owned property assessed at a value of at least $200. In 1901, there were just 330 names on the voters' list. The census of that year showed the town's population was 2249, consisting of 1208 males and 1041 females. Well over 70 per cent were of British origin, but an ethnic community had established itself in the east end. It was known as Germantown, and was populated not only by Germans, but by Ukrainians and a handful of Indians and Chinese.

There were lots of organizations and activities in the town. These included cycling, tennis, golf, baseball, curling, lacrosse and both men's and women's hockey teams, as well as the Assiniboia Club, the Orange Lodge, the Odd Fellows, the Masons, the YMCA, the Women's Christian Temperance Union, the Royal Templars of Temperance and the Regina Musical Society, which put on Gilbert and Sullivan's *HMS Pinafore* at Christmas in 1900.

There were three weekly newspapers, all lively and opinionated, which helped make the town an interesting place to live. But the town's water supply and sewage system left a lot to be desired. The water came from the creek and three wells. Outdoor toilets were the norm. They were cleaned out by a man known as the scavenger, who dumped the waste at the edge of town.

There was a 25-bed hospital, public and Catholic schools, a teachers' college, telephone service, several banks, half a dozen land investment companies, Anglican, Methodist, Presbyterian, Baptist and Roman Catholic churches, several lawyers and doctors, blacksmiths, wagon makers, brewers and other craftsmen, a couple of dozen stores, several hotels and bars, including the Landsdowne, the Waverly, the Windsor and the Palmer, and a Chinese laundry operated by Mack and Sam Sing.

All in all, Regina was doing all right, but its progress had been retarded by a stubborn economic depression in Canada during the 1890s. As it happened, recovery coincided with the start of the new century, and that was good news for Regina. By late 1901, things had picked up considerably. Less than two years before, the Regina *Leader* reported, "a person house-hunting could have a choice of several houses on each street, and could offer a rate of rent instead of accepting one. All this is now changing. There is not a vacant house in the whole town, and rents are being gradually raised .... Several houses have been built averaging $3,000 each."

The Leader said there was a one-word explanation for this great change. Wheat. That fall, the fields were yielding twice as much wheat as they had in the previous year. Farmers were averaging 35.5 bushels to the acre. This was generating so much money, that "debts are being paid, sound investments are being made, trade is stimulated, and there is a general increase in comfort, luxury, elegances, and all around is that air of cheeriness that is the surest sign of affluence and prosperity."

Newcomers were arriving in the town each day, and while some of them were part of the great wave of central Europeans which had started coming to Canada, most were of British origin. As *The Leader* put it:

> "All are of a very desirable class. Not a few are Canadians returning from the States; experienced farmers from Ontario with means are also in evidence and there is a good sprinkling of the best sort of men from other nationalities who are establishing excellent farms."

But as the community looked forward to its bright future, there was an interesting development which shed light on its not-too-distant past. In early 1901, the federal government released the results of an inquiry it had conducted into the sale of building lots when Regina was first established. The trustees appointed to look after the sale of the lots turned out to be sharpies. They took money from purchasers of the lots and used it to erect a large building to house stores and offices. Some of those offices were rented to the government, which paid what the report called "enormous rent." Then the trustees sold the building to the government for much more than it was worth.

They also paid themselves fat salaries for their work as trustees, and were involved in a kickback scheme through their connections with companies operating in Manitoba and Scotland. "That the trustees should make such an enormous profit out of the Government would seem most improper," the report concluded. But the report didn't recommended that the trustees be prosecuted. It simply said they should be required to repay the money they stole.

Interestingly, four downtown streets in Regina are named after the discredited trustees, whose names were R. B. Angus, Sir Donald Smith, E. B. Osler and William B. Scarth. When people drive down these streets today, few of them realize that these founding fathers of the city were crooks.

Life, death and trivia – it was all in *The Leader*

You certainly got a lot for your nickel when you bought a newspaper a hundred years ago. Consider *The Leader*, one of the three weekly newspapers published in Regina at the start of the 20th century. The 10-page paper contains a great deal of information – everything from world events and wonder cures to social news and advertising. It gives a good idea of what life was like in the small prairie town. Here's a summary of the contents of the first issue published in the new century, printed on Thursday, Jan. 3, 1901:

The top story is on the Boer War, and while the newspaper supports the war effort, it takes an aggressive angle in this story. It points out that the commanding general, Lord Kitchener, is "gagging the press" to hide the fact that the British are having trouble repelling the Boer invasion of the Cape Colony. In one action, the Boers were mistaken for British troops,

Leader office.
SPA R-B 9884

and "the result was the Boers were able to occupy all the commanding positions and the British had to retire." The story also says the British War Office will pay a bonus to troops. This "gratuity" will be 2500 pounds sterling for field marshals, with lesser amounts down through the ranks. Captains will get 60 pounds, and privates just five pounds.

The Regina Musical Society did a fine job during its recent performance of Gilbert and Sullivan's operetta *H.M.S. Pinafore*. A recent meeting of the Liberal party was a great success. "The room was well filled and the proceedings were enthusiastic." A coal shortage in nearby Lumsden is being slowly relieved "by the arrival of the occasional car." Settlers in Yellowgrass are "availing themselves of excursion rates to take a trip to the east." Indian Head has a new skating and curling rink, but still needs a watchmaker, undertaker, bank and, following a series of burglaries, a policeman who is "not afraid to attend to duty."

A big ad on the front page urges people to buy Slater shoes, which can be distinguished "from the hordes of nameless shoes" by a student's chalk slate engraved on the sole. The shoes sell for $4 and $5. Another ad says Dr. Chase's Syrup of Linseed and Turpentine is good for treating asthma, especially if taken along with Dr. Chase's Nerve Food. How do you know if you needed Dr. Chase's help? "The victim is suddenly aroused by an intense anguish in the chest, the breathing is accompanied by a loud wheezing, the face becomes flushed, and bathed in perspiration; he gasps for air, believing that each moment may be his last."

In the trivia department, *The Leader* reports that Queen Victoria "rarely sends any telegrams to any member of the Royal Family, or to her intimate friends, otherwise than in cypher, a system of figure cyphers having been carefully arranged for her and their use." The income of the Emperor of Russia for one day is 5000 pounds sterling. A well near Pittsburgh,

Penn., has been dug 5532 feet deep. To wash woolens without shrinking them, squeeze the water out, don't twist it out.

An ad for Canada Permanent and Western Canada Mortgage Corporation has this advice on how to get ahead: "Some of our best deposit accounts were begun in a modest way. By adding small sums at regular intervals, and by the accumulation of interest, they have grown till they now show handsome balances." The interest rate is three per cent.

On the lighter side, William's girlfriend asks if he really loves her. William replies: "Course I does. Think I been walkin' six miles a week ter see you fur the las' year 'cause I hated you?"

The Leader reminds its readers that a yearly subscription costs just $1 if paid in advance. *The Leader* claims it's better than the other two newspapers in Regina. It says *The Standard* makes up the news, while *The West* is anti-French and racist. *The Leader* "has undoubtedly a larger circulation than any other North-West newspaper, and is correspondingly the most valuable advertising medium."

When the Prince of Wales visited Canada in 1860, it was "one of the greatest events in the history of this country." Now that his son, the Duke of York, is coming to Canada later this year, "he will find the grand opening up of the great North-West," which is part of "a budding nation inhabited by an intelligent and enterprising people."

When the students at the teachers' college, known as the Normal School, arrived a few months ago, "Regina was taken by storm" by young scholars from across the country. Now they're graduating, and so it's farewell to "the honor graduate from eastern colleges and the ambitious student from the public schools; the young man making his first venture in the wild west and the young lady whose entire life had been spent in a prairie home."

Henriette Forget, wife of the lieutenant governor, has a message for the women of Canada at the dawn of the 20th century:

> "Surely the lesson to be learnt from the war is the evil that arises from racial prejudices and racial animosities. That in this our beloved country we shall avoid such feelings, is my message to the women of Canada. Let

Walter Scott, editor of the <u>Leader</u>, and wife. SPA R-A 6125.

us remember that whether we be English, Scotch, Irish, French, Teutonics or Slavics, we are yet all Canadians, and being Canadians we are British too, and as British women we shall have great influence in the homes of the empire. Let that influence be directed to the promoting of harmony among all classes, races and creeds and to creating that good will among men which is the safest and surest way of securing peace on earth."

Atlantic Steam Shop Lines offers passage to Britain from Halifax, St. John, Portland and New York. Cabins are available for $42.50 to $80 and upward. Intermediate fares are $32 and upward. Steerage is $22 and upward. The CPR excursion fare to Montreal and Toronto is $43.70.

From *Pall Mall* magazine:

"At the start of the 19th century, English was spoken by only 21 million people and was surpassed by French, German, Spanish and probably Italian. Today English is the language of 130 million people, or nearly twice as many as any of the others mentioned . . . . It looks very much as if English will, during the next century, become the universal language of mankind."

Arthur J. Reed, who used false names and phony cheques in a forgery scheme, is going to prison for 18 months. The judge told Reed that he was a deadbeat.

An ad that looks like a news story reads as follows: "I had vascular disease of the heart," writes Mrs. J. S. Goode of Truro, N.S. "I suffered terribly and was speechless and partially paralyzed. One dose of Dr. Agnew's Cure for the Heart gave me relief, and before I finished one bottle I was able to go about. Today I am a well woman."

"Mr. Jas. Hudson of the Coventry settlement (near Moose Jaw) while driving on Wednesday afternoon with Mr. Jonathan, saw a badger and discharged one barrel of his gun at the animal. He then went over to it and either struck it with the butt of the gun or poked it while it was in a hole and discharged the other barrel, the contents lodging in his breast. He lived one hour."

Even though it was 40 below zero on New Year's Day, there were "a large number of callers" at Government House for the first levee of the new century.

"The house of Const. Main NWMP and all the contents including $345.00 in money was destroyed by fire on Wednesday. The fire was caused by one of the children lighting a match which set fire to a curtain and in a very few moments the building was in flames. Mr. Main is at present in the Yukon. There was no insurance."

How a Yankee outsmarted Canadian sharpies

How can you use a little vinegar to make a lot of money? Emil Meilicke knew the answer to that question when he went to the Dundurn area in Canada's North-West Territories in the summer of 1901. The resourceful American put a little prairie soil on the saucer and poured the vinegar on top. When it fizzed, he knew the land was good for growing wheat. The test showed the clay contained carbonate of lime. Meilicke knew this kind of soil would support a good crop of grain.

Meilicke hid behind a bush to perform his test. He didn't want the opportunistic Canadians travelling with him to see what he was up to. His companions tried to pass themselves off as friends, but the 50-year-old Meilicke, an experienced farmer and businessman, knew they were speculators who would snap up vacant land if they thought they could resell it and make a quick buck.

Meilicke was too smart for them. He threw them off the scent by saying he intended to go elsewhere to look at property. Then he quietly bought 24 000 acres near Dundurn, south of Saskatoon, and invited his friends and relatives in the U.S. to take up homesteads on neighboring plots. Together, they acquired a large block of land which turned out to be one of the nation's finest wheat-producing districts.

Many others before Meilicke had looked at the same land and concluded it was useless for agriculture. To the untrained eye, it seemed like a desert. But Meilicke's vinegar test revealed that it was not too alkali, as the others who came before him had assumed. He also determined that the soil was "warm," meaning that it would foster quick wheat growth and the crop could be harvested before the first frost.

Meilicke was a German who immigrated to the United States in the 1860s. He had previously developed farm land and sold it at a good profit in Minnesota. He hoped to do the same thing in Canada. He was aided in this business venture by the federal government, which hoped to develop the national economy by building up population and agriculture in the West. Ottawa dispatched agents to the United States, Britain and Europe to persuade people to come to Canada. Up to that point, many immigrants had come, but a lot of them had subsequently left. Most went to the States, where the climate was warmer and the opportunities for success were greater.

But by the late 1890s, all the free farm land south of the border had been taken up. Now it was Canada's turn. Ottawa's public relations campaign sold the North-West Territories as "the last, best West." The government offered homesteaders 160-acre plots. It was a terrific deal. All the settlers had to do was pay a $10 registration fee, build a home, and farm the land. If they did that, they were granted legal title to the property. Meilicke's interest in Canada was sparked by a government agent he met at the Minnesota State Fair. The agent showed him samples of wheat grown in the Territories, together with good soil reports and predictions of strong wheat sales to the United Kingdom.

"I wondered if good wheat could actually be grown a distance of five or six hundred miles from us, toward the North Pole," Meilicke wrote later in his autobiography. "When I hinted that land agents had not been above exhibiting unauthentic samples, he pointed out that he was no ordinary land agent but an employee of the Canadian government, and that the samples shown had been supplied by that government itself."

When the agent offered to provide free transportation to Canada so he could assess the West's potential, Meilicke accepted. Once he saw the fertile soil and the low price of land in the Dundurn area, he decided to acquire far more than a single homesteader's farm of 160 acres. He had a good deal of cash, and was in a position to buy land. The land around Dundurn was owned by the Temperance Colonization Society, a group of teatotallers who had received a huge land grant from the government two decades earlier. They planned to establish an alcohol-free community in Saskatoon, and then spread south. But their venture had not prospered.

While other towns at the start of the century were doing fairly well – Regina had 2249 people, Prince Albert had 1785 and Moose Jaw had 1585 – Saskatoon could barely scrape together 100 bodies to qualify as a village. At that point, there was little reason to believe Saskatoon would eventually grow to become Saskatchewan's largest city, with a population near the end of the 20th century of about 190 000.

In one pessimistic account written in 1901, Saskatoon was described as

> *"a sprinkling of rude shacks dotted upon a raw prairie and housing a mere 113 sanguine souls; one wretched railway over which a most miserable mixed passenger and freight train came and went upon no schedule, but merely as convenience dictated; one tiny single-room school; no streets; no sidewalks; neither sewers nor waterworks; no light; no newspaper, no telephone – in fact, nothing that bore the faintest semblance of simplest comfort."*

But Meilicke wasn't concerned about the inadequacies of poor little Saskatoon. In fact, he felt that his newly acquired property's closeness to the village "would be a great advantage in the early stages of settlement. But we made a point of keeping our own council," he continued, "fearful of what our companions, through their scrip, might do to injure our plans."

The "companions" he was talking about were the Canadian hustlers who tagged along, watching Meilicke to see what he would do, and the "scrip" he mentioned was written permission issued by the government giving the possessor the right to acquire 240 acres, anywhere in the Territories. Originally, this scrip had been issued to the Metis to settle land claims they had against the government, but many of the Metis sold their scrip to speculators to acquire cash, and the speculators used the scrip to make fast profits.

"My companions' plan," Meilicke recalled in his autobiography, "was to buy scrip at one dollar and fifty cents per acre and secure with it the homesteads beside the land purchased by us, and sell at a large profit to the people I hoped to bring in. This would, of course, prevent those whom I would bring in from getting the free homesteads beside us."

But the crafty Meilicke outfoxed the Canadians. He appointed a trustworthy Scotsman in Saskatoon as his agent. After returning to Minnesota and lining up the Americans who would join him in his venture in Canada, Meilicke sent his agent $15 for each of them – $10 to register their homestead and a $5 commission. The agent duly registered the homelands, on the proviso that the Americans would soon arrive to settle on the land.

And so it was that the American who helped settle the Canadian West outsmarted the local sharpies. Meilicke bragged later in his autobiography that the Canadians "were waiting like cats watching mice," but the mouse from Minnesota was too quick for them.

From political hack to great journalist

One of the best journalists Canada has ever produced started the new century with a new job. John Wesley Dafoe became editor of the Manitoba *Free Press* in 1901. He held that job for 43 years, and made a name for himself not only as a thundering partisan journalist and an ardent spokesman for the West, but also as a great Canadian patriot.

Dafoe was born in 1866, the son of a farmer in Eastern Ontario. He received little education, but he had a gift for words and at the age of 17 got a job on the *Weekly Star* in Montreal. In one of his first assignments, the big, redheaded kid who looked like a country bumpkin went undercover to expose a racket in which young men were sold expensive clothes in a store, only to find cheap imitations in the package when they got home.

Dafoe soon became the *Star*'s correspondent in Ottawa. It was a big job for the young reporter, but he had natural talent as a journalist. He broke a major story in 1885 when he overheard in the corridors of Parliament that the government of Sir John A. Macdonald intended to hang Louis Riel.

In those days, politics got even bigger play in Canadian newspapers than it does today. The stories were a combination of government affairs, party propaganda and

J. W. Dafoe in 1927.

entertainment. Many publishers and journalists were blatantly partisan. Dafoe soon decided which side of the political fence he was on. He became a Liberal and stayed one for the rest of his life. He worked on various papers over the next 15 years, including six years as a reporter at *The Free Press* in Winnipeg, where he grew to know and love the West.

In the early 1890s, he honed his skills as the Tory-bashing editor of the Montreal *Herald*. He developed a technique of hammering away at one topic, day after day, week after week. Years later, he compared this heavy-handed method of swaying public opinion to building a bridge by tossing weighty stones into a swift-moving stream, and gradually making a path across the channel.

When the Montreal *Herald* folded in 1895, Dafoe's broadside-writing days were over, temporarily. He became editor of the *Family Herald*. It was owned by Hugh Graham, a prominent Conservative publisher, but the *Family Herald* was non-partisan in order to appeal to the largest-possible number of rural readers. Graham decreed that the paper must carry innocuous human interest stories and features on such subjects as prize-winning cows. Dafoe found the job dull, but he was good at it, and over the next six years he doubled the circulation to 100 000.

By 1901, he had a wife and four children, and was looking for a challenge. That's when Sir Clifford Sifton came looking for an editor with fire in his belly to run the Manitoba *Free Press*. Sifton, a member of the federal cabinet, had purchased the paper to be the voice of Liberalism in the West. He wanted the editorials to be consistently pro-Liberal, and the news to be written with a Liberal bias. If the news was craftily slanted, Sifton said slyly, "the simple-minded farmer will swallow it, and a great many who are not farmers and who ought to know better."

Sifton sent letters to Dafoe from Ottawa supplying information whenever he wanted an attack mounted in the *Free Press*. The politician-publisher also had Dafoe keep tabs on the province's weekly newspapers so loyal Liberals could be rewarded with government advertising.

Dafoe got a chance to unleash a political broadside soon after his arrival, when the royal tour of 1901 stopped in Winnipeg. The Duke and Duchess of York were accompanied by the governor general, Lord Minto. Dafoe wrote an editorial attacking Minto. He accused the British aristocrat of being a representative of the British colonial office and a spokesman for imperialism. The governor general was a symbol of servitude in Dafoe's mind. He felt Canada should assert itself as an independent nation rather than remain a British subordinate. Sir Wilfrid Laurier wrote a letter rebuking Dafoe for this editorial and asking him to "correct this very inaccurate account," but Dafoe did not publish a correction.

One of his assignments from Sifton was to use the newspaper to get rid of the Conservative government then in power in Manitoba. When Premier R. P. Roblin called an election in 1903, Dafoe eagerly went on the attack. He recalled that when the Tories had taken power in 1899, they had fired all the Liberals holding government jobs and replaced them with Conservatives. Although this form of patronage was standard practice in Ottawa and in every province, Dafoe called the Manitoba Tories "a predatory gang of headhunters and blood suckers."

He went so far as to claim the Tories were corrupting the justice system. He said the Tories had instructed magistrates not to jail horse thieves, bootleggers and whore house operators if they promised to vote Conservative. And he characterized Premier Roblin as a man who "does not hesitate to lie in order to deceive the electors."

Despite Dafoe's efforts, the Tories were re-elected. He had better luck in the federal election the following year. He consistently twisted the news to make the Liberals look good and the Tories look bad. If what he wrote was not always true, at least it was lively. As author Murray Donnelly points out in his book, *Dafoe of the Free Press*:

> "Conservative meetings were always reported as dismal flops, wakes, or groups of lost sheep huddling together for mutual warmth, but Liberal gatherings were characterized as enthusiastic, eager, enlightened, and dynamic. As expected by nearly everyone, the election resulted in a Liberal landslide."

If he had remained at that partisan level, Dafoe would have gone down in history as just another partisan hack. But as the 20th century progressed, Dafoe developed into a less-partisan and more farsighted journalist. He turned the *Free Press* into a paper with a national outlook and a national reputation for excellence.

By 1911, his stature and strength as editor had reached the point that he could take on Sifton over a matter of principle, and win. In the election of that year, the *Free Press* came out in favor of free trade with the U.S. because it was good for the West, even though Sifton was against it. In 1914, Dafoe used the paper to further his campaign for Canadian independence from Britain. Even though the Canadian colony automatically was at war when Britain went to war, Dafoe headlined the story this way: "Canada in a State of War for the First Time Since Becoming a Nation."

As the century continued, Dafoe was ahead of his time in calling for a national flag. He spoke out against hyphenated-Canadianism, saying he didn't see how immigrants could stay loyal to their old countries and be loyal to their new one.

After Sifton died in 1929, Dafoe became undisputed chief of the paper until his death 15 years later. The fiery journalist who had been hired in 1901 as Sir Clifford Sifton's mudslinger had risen to the heights of Canadian journalism. He became chancellor of the University of Manitoba, and hob-nobbed with prime ministers. He turned down an invitation to become ambassador to Washington, but accepted an honorary degree from New York City's prestigious Columbia University.

By the time he died in 1944, Dafoe was regarded as one of the best journalists Canada had ever produced. Today, more than half a century later, many people still rank him up there with the great ones.

Flamboyant former MP took his own life

Nicholas Flood Davin walked into a Winnipeg hardware store on Oct. 18, 1901, and bought a .32-calibre revolver for $2.50. In those days you didn't need to have a permit or come up with an explanation as to why you wanted a gun, but Davin offered one anyway. He said he wanted to get some target practice and shoot some cats which had been annoying him.

He took a cab to the Clarendon Hotel, told the driver to wait while he collected his luggage, went up to his room and locked the door. Half an hour later, the hotel porter went to tell Davin it was time to go to the station to catch the train home to Regina. When Davin didn't respond, the porter climbed through the transom and found him lying on the bed with the gun in his hand, the barrel in his mouth, and blood soaking the pillow. Nicholas Flood Davin, ex-MP, had taken his own life. His political death had occurred the previous year, when the voters of Assiniboia West in the North-West Territories turned Davin out of office. He had held the seat since the constituency was established in 1887.

The news of Davin's suicide quickly reached Regina, 370 miles to the west, by telegraph. "It is impossible to describe the shock felt by the town of Regina on Friday afternoon," said one of the town's weekly newspapers, *The Leader*. "Persons of all shades of politics, members of every church, citizens of every nationality recognized that a gloom had fallen over the town so closely associated with Mr. Davin's name and Mr. Davin's career."

Nicholas Flood Davin. SPA R-B 638.

Until his defeat in the election of 1900, he had been one of the most prominent men in the Territories. But after his defeat he fell so far in importance that he didn't even receive an invitation to the reception when the Duke and Duchess of York passed through Regina on the 1901 royal tour. It was a snub which hit him hard. Davin was a political gadfly whose sense of self-importance was one of his most distinctive traits.

The 61-year-old Davin didn't leave a note explaining why he killed himself, but an explanation wasn't really needed. He had lost his role in life and his place on the public stage. To Davin, who loved to be at the political centre of things, the loss of his position as an MP was a great blow to his ego. He had wandered aimlessly through life since his defeat a year earlier, and was said to be having money troubles because he no longer had an income from the government. Pensions for veteran MPs were not introduced until many years later.

Davin was an Irishman who came to Canada in 1872, just before he turned 30. He practised law and worked as a journalist and political operative in Toronto for a decade. In 1882, he was invited to have a look at the new town of Regina by W. B. Scarth of the Canada North-West Land Company. When Scarth and others suggested that what the young community needed was a newspaper to support the Conservative government, Davin saw a chance to improve his fortunes in life. He put out the first issue of his weekly paper, *The Leader*, on March 1, 1883, and quickly established himself as a leader in the community and throughout the Territories.

Davin stood out, not only because the newspaper gave him a public forum, but also because of his Irish wit and charm, along with his flamboyant dress and boisterous manner. He strutted around in a pearl-grey suit and cutaway coat, toting a cane and wearing a pair of glasses on a black ribbon around his neck. The impetuous and outspoken Davin stood out from the crowd, which in Regina consisted mainly of straight-laced men and women, most of whom had come from Ontario and Manitoba to invest in the new town and hopefully get rich.

He won the Tory nomination when Assiniboia West was created, along with three other new federal ridings, to represent the growing population of the Territories. He took the seat by a good margin in the elections of 1887 and 1891, sitting in Parliament with the governing Conservatives and enjoying the power and privileges his position afforded him. Davin had a high opinion of himself and hoped to obtain a position in the cabinet, but he never achieved that goal.

People told jokes about the way he dispensed political patronage. According to one story, Davin met a man on the street and struck up a conversation. When Davin asked about his employment, the man, who had recently been released from the penitentiary, diplomatically said he'd just been let go by the government. Davin flew into a rage because he had not been consulted before the man was fired from a government job.

But while many people found their MP a bit strange, he was popular enough to retain his seat the third time he stood for office in 1896, although he held the seat by the narrowest of margins, winning by just one vote after the election ended up in a tie. The returning officer, Dixie Watson, cast the deciding vote in Davin's favor. After that, Davin was jokingly known as the honorable Member for Dixie in the House of Commons. That was the year the Liberals took power, and Davin found himself in opposition.

He did a good job during his last term, blasting the government for its failure to control the railways more tightly and its lack of vigor in recruiting more immigrants from Great Britain. He spoke so often in the House of Commons that a fellow MP joked that "it seems there are only two parties in this House, the government and Mr. Davin."

But the fiery Irishman kept at it, sometimes with a too-sharp tongue. Once he threatened to take a whip to T. O. Davis, the Liberal MP for the neighboring riding of Saskatchewan. On another occasion he called a political opponent a "bleached negro." When he ran for a fourth time in the election of 1900, his Liberal opponent was Walter Scott, a former printer at *The Leader* who had purchased the paper in 1895. Davin had short-sightedly let it go so he could spend more time on government business.

Conservative Regina businessmen started a rival weekly called *The West* in 1899, after it became clear the Tories would need a propaganda organ to respond to Scott and the much-changed *Leader*. Davin and Scott fought the election of 1900 in their newspapers as well as on the hustings. In the week before the vote, both papers ran headlines saying their man would win, but only one could be right. Scott was elected by a healthy margin in a national Liberal sweep, and Davin was out of a job. He went to Ottawa in 1901 as a journalist, but found little satisfaction in covering Parliament from the press gallery. He even sent notes down to the floor of the House of Commons giving advice to Tory MPs on what to say.

The frustrated Davin worked on an unpublished old novel he had written years earlier, but his heart wasn't in it. His final trip to Winnipeg was an effort to cash in political favors, since the Conservatives had recently won the Manitoba provincial election. But Davin's request to see the new premier was politely refused, and at that point he reached the end of the line and took his own life. His widow Eliza Jane took the train to Winnipeg on the evening of Davin's death, and took his body to Ottawa, where Davin had taken so much pleasure in being a member of the House of Commons. A large headstone and a bust mark the place where he is buried in Beechwood Cemetery.

He died believing his life had been a failure, but the press across Canada hailed him as a significant figure. *The Globe* of Toronto said that "although in political debate and declamation no one could be more scathing, opponents could always feel that beneath the sweeping torrents of rhetoric there was an undercurrent of good nature and human sympathy." The Calgary *Herald* said Davin was right when he bragged that "the history of the west can never be written without being closely associated with my name." The Manitoba *Free Press* said that "few men were more widely known or better liked than the breezy, friendly, companionable Irishman, with his ready wit, his charming manners, and his persuasive and magnetic personality."

The Leader had the toughest obituary to write, since the paper that was founded by Davin had become such a bitter enemy. Walter Scott said he wouldn't be a hypocrite and pretend to have been Davin's friend, but suggested that "in the presence of Death we forget the shafts that we aimed and the shafts that we had to ward alike." Still, the combative Scott could not resist a final shot. He said the reason for Davin's suicide would never be known for certain, but speculated that Davin's loss of his seat in Parliament was too much for him, because "public applause was even more essential to him than eat or drink."

Axe-murderer hanged for killing parents, 3 children

We don't hang murderers anymore. That's one of the big differences between the way we punished killers at the start of the century, and the kinder, gentler way we treat them now. There hasn't been a judicial execution in Canada since the early 1960s, and today even mass murderers escape the gallows, while killers who act in a fit of passion or in an outburst of rage often get off with a manslaughter conviction, and are released from jail after serving only a few years.

Things were much different after John Morrison went on a rampage on June 9, 1900. He paid for his vicious crime with his own life, and nobody at the time felt the price was too high, given the horrid nature of the deed he committed.

Shortly after midnight on that fateful night, Morrison slipped into an unlocked prairie farmhouse near Moosomin, about 200 miles west of Winnipeg. He was carrying an axe. He systematically went from bedroom to bedroom, bashing and hacking the members of the sleeping family. Within minutes, he had killed Alexander McArthur, his wife, and three of their children. The viciousness of the attack can be gauged from a report in *The Leader*. It said that Mrs. McArthur's "right ear was partially cut," and that "there is a gash on her head, another over the right eye, and a deep cut on the skull."

Morrison chopped up three other children, who somehow managed to survive, but he left the seventh and oldest child untouched. She was the McArthurs' 15-year-old daughter. The killer calmly told the stunned girl that he had wiped out her entire family, but that she would be spared if she would have sex with him. When the horror-stricken girl refused, Morrison threatened to take his own life. He went out to the stable and turned a shotgun on himself. Unfortunately, he wasn't as efficient at killing himself as he was at killing others, and his wound was superficial. The girl ran to the home of a neighbor, who quickly informed the North-West Mounted Police that a mass-murder had been committed. Morrison was found bleeding in the barn. He was arrested and his wound was attended to.

He refused to reveal why he had committed this vicious and apparently senseless crime, but there was plenty of speculation. One theory was that he had fallen in love with the 15-year-old girl, and that her parents had forbidden him to have anything to do with her, sending him into a violent fit of anger and lust. Another theory was that he had simply "snapped." But a medical specialist who examined him concluded that he was sane enough to stand trial, and a few months later, after he entered a guilty plea, Morrison was sentenced to hang.

There were no appeals, no pleas for mercy, no suggestions that society was responsible for the vicious thing that Morrison had done. The condemned man sat quietly in his cell, day after day, waiting for his appointment with the hangman on Jan. 17, 1901. He did not even read, since he was illiterate, but he ate heartily and slept soundly. "He has exhibited the utmost indifference," *The Leader* reported. "He has not been callous or flippant, but has simply appeared insensible of or unconcerned about everything and everybody."

A few days before the execution, a scaffold was erected in the Regina jail yard. A hole was dug in the earth beneath the trap door so that the distance Morrison would drop would be precisely eight feet. This would ensure that his fall would be great enough to break his neck, but not so great that his head would be torn from his body. The scaffold had been used seven times previously. Its most famous "customer" was Louis Riel, who was hanged in 1885 after being convicted for treason in the North-West Rebellion. The scaffold's most recent victim was a peddler named Antonio Lucianio, who was hanged in 1897 for killing a travelling scissors grinder.

The arrival of the executioner in Regina for Morrison's hanging a few days before the event generated considerable public interest. "Mr. Radclive" was the name always used by the hangman. *The Leader* reported that he was a sociable fellow, spending his time in a bar and "making free with whomsoever sought his acquaintance. He says he has hanged over 100 murderers, representing 14 different nationalities."

Morrison passed a restless final night in his cell, and refused to eat his breakfast. The sheriff led the condemned man up the scaffold steps early on that frigid Thursday morning. After Mr. Radclive put the noose around his neck, Morrison said he wanted to make a statement. "Then be quick about it!" the merciless Mr. Radclive replied harshly. In a calm, quiet voice, Morrison spoke his final words: "I have lived a sinful life. It is foolish to do this, and I hope my life will be a warning to others . . . . Goodbye and God bless you all."

As a Salvation Army captain recited the Lord's Prayer, Radclive thrust a black hood over Morrison's face and stepped back from the scaffold's trap door. He pulled the bolt which held the door shut. Morrison plunged through the hole. There was a sickening snap of his neck. He was left dangling at the end of the rope. A doctor checked his heartbeat from time to time. After 13 minutes, the doctor announced that Morrison's heart had stopped. His body was taken down. A black flag was raised from the top of the jail to tell the curious that justice had been carried out.

Six citizens had been assembled to form a coroner's jury for the required inquest. After hearing sworn testimony from those who had taken part in the execution, the jurors retired and quickly returned with the unsurprising verdict that Morrison's death "had been caused by hanging during the process of a legal sentence legally carried out." Morrison's body was buried in the jail yard. *The Leader* dramatically concluded its story with these words: "Thus ends the most frightful series of tragedies that ever took place in the Dominion of Canada, and one of the most fearful that ever occurred in the world."

The deadly side of train travel

In the summer of 1901, two men who had hoped to go home with their pockets full of money went home in coffins instead. They were victims of a railway accident. It was a terrible but common way for Canadians to die at the beginning of the 20th century. Such tragedies were almost as common in those days as automobile accidents are today.

Dan LeBlanc and Don McKegan were among the thousands of men from the Maritimes, Quebec and Ontario who made their way by rail each year to Manitoba and the North-West Territories. They were part of an army of laborers who joined the annual trek west in what were known as "harvest trains." There was a bumper wheat crop in 1901, and the two men were hoping to find grain farmers who were willing to pay $40 or $50 a month plus room and board. In exchange, LeBlanc and McKegan were willing to work from dawn to dusk, seven days a week, until the harvest was completed.

The 17-car train was packed with 750 men. The train was travelling through rough and rocky terrain near a place called Ingolf, about 100 miles west of Winnipeg, when the engine, tender and the first five passenger cars went flying off the tracks. All kinds of people were hurt, and it's amazing that LeBlanc and McKegan were the only two who lost their lives.

It didn't take the nearest daily newspaper long to send a reporter to the scene to get the story. "The wreck presents a most sensational sight, with debris of the derailed locomotive, cars broken and other signs of mishap," a Manitoba *Free Press* reporter said the next day in the first written account of the disaster.

LeBlanc and McKegan had the bad luck to be outside the train car's compartment when the mishap occurred. They were standing on the platform of the first car. "Had they been inside the car they probably would not have lost their lives," the newspaper's reporter learned when he talked to survivors and railway officials. "There were some 75 men in the car, which was all smashed up, and the wonder is that more of the passengers were not killed or injured, as the car went clear over an embankment of about 30 feet in height."

Lacking photographs, the reporter used graphic language to describe what was left of the railway car. "It is now nothing more than a mass of kindling wood. It resembles nothing so much as a discarded fruit cake which has been broken up and stamped on." The story went on to say that the train's fireman, Jack Corwin, might well have been the third fatality, but he managed to survive after being pinned to the ground by one of the locomotive's driving wheels.

Doctors were only able to free him by amputating his left leg just above the knee. He underwent the ordeal "with great fortitude," the *Free Press* noted, telling its readers that Corwin "had been firing on the CPR for several years past and is a great favorite with railroad men, who deeply regret his deplorable accident."

The unhappy fate which befell LeBlanc, McKegan and Corwin was tragic, but not unusual. Train accidents were common in Canada at the turn of the century, when safety standards were much lower than they are today, and when the trains were the only way for people to travel across the long, narrow country at speed and in comfort.

According to initial reports, the cause of the wreck at Ingolf was a loose rail, but the interesting thing from a modern perspective is how deferential the news media were to the CPR. The paper wasn't quick to find fault with the company, as the modern media might be inclined to do under these circumstances. The *Free Press* reporter seems to have assumed that the railway company would look into the tragedy in great detail, and take whatever steps were necessary to prevent a similar mishap from occurring in the future.

Rather than demanding to know who was to blame for the accident and calling for an independent inquiry, the *Free Press* seemed determined to put the railway in the best light. In fact, when the Crown attorney announced that he "would not ask for an inquest unless some of the parties interested demanded it," the newspaper made no effort to encourage such an investigation. Rather, the *Free Press* used the opportunity to curry favor with the company and boost the morale of employees.

The CPR's general superintendent in Winnipeg was given credit for taking "immediate and energetic steps to clear the line of obstructions and give the injured all the medical help and relief possible." The train's brakemen were praised for their promptness in applying the air brakes, and thus preventing the last 12 cars of the train from going off the tracks and becoming part of the wreck. And the train's engineer was praised for not jumping off the engine sooner than he did to save his own life. He "pluckily stuck to his brakes until the last moment, and the universal comment is that had he not played a heroic part, the accident would have been much worse."

The newspaper never raised the question of whether the train was going too fast for the treacherous conditions at Ingolf, or asked why the loose rail was not spotted by an inspection crew before a train carrying 750 people came barrelling along the tracks.

The kind of news coverage given to the Ingolf rail disaster was not unusual. In those days, the reporting of such tragedies was a blend of the gory and the sentimental, rather than being adversarial and accusatory in nature. It was as if the newspaper and the company were on the same team. Since there were so many railway mishaps, examples of this sort of sensational but uncritical news coverage abounded. A story from the *People's Press*, a small paper in Welland, Ont., is a typical example.

It reported that a man named Delos Rowe, a rail car inspector, was walking with a lantern along the track early one morning in October, 1901. A train came along. According to the newspaper, the engineer "pulled the whistle but it was too late, and the man went down and under the wheels." But poor Rowe, who had a wife and six young children, didn't die instantly.

"The train was stopped in a car's length, and the poor, mangled body was taken from under the tender," the newspaper said. "A spark of life still remained, and in a few minutes a special engine and caboose were bearing the dying man to Niagara Falls. At the depot there, Dr. J. H. McGarry did what he could to allay the torture of approaching death. Rowe regained consciousness and asked for Archdeacon Houston. In a few minutes the venerable clergyman was administering spiritual consolation, and a short time after Rowe drew his last breath."

There wasn't a single word about why there was such an appalling lack of safety regulations that this sort of tragedy could have happened. Rather, it was assumed that Rowe was either daydreaming or simply too stupid to stay out of the way of the oncoming train. The assumption was that when a man worked for the railway, he took his own risks, and he was responsible for looking out for his own safety.

Canada's "Titanic" struck an iceberg

A satchel of gold makes a lousy life preserver. A Klondike adventurer found that out the hard way early on the morning of Aug 15, 1901. The man was a passenger on a ship making its way south from Skagway toward Victoria, B.C., when it hit an iceberg and went down in frigid water. While other miners with heavy loads of gold abandoned their treasure to save their lives, one foolish man carried his precious satchel with him when he jumped overboard. He was one of 42 passengers and crew members who died that night.

The story of the sourdough who loved his money more than his life was one of many tales told in the days after the ship sank in 140 feet of water in a treacherous channel known as the Lynn Canal. It's a remarkable but little-known tale which bears a stark resemblance to the sinking of the Titanic 11 years later.

The *Islander* was the flagship of Canadian Pacific Navigation Ltd., the seagoing arm of the giant CPR consortium. It was a fast and handsome vessel which had made the run down the Pacific coast from Skagway to the capital of British Columbia many times. On its final journey the ship was carrying 107 passengers and 71 crew members.

Although the channel was the most dangerous part of the voyage because its waters frequently contained icebergs broken off from a nearby glacier, the ship was travelling in the dark at its top speed of 10 knots. Hamilton Foote, the captain, was in the ship's saloon, entertaining a group of prospectors on their way home from the Klondike. Several of them had struck it rich, and were bringing their gold home in satchels.

Captain Foote had left Edmund LeBlanc, a veteran pilot, in charge of the bridge. Equipped with night glasses, LeBlanc scanned the water ahead to watch out for icebergs, while another sailor was at the helm. LeBlanc, interviewed by a reporter in Victoria a few days after the tragedy, said this is what happened:

"The night was fine and as we always expect to meet ice, a sharp lookout was kept. About 2:48 a.m. the crash came. The boat was under full speed, and no ice was in sight and there was no fog, but the wind was blowing and it was dark and cloudy. The fatal berg was no doubt even with the water. After she struck, I stopped the engines, when Captain Foote appeared with the night watchman who reported the ship leaking forward. I told Captain Foote that

we had better head for the beach, but he demurred and when he decided to do so the ship was taking water so fast she would not answer to the helm.

"Then I called the mate and ordered the life boats out. This was done and they were loaded with passengers. Many passengers jumped overboard with life preservers on. I jumped overboard and was in the water two and a quarter hours before securing a piece of wreckage."

An American prospector named Brumbauer abandoned a satchel containing $14 000 in gold and lived to tell the tale. He rushed to the upper deck when the ship started sinking. He was afraid to toss his heavy satchel from the deck into a life boat before sliding down a rope because he feared the weight of the gold would knock a hole through the bottom of the life boat. Brumbauer wisely dropped the satchel on the *Islander*'s deck before sliding down and being hauled into the boat.

A couple of other prospectors did the same, but one man couldn't bring himself to let go of his fortune. According to a report in the Manitoba *Free Press*, the man was carrying $40 000 in gold dust. He grasped his satchel and jumped from the sinking ship toward a life boat, but landed in the water and went down with his treasure.

The most prominent person to die that night was Barbara Ross, the wife of the newly-appointed governor of the Yukon Territory. She had come north on the *Islander* just a few weeks earlier with her seven children to join the governor in Whitehorse, the territorial capital. Mrs. Ross had reboarded the ship just a few weeks later to buy furnishings in Victoria for the new government house.

J. W. MacFarlane, a mining engineer, told reporters about the last moments of Mrs. Ross's life. MacFarlane helped the woman and two other passengers put on their life belts. It was pitch black and all the boats were gone.

"We walked along the promenade deck," said MacFarlane, "hoping to find some means of assistance. By this time the ship was pretty well down by the head, and as we walked she gave a sudden lurch forward. I said to Mrs. Ross it was time to jump, and told her to follow me. I jumped clear of the ship but they did not have time, and as I leapt I saw them running up the quickly increasing incline of the steamer's deck. Just at that moment the vessel took an awful plunge and the compressed air, which was forced from the ship, rent the deck, which burst with considerable noise."

MacFarlane's story continued to a dramatic conclusion:

"In leaping over I sprang well out from the vessel, realizing that she was going down. I swam about for some time and saw the steamer go down as I swam. I came across Captain Foote also swimming, and together we made our way to a raft, which showed up in the darkness. There were 20 or 30 men on it at the time. The captain and I reached the raft at the same time, and he held on, I should judge, about 10 minutes. Finally he said, 'Boys, I have seen the last of my ship,' and a few minutes after that he said, 'I think I am done for.' He left the raft and

swam away five or six yards, when he threw up his hands and went down."

In a subsequent legal inquiry, the dead Captain Foote was held negligent for leaving the bridge without giving his officers instructions to reduce speed in view of the iceberg hazard. His error was especially bad because two years earlier, Foote had been in command of another ship in the Lynn Canal when it had struck an iceberg. He got away with it that time, managing to get the damaged ship into the harbor at Juneau.

Soon after the *Islander* tragedy, rumor started flying that the ship had gone down carrying a lot of gold. Some estimates put the figure as high as $3 million. Several attempts were made to salvage the ship, but the channel's deep and icy water made it a difficult task.

It wasn't until 1934 that the rusted remains of the *Islander* were finally raised and hauled ashore. About $8000 in cash was recovered from the ship's safe. Some gold was also recovered, but the salvage company refused to say how much. The hulk remained on the beach until 1952, when the *Islander* was cut up for scrap. The ill-fated ship was finally gone, but her legend lives on in Canada's maritime history.

Chapter 4
How About Those Easterners?

She was the Indian princess of poetry

With no radios, TVs, VCRs, movies, video games or Internet chat groups, what did turn-of-the-century Canadians do for entertainment? Whenever they could, they went to live performances. Groups of entertainers criss-crossed the land, putting on one-night shows which drew appreciative audiences from coast to coast.

In the more isolated places – and there were a lot of them in Canada – people were starved for entertainment. An evening of poetry and piano playing might not sound very entertaining today, but it drew a lot of interest in the old days, and people would travel for hours to attend.

One of the liveliest shows on the circuit was headlined by Pauline Johnson, a Mohawk Indian princess who recited her own poetry, gave talks on the beauty of nature and dramatically scolded Canadians for their shabby treatment of aboriginal people. Johnson was not only popular in her own day. She has stood the test of time, and become a legend. The aboriginal community venerates her, and she is now one of Canada's best-known poets.

Johnson turned to show business because poetry paid poorly 100 years ago, and there were no Canada Council grants to support creative artists. *Saturday Night*

Pauline Johnson with bear claw necklace.
NAC c-85215

magazine paid her only $3 for "The Song My Paddle Sings," her most-often-quoted poem. *Rod and Gun* magazine sent her just 70 cents for another poem, "The Train Dogs." She returned the money with a note consoling them on their poverty.

She became part of a band of singers, musicians, lecturers, monologists, comedians and reciters who crossed the land bringing entertainment not only to the cities, but to almost every little town and village. She was a striking figure in her buckskin dress trimmed with ermine. Her costume was accented with silver decorations hammered from old coins and a bear-claw necklace. Her wrist bracelets were made out of wampum beads. She wore an eagle feather in her long, dark hair and covered her shoulders with a red blanket once used by a duke when he was made an honorary Indian chief. Sometimes she also wore a couple of scalps tied to her belt.

Her black eyes, high cheek bones and olive coloring gave her an Indian-like appearance, but she was held in much higher esteem in the white community than a typical aboriginal woman. In part, her popularity was due to the fact that she was an "acceptable" Indian. White people could relate to this charming and articulate figure, especially when she appeared in traditional western dress during the second half of her show. The contrast between her Indian and white costumes was striking, and people were intrigued by the way she blended the two cultures.

Her father was a chief of the Mohawk tribe, which had been an ally of the British since the war with the French in the 18th century. Her mother was a member of prominent English family who shocked her relatives when she married a Canadian Indian. Pauline grew up in a fine stone house on the Brant reserve near Brantford, Ont., and used her skills in English to translate the songs of the Mohawk into poetry. She gained acceptance in the Canadian literary establishment and won popular acclaim from white society. The prime minister and the governor general were among her patrons. When she went to London in the mid-1890s, she was lionized by fashionable British society.

Back in Canada, she performed in libraries, lodges, schools, churches, town halls, pool rooms bars and even grain elevators – anywhere an audience could be assembled. The admission charge was anywhere from 50 cents to $2.50, depending on what the traffic would bear. Her reputation was so great that all she had to do was send out post cards giving details of her itinerary, and local people would get busy and arrange halls, refreshments and the like.

Sometimes she and her colleagues put on benefits for local charities. In one Ontario community, they helped buy a wooden leg for the town constable. In an isolated British Columbia town they helped raise money to build a church. At the height of her fame in the early 20th century, she acquired a reputation as "a well-loved vagabond" whose talent and charm won the hearts of audiences from coast to coast, and who was as at home in the company of farmers and miners as with the elite of the Canadian establishment.

As her friend and fellow entertainer Walter McRaye wrote many years after Johnson's death: "Canada was her creed and religion, and her work, prose and verse, has a real breath of Canadian air, whether treating of the plains, of the never coming herd of buffalo, of Halifax on its hill, of Calgary at sunset, of the Qu'Appelle Valley, of gold, of the Selkirks, or of Shadow River in Muskoka. It is all Canadian, and full of a passionate love of country."

Connor and Watson, Canadian myth-makers

If you were asked to name Canada's top adventure writer, you could pick from a dozen contenders. And if you were asked to identify Canada's greatest landscape artist, you could chose from an equally large selection. But at the start of the 20th century, when there were far fewer contenders to choose from, there was little doubt that Ralph Connor was the nation's leading action novelist, and Homer Watson was its finest landscape painter.

Both won fame by portraying Canadian heroes. In Connor's case, the hero was a man of God who won souls for the Lord in the rugged West, while Watson's hero was a more terrestial sort who pitted his strength against the forces of nature in rural Ontario. They were as different as chalk and cheese, yet each in his own way helped to create the distinctive identity of the Canadian nation, and each stood at the summit of accomplishment in his artistic area as the new century dawned.

In 1901, Connor's latest book, *The Sky Pilot*, was a smash hit in Canada, and was selling thousands of copies a week in the United States and Great Britain, while Watson's great painting, *The Flood Gate*, was being recognized as a masterpiece.

Connor's novel was the inspirational story of a frontier minister who arrives in the foothills of the Rocky Mountains and brings Christianity to the people of Swan Creek. The book combined the features of a morality saga and a rip-roaring western. According to a review of *The Sky Pilot* in *The New York Times*, Connor "writes of the cowboy and frontier trader as living realities . . . There is no novel dealing with the rough existence of the seemingly rough cowboys which can approach it in the charm of its telling, its pathos and its beautiful descriptions."

Connor was one of the first Canadians to make a splash in literary circles in the States and in England, but unlike many who were to follow his lead later in the 20th century, he didn't leave Canada to capitalize on his success. Connor remained in Winnipeg doing what he considered to be his primary work, ministering to the members of his congregation. Ralph Connor, like the hero of his novel, was a Presbyterian minister. His real name was Rev. Charles William Gordon.

How did a man of the cloth become a best-selling writer? He based his writing on personal experience. After completing his theological studies in Ontario in the early 1890s, Gordon served as a missionary in the mining and lumber camps of the Rocky Mountains. He had plenty of work. The camps were full of men suffering from the problems associated with alcoholism, loneliness and despair.

After four years in the camps, Gordon moved to a church in Winnipeg, but kept in touch with the missions, and in the late 1890s he wrote an article to help publicize the church's work in the Rockies. He prepared an article about Christmas Eve in a lumber camp and sent it to a magazine in Toronto. Gordon didn't sign the article, so the editor sent him a telegram asking for a pen name. Gordon came up with "Cannor," an abbreviation of "Canadian Northwest," part of the title of the church's Royal Canadian Northwest Mission.

The telegraph operator assumed a spelling mistake had been made, and changed the name from "Cannor" to "Connor" before sending the message to Toronto. The editor pulled the first name "Ralph" out of the air, thinking that it went well with "Connor," and so the pen-name "Ralph Connor" was born.

The article about Christmas in the lumber camps was a success, and the editor persuaded the author to expand it into a novel. Titled *Black Rock*, the book sold 5000 copies, a phenomenal number for Canada at the turn of the century, where even today sales of 10 000 make a book a best-seller. An American publisher bought the rights to *Black Rock* and sold hundreds of thousands of copies in the States. The clergyman from Winnipeg was on his way to international literary stardom.

His rugged writing style was a refreshing change from the placid and reflective tales typical of novels written by other Canadians of the time. Connor wrote with humor and dramatic realism. His books captured the beauty and spiritualism of the mountains. His themes were the nobility of sacrifice, personal regeneration and the way in which strongly moral characters can influence others to improve their own lives.

Connor ended up writing 25 books during his long and prolific career. His sales ran into the millions, and while his work seems dated today, it provides us with graphic portrayals of the social conditions and the attitudes of people of their day. Here, for example, is how Connor describes the way in which the rough men of Swan Creek in the Rockies got around the territorial law prohibiting alcohol.

"When one of the boys feels as if he were going to have a spell of sickness he gets a permit to bring in a few gallons for medicinal purposes; and of course, the other boys being similarly exposed, he invites them to assist him in taking preventive measure. And it is remarkable, in a healthy country like this, how many epidemics come near ketching us."

Today, Connor's books seem simplistic and preachy, but they reflected the prevailing morality of their times, in which the Christian church was one of the major pillars of Canadian society, and a rugged frontier minister could be seen as a genuine hero. Many people in those days would have agreed with *The Sky Pilot*'s title character, who felt there was more to life than having fun. He said that Jesus had to play a key part. As the writer put it: "Men cannot live without Him, and be men."

Despite the urging of his publisher, Connor didn't devote his full time to writing. He continued his work as a minister in his Winnipeg church, and went on to become moderator of the Presbyterian Church and one of the founders of the United Church of Canada. Yet he always found time to write, and managed to churn out a book almost every year until his death in the 1930s.

Meanwhile, in another province and in another area of the arts, Homer Watson had made quite a reputation for himself. The people in his home town of Doon in Southern Ontario thought Watson was an oddball until Queen Victoria ordered one of his paintings in the early 1880s. Then they decided that the young artist in their midst wasn't such a strange fellow after all, and they looked upon the gifted painter with appreciative new eyes.

By the dawn of the 20th century, Homer Watson had become Canada's leading landscape artist. Sharp investors in Montreal who collected old masters were snapping up Watson's paintings, knowing that his work was so good that it would make large profits for them.

The artist was born in 1855. At the age of 11, he was recognized as having talent when he drew a fine sketch of the Battle of Ridgeway showing British troops battling Fenian invaders. Watson was only in his mid-20s when he created a sensation at the first Royal Canadian Academy exhibit in Ottawa in 1880. He submitted a painting of a waterwheel. The governor general bought it and sent it to the Queen as a gift. She liked it so much she immediately ordered another painting by the brilliant young Canadian artist.

Several years later, Oscar Wilde, the British author and wit, befriended Watson on a visit to Canada and called him "the Canadian Constable," a flattering reference to John Constable, the master painter of English landscapes. Both Constable and Watson painted rural scenes romanticizing the land and celebrating the superiority of village life over that of the cities. This was a popular theme at the start of the century not only in painting, but also in literature. The city, it was felt, was crass and corrupting, while country life was nostalgically seen as physically and morally healthy.

The patronage of the Queen, and the comparison to Constable, put Watson in the big leagues of not only the Canadian but the international art scene. To be judged favorably by imperial standards, rather than just by colonial standards, was the ultimate tribute. But on a tour of England, Watson rejected suggestions that he further his career by moving to Britain. He felt that in order to produce the truest form of his art, the artist must have a genuine connection with his subject – and in his case, that connection was rooted in the Canada of his birth and his forefathers.

Watson believed that painters should address noble themes, rather than simply be illustrators or abstractionists. He scorned those who painted pictures of trivial objects, which he termed "pots and pans." He believed that "no immortal work has been done which has not had as one of its promptings for its creation a feeling its creator had of having roots in his native land and being a product of its soil."

Watson has been compared to Sir John A. Macdonald, in the sense that just as Canada's first prime minister sought to build a distinctive Canadian nation, Watson tried to create a distinctive Canadian painting style. In the early 1900s, he focused on what was to turn out to be the major project of his career. It was a series of pictures portraying the settlement of his home area, Ontario's Waterloo County. The works paid tribute to the settlers from Pennsylvania who arrived in Conestoga wagons, cut the forest, broke the soil and built log cabins.

Watson produced his finest individual painting in 1900. It was titled *The Flood Gate*, and it was enormously popular. It shows a farmer struggling to close a gate in a flood. As the trees bend and the horses cower before nature's fury, the farmer puts all his strength into his fight against the raging torrent. This reflects a basic theme of the Canadian experience – the pioneers' classic struggle to tame nature and make a living from the rugged land.

Watson was one of the first Canadian artists to break away from European conventions and present the Canadian landscape in a distinctively Canadian way. He was a forerunner of the Group of Seven, who later in the century were to become even more famous as landscape artists. But in his day, no Canadian landscape artist was better than Homer Watson, just as no Canadian adventure writer was better than Ralph Connor.

Annie conquered Niagara Falls in a barrel

Was Annie Taylor incredibly brave, just greedy or stark raving mad? Those were the questions Canadians asked in the fall of 1901 about the woman who went over Niagara Falls in a barrel. Annie was a short, stout widow who took on the thundering cataract in a poorly-thought-out scheme to make herself rich.

She came up with the idea one day as she contemplated retirement from her teaching job with no pension, and concluded that going over the falls would give her instant fame, which in turn would translate into a fortune. Naively, she assumed that people would shower her with money if she pulled off the dangerous feat. She turned out to be a better marine engineer than a businesswoman. Her barrel worked, but her financial scheme flopped.

Annie sketched out the barrel on a sheet of paper and had it built of 1-1/2-inch-thick maple staves bound by 10 iron hoops. She shipped the 160-pound barrel from her home in Bay City, Michigan, to Niagara Falls, hired a publicist, and arrived in the Falls a few days before her date with destiny. She painted the words "Queen of the Mist" on the side of the barrel and billed herself as a woman of "mistery."

"I am doing it for the money," she told reporters with forthright honesty. "I don't know how the money is to be made from the venture, but my manager is sanguine that there is money in it, and I have faith in him." She claimed to be only 42 years old, when in fact she was 62. The press went along with the lie, even though it was obvious from grey hair and wrinkled skin that she was much older than she claimed to be. Annie explained later that she under-reported her age because "youth sells better than agedness," failing to see that a senior citizen attempting the feat added an extra element of the unusual to her stunt.

Annie knew she was taking a big risk with her life, but she never showed any sign of changing her mind, even after she saw that the thundering falls could easily break her barrel or submerge it for a long period of time. There are two big drops of water at Niagara. The one on the American side would spell certain death for Annie, since the huge rocks strewn across the base would shatter even the strongest barrel.

But the falls on the Canadian side – known as the Horseshoe Falls – offered hope of a softer landing, since there's a deep pool of turbulent water at the base of the 167-foot cataract. The Horseshoe Falls were also much wider, making for a more spectacular show. The biggest danger of the Horseshoe Falls would be that the barrel would plunge under the water and stay there, caught in the currents and undertows whirling around the gorge.

On the afternoon of Oct. 24, 1901, Annie arrived at the place where the barrel was hidden on the American side of the river. Secrecy was necessary because the police had threatened to prosecute Annie if they caught her trying to perform the stunt. Still, thanks to her publicity agent, the shores of the river were lined with people who knew that the unusual spectacle was about to take place.

Wearing a blue and white blouse open at the neck, a loose black skirt, black cotton stockings and dark tan shoes, Annie got on her hands and knees and backed into the barrel through its 10-by-14-inch hatch. A 150-pound anvil had been fastened beneath the barrel to keep it upright, no matter how the waters tried to spin and rotate the craft. Annie took with her a small container of brandy "to sustain me if I should feel faint," and promised she would see everyone soon, after she had successfully carried out her mission.

She fastened a belt around her waist, then hooked up a harness designed to keep her feet on the floor and prevent her head from striking the lid. She positioned cushions to protect herself front and rear. Then she put a pillow behind her head and stuck an air tube in her mouth. The tube was hooked up to a valve which would close when the barrel was under water.

She ordered the hatch to be sealed, and she sat back to await her fate. The barrel was put in the stern of a boat by two men who rowed upstream and then across the river to the Canadian side. It was released at the mouth of the Chippawa River, about a mile and a half above the falls, and began its trip down the swiftly moving water toward the brink. It dodged its way around the many rocks in its path as it pitched and rolled closer and closer to the brink of the Horseshoe Falls.

It shot over the edge and plunged into the gorge, where it disappeared in the foam and the mist. Two steamer boats waited a couple of hundred yards below the falls in relatively calm waters. They were from the *Maid of the Mist* fleet, which took thrill-seeking tourists on trips up the river as close as they could safely come to the pounding waters. Those on board on this occasion held their breath until they saw the barrel emerge safely from the base of the falls.

A rope was attached to the barrel, which was pulled out of the water onto a nearby rock. The barrel's cover was pulled off to reveal Annie's starkly white face, her eyes turned upward and blinking at the sudden flood of daylight. Annie extended a hand, waved feebly, moaned and asked where she was.

She was taken to the Niagara Falls hospital, where it was found that the only injury she sustained was a small gash on her forehead. As the word went out that she had accomplished a feat no other person in the world had accomplished, bells rang, horns blew and whistles tooted in her honor.

But the woman who was smart enough to find a way to beat Niagara Falls proved remarkably inept at turning her fame into a fortune. Her unrealistic hopes that people would shower her with cash proved false, and she quickly disappeared from public attention, turning up from time to time on the street trying to beg a few cents from passers-by. Annie died in obscurity and poverty, but she is remembered today in the tourist traps of Niagara, which celebrate her accomplishment and recall that she was the first of what soon turned out to be a parade of dare-devils who went over Niagara Falls in a barrel.

Canada strutted its stuff in Paris

Snow, ice, Canada. Do those three words seem to go together? They did to a lot of Europeans at the turn of the century, but an eye-opening Canadian display at the Paris Exposition of 1900 helped dispel the myth that this country was nothing more than a few acres of snow.

The big French show was an international coming-of-age party for the young country. It revealed that Canada was a rich nation producing a wide variety of agricultural crops, forestry products, minerals, manufactured goods and other items. We weren't in Britain's league when it came to manufacturing, and we were overshadowed by the huge agricultural economy of the United States, but we were far beyond the primitive stage. We were coming into our own as a major producing nation. Our future was much brighter than what might be expected for a country supposedly trapped in a perpetual blizzard.

"Canada now has a reputation," proclaimed *The Canadian Magazine* in an article describing the Paris Exposition. International fairs were more important and impressive than they are today. Newspapers and magazines had not yet developed to the point where their photos could show off products in all their wondrous detail, and there was, of course, no TV. So people had to go and see for themselves what the world had to offer, and our part of the world looked pretty good with its lush apples, magnificent wheat, solidly crafted canoes, modern farm machinery and natural wonders.

"Canada heretofore, as even the most patriotic of Canadians must admit, has been but little known in Europe, and that little generally wrong," *The Canadian Magazine* observed. "It is not the fault of the present-day Canadian that his country is popularly regarded abroad as a land of all but perpetual snow and ice. That is a legacy from the past, a fallacy which only time and knowledge can correct."

The Canadian display included 1800 exhibits and occupied 27 000 square feet of floor space. It consisted of sections devoted to natural history, food, minerals, agriculture, lumbering, manufacturing and intellectual life. A giant stuffed moose greeted visitors at the entrance. Inside was a virtual zoo of Canadian wildlife, including buffalo, caribou, deer, wolves, foxes, beavers, wolverines, lynxes, otters, skunks, antelope and Rocky Mountain sheep.

In the food section, glass cylinders full of maple syrup and jars of preserved pears stood along side canned fish and lobsters, dried cod and mackerel, honey in comb and liquid form, and a variety of beers and spirits. There was even an exhibit of wine from Pelee Island in Southern Ontario, but Frenchmen wishing to compare it to Parisian wine were disappointed. The government felt that the consumption of food and drink on the premises would take away from the dignity of the Canadian presentation. But thanks to a refrigerating plant below the flooring, people could at least see fresh Canadian fruit, cheese, butter and eggs.

Prices for typical products showed that food in Canada was a bargain. Parisians were paying the equivalent of 28 cents a dozen for eggs. In Canada they sold for 15 cents. A pound of butter, which cost 40 Canadian cents in Paris, sold for just 18 cents in Canada. The opportunities for Canadian exporters were obvious, particularly since steamers with cold-storage facilities were regularly crossing the Atlantic.

Gold from the Klondike was displayed in cases protected by steel bars. One tray showed 61 ounces of gold which had been washed from a 20-pound pan of gravel. Another showed $301 worth of gold, said to represent just one-sixteenth of the amount of gold that could be obtained in a single day by a team of four men. Samples of Canadian iron, lead, coal, mica, chrome and phosphate were also shown. A 100-pound chunk of copper ore was protected by a railing made of solid nickel.

The agriculture section featured artistic arrangements of the sheaves of cereals and fodder plants, along with pillars, urns and glass globes of threshed grains. Samples of wheat, oats, rye, barley, buckwheat, corn, peas, beans and flax were arranged in arches, pillars and monuments. A chandelier formed of various grains in the sheaf hung from the ceiling. Cross-sections of trees, polished boards and wood products such as clothespins, cigar boxes, broom handles and chairs were surrounded by 200 photos showing the various stages of lumbering operations.

An assortment of carriages, wagons, bicycles, sleighs, boats, stoves, plows, harvesters, reaping and mowing machines, pulleys, pianos and organs demonstrated Canada's manufacturing ability, while the Canadian Pacific Railway showed off one of its sleeping compartments. Quebec, anxious to show Old France that intellectual life in New France was thriving, displayed samples of pupils' work, arranged and graded according to age and class. Laval and McGill universities showed pictures of their modern science labs and other facilities.

Interior of the Canadian Building at the Pan. The Canadian Magazine, July 1900.

Canada had a similar display at the Pan American Exhibition in Buffalo, N.Y., in 1901, but the limelight was stolen by the flashy Americans, who put the accent on modern technology. The Canadian exhibit, with its stuffed animals and jars of wheat, drew little interest.

We did better at an exposition in 1901 in Scotland. The Glasgow *Herald* said the exterior of the Canadian pavilion "shines out in white and gold like a temple of Greece." The newspaper was impressed by Canadian plows which were lighter, sharper and stronger than those used in the United Kingdom, and by a harrower which picked up clods of earth between discs and pulverized them. Canadian seed drills, mowers and reapers drew praise for their ingenuity, size and strength.

And rather than dwell on Canada's reputation for ice and snow, the *Herald* praised the nation's display of stoves, which it said were "of many sizes and shapes, beautifully moulded and ornamented." Those stoves, the paper concluded, "do credit to the iron-moulding and steel-working trades of Canada."

Ontario farmers were sure to succeed

A little capital, a few brains and a lot of work – that's what it took to become a successful farmer in Ontario at the turn of the century, according to Thomas Conant, a popular writer who typified the upbeat mood of the times. In his book, *Life in Canada*, Conant laid out the details of how to succeed in agriculture in Canada's richest province.

Almost everyone was bullish on Canada in those happy days. The nation had embarked on a period of such strong economic growth that it later became known in history as the Big Boom. Government officials, newspaper editors and others cited impressive figures which showed terrific growth in Canadian farming, manufacturing, population and other measures of success.

In those days there was no United Nations to declare that Canadians enjoyed the best quality of life in the world, but people were figuring it out, and the figures spoke for themselves. Canada was the fastest-growing country on earth. The optimistic mood was summed up a few years later when the prime minister, Sir Wilfrid Laurier, declared that while the 19th century was the century of the United States, the 20th century belonged to Canada.

Agriculture was the backbone of the Canadian economy, and Ontario was the heartland of agriculture, so if you were going to join in the prosperity of Canada, a farm in Ontario was a good place to do it. Thomas Conant highlighted the terrific opportunities available in farming in Canada's most populous and prosperous province. He mapped the road to success in a clear and concrete manner, offering specifics to show how to get rich off the land.

He said there was plenty of good land available in the province for $80 an acre, so a typical 100-acre farm would cost $8000. Stock, implements, seed and other essentials would add another $2000, but the $10 000 deal could be done mainly on credit. A bright young farmer could take out a mortgage at an annual interest rate of five or six per cent. According to Conant, a hard-worker could earn enough each year to pay the interest, support himself and his family, and whittle a chunk off the mortgage.

Eventually he would own the farm, debt-free. At that point, Conant confidently predicted, the farmer would be set for life. His farm could generate an income of $1200 a year, which was enough to provide a comfortable living. The farmer would be "as free and independent as any king upon a throne." It was a sure-fire recipe for success, said Conant, because "very few farmers in Ontario fail." The land was rich, the climate mild, and the variety of farm products so great that the farmer could always find a way to make money. "Everything he can grow will sell for money, and with his family's help, and increase of his stock, he is bound to succeed."

The author filled his buoyant-hearted book with Horatio Alger-like stories. There was the boy, for instance, who was just 12 when his father died. The plucky lad went to work as a farm hand and saved $400 by the time he was 19. Then he went to school and became a teacher, bought 50 acres, worked the land when he wasn't in the classroom, and soon paid off his mortgage. He bought another 50 acres, hired farm hands, earned a university degree and eventually ended up owning 500 acres. The man was rich, and his family was sure to get even richer, because they "have all been taught to labor, and have been brought up to industrious habits, and the individual members cannot fail to make their mark in our midst."

Conant said this was not an isolated case. "Many more might be mentioned, but this is sufficient to show what push, determination and brains will accomplish in rural Ontario." Conant said those who thought farming was too much work and opted for the easier life as a factory worker in the city weren't taking a long-range view of things. While the city man finished work at 6 p.m. and went through life "with tolerable ease upon his day's wages, as a rule he is not saving much for his declining days; but his farmer brother invariably is . . . . His farmer brother will have soiled hands, and wear his working clothes the whole day through, and cannot go about the streets in the evenings, nor attend many of places of amusement, but he enjoys himself just as well at home, and he is saving for a rainy day."

Conant said Ontario was a place where the opportunities to succeed were as great as, if not greater than, anywhere else in the world. He told the story of the Irish immigrant who

"began by chopping wood by the cord. Saving enough thereby, he bought a team, and then bought wood by the lump and hauled it to town to sell. Then he bought a wood lot, and proceeded to haul the cord-wood from it, which he sold to manufacturers in the town. After a time he got his lot cleared of wood, and put fall wheat on it, seeding the land down to clover and timothy at the same time."

The story goes on in this step-by-step manner until the immigrant learns how to make real money in the cattle business, just by keeping his ears open.

"Unlettered as he was, and unable even to write his own name, he seemed to take in all knowledge intuitively, as it were. In a word, he seemed to drink in knowledge as a sponge takes up moisture. He could often be seen standing listening to groups of men who were talking, saying but little himself, but treasuring up every word dropped by them."

But everything was not rosy in Thomas Conant's world. He interlaced his stories of success with tales of predators and sharpies who preyed on hard-working farmers and tried to cheat them out of their money. There were, for instance, the "Shylocks," men who came from Britain in the old days, when money was scarce, and were able to demand outrageous rates of interest. They lent out money to farmers at 15 per cent, then collected a 10-per-cent bonus. When borrowers fell behind, these greedy money-lenders took yet another 10-per-cent bonus, and soon doubled or tripled their wealth.

But as always in Conant's work, the story has a happy ending. The children of these "Shylocks" didn't learn to work hard. They squandered their parents' ill-gotten gains, while the children of the farmers who paid the high interest rates learned to be frugal. In succeeding generations, those who worked the land came out all right. Today, Conant said in his Bible-like fashion, they "are still at the fore, and their descendants will inherit many broad acres."

Original Parliament Buildings lost in fire

When you look at the stately old Parliament Buildings in Ottawa, you'd swear they've been there all through the 20th century, but you'd be wrong. Only the library dates back that far. The rest of the structures, including the Peace Tower, are relatively recent creations.

The current buildings are replacements erected after a fire burned down the original Parliament Buildings in 1916. The new ones are in the same location, on a 29-acre site overlooking the Ottawa River. They were built there in the 1860s after Ottawa was chosen as the seat of government by Queen Victoria. At that time, Canada consisted of just Ontario and Quebec, formerly known as Upper and Lower Canada. Although the two colonies had been politically united for some time, they couldn't agree on where to establish their permanent capital. Toronto, Montreal and Kingston vied for the honor, but the wise Queen chose Ottawa because it was on the Ontario-Quebec border.

The impressive buildings, said to be the most beautiful government structures in North America, were completed in 1865, and inherited two years later by the government of the new Dominion of Canada. Those buildings were the scene of all the great parliamentary debates of the 19th century. This is where Sir John A. Macdonald made his famous speeches, and where Sir Wilfrid Laurier spent his career as Canada's greatest prime minister.

But five explosions of mysterious origin rocked the structures in 1916, leading to a spectacular fire which killed seven people and tore through the old buildings. Since they were made of stone they weren't burned to the ground, but they had to be torn down because they were so badly damaged. Everything but the library was replaced. The reconstruction was completed in 1920.

The new Parliament Buildings look a lot like the old ones, but there are some differences. Today's Peace Tower soars to a height of 300 feet, while the old Victoria Tower rose only 180 feet. The roofs of the modern buildings are covered with copper, while the old roofs were covered with grey and green slate. A lot of the stone carvings are different, and the interior is brighter and more spacious. But in most respects the new buildings resemble the

Parliament buildings draped for the death of Queen Victoria. PAC PA 8988.

original, and remain an impressive sight. People who visited Ottawa at the start of this century said that viewing the Parliament Buildings sparked feelings of national pride. It's the same today for modern Canadians.

The buildings were created in the urban Gothic style. It was popular in the mid-18th century and was based on medieval ecclesiastical architecture, which was distinguished by pointed arches, lancet windows with tracery, pinnacles with crockets and prominent, exposed buttresses. In less technical terms, the Parliament Buildings have many of the features of old European churches. The architects who won the competition to design Canada's first Parliament Buildings based their proposal on the British Houses of Parliament, known as the Palace of Westminster and erected in London in 1853. The similarity was appropriate, since all things British were much admired in Canada at the time, and the colony's parliamentary system was based on Britain's.

There were three buildings. The centre block included the House of Commons and the Senate, plus living quarters for the Speaker. The centre block was flanked at right angles by office buildings on each side, creating an enclosed grassy area which formed an inviting entranceway and courtyard. The buildings were covered with buff-colored sandstone from a quarry near Ottawa. Lighter Ohio sandstone was used for the dressings, gablets and pinnacles, while red sandstone from Potsdam, N.Y., trimmed the windows and doors. The red stone gave the old buildings an incongruous and slightly harsh look which was eliminated in the new buildings by using stone of a more harmonious color.

The library, built nine years after Confederation, survived the fire thanks to its isolated location and an iron door which held back the flames which shot down the passageway connecting the library to the centre block. The library was modelled after the reading room of the British Museum in London. It was circular in shape and featured a dome 140 feet above the floor. A. G. Bradley, a British writer who visited Ottawa early in the 20th century, felt that the library was the most impressive building on Parliament Hill. "It contains nearly a quarter of a million books beautifully shelved on the choicest Canadian woods, and has for long possessed an eminent librarian. To this delightful and spacious treasure-house the fortunate citizens of Ottawa have virtually free access."

Bradley was also impressed by the view from Parliament Hill:

"I hardly know whether the outlook is the more striking when the far-spreading prospect beneath is locked in the white rigours of winter, from the frozen river at your feet to the snowy undulations of the distant Laurentian hills, or whether in summer, when you may sit on a garden seat at the verge of the leafy precipice and absorb the glorious outlook at your leisure."

The Union Jack flew over the old Parliament Buildings, and over the new buildings as well, for many years. It wasn't until 1965 that Canada's distinctive Red Maple Leaf flag was adopted by Parliament, following a long and emotional debate. Today that flag looks so appropriate that one might think it has always been there, but if anyone had suggested the idea in Parliament at the turn of the century, he would have received little support. At that time, most people believed that Canada would be flying the Union Jack for as long as the nation existed.

Hull and Ottawa were engulfed by a massive fire

It was close to lunch time on Thursday, April 26, 1900, in Hull, Quebec, when Alphonse Kirouac's wife loaded dry kindling into the kitchen stove to prepare the noontime meal. She lit the match. A few seconds later, flames belched from the chimney, setting the cedar roof on fire. Jacques Blais, a neighbor, saw the flames. He ran to the nearest fire call box and turned in the alarm.

Fire was always a danger in Hull. The city, which had a population of about 14 000, was located directly across the river from Ottawa. A working-class community, Hull was the national capital's poor cousin. Hull was a lumber town, built largely of its own product. At the beginning of the 20th century, Ottawa-Hull was the largest lumber-producing centre in Eastern Canada. Vast quantities of logs from Ontario and Quebec forests were carried down the Ottawa River to be processed and turned into lumber, most notably at the E. B. Eddy complex in Hull and the Booth and Bronson lumber yards in Ottawa. Huge piles of wood were stored in these industrial areas, spread out so the sun and the air could dry them, making them particularly vulnerable to fire.

Despite warnings from insurance companies and safety experts, the city of Hull's lax building codes put more emphasis on profit than on safety. Most of its citizens lived on narrow streets packed tightly with wooden houses. Hull was, in essence, a fire trap. On top of that, the weather was unseasonably warm that spring, and there had been no rain for three weeks. Everything was as dry as tinder. It was a conflagration waiting to happen.

By the time the dozen men and two hose reels which constituted Hull's tiny fire department arrived, the Kirouac house and three adjoining houses were on fire. The flames, whipped by a strong wind, were spreading rapidly. Within 15 minutes, the whole block was ablaze, and the inferno was moving south toward the business district and the volatile forest industry facilities along the river.

"A tremendous column of black smoke struggled 30 feet high, and then was whipped horizontally south by the fierce north wind that was blowing 30 miles an hour," *The Globe* reported in its front-page story the following day.

"The Ottawa fire brigade was telephoned for, and in a few minutes Chief Prevost with two fire engines, eight hose reels and an aerial truck was on the way to the conflagration. By the time they arrived, billows of flame faced them. So fierce was the heat, even when the firemen were standing 100 feet from the burning houses, that Chief Prevost dropped in a swoon, as though he had been hit on the head

Queen Street in Ottawa as the flames approach. PAC Booth Family, C120334.

with a sandbag, and his men, some of whom were incapacitated, had to carry him to cooler quarters. It was apparent that, so far as Hull was concerned, the firemen had a hopeless task before them."

The flames leapt from roof to roof, setting block after block ablaze. Occasionally a place was spared as the fire advanced at a rapid pace. "Families carried their household effects into the street, and threw bedding and large pieces of furniture from the upper windows," *The Globe* reported. "Some were fortunate to have horses to remove their goods to a place of safety, but, in the large majority of cases, effects were simply saved from the flames in the buildings to be destroyed in the streets."

The conflagration cut a wide swath as it worked its way through the central and southern part of the city, taking out much of the downtown area. Then it moved toward the Eddy complex on the north shore of the Ottawa River. "If one could imagine a snow storm of particles of fire instead of snow," Mr. Eddy recounted later, "it would give some idea of the intensity." Despite the efforts of the company fire brigade and part of the Ottawa fire department, the Eddy complex was destroyed, with damage totalling some $3 million.

By the time the fire fiend had finished ravishing Hull, 276 acres of the city were blackened, 1300 homes and buildings were wiped out, and 42 per cent of the population was left homeless.

It was a spectacular sight from across the river, but it was soon much more than that. Within a few hours of the outbreak of the fire, the 58 000 citizens of Ottawa joined their brothers and sisters across the river in facing the disaster. The 1000-foot-wide Ottawa River proved to be no barrier to the blaze. Thousands of burning embers were whipped across the river by the strong north winds, and the strength of the fire was so great that flames marched across the wooden deck of the bridge which joined the two cities.

The flames soon spread into the flatland along the river on the Ottawa side. They consumed the Booth and Bronson lumber yards, and worked their way through houses, flour mills, the railway station and the hydro electric stations which provided power for Ottawa's street railway and electric lighting. Officials desperately tried to create a fire break by using dynamite, but the explosion sent embers flying and ignited more blazes. The Chaudière district in the city's northwest end was wiped out. The fire cut a 440-acre swath, half a mile wide and two and a half miles long, from the river all the way to Carling Avenue near the city limits.

Bad as it was, the disaster could have been worse. Parliament and the central business district in the east end of Ottawa were spared, thanks to the fact that they were located on a high bluff, which acted as a wall. But the west end was devasted. The fire destroyed 400 buildings and left 14 per cent of Ottawa's population homeless. By the time the blaze finally died out about midnight, it was one of the worst fires in Canadian history. Fortunately, only seven people died, but damage amounted to more than $10 million, and some 15 000 people lost their homes.

A massive relief and reconstruction effort was undertaken, and the spirits of the people of Hull and Ottawa were high.

Queen Victoria sent a message of sympathy and support. The weather remained warm and sunny. People were soon going through the ashes looking for nails to be used in rebuilding. Temporary shelters were thrown up with lumber which had escaped the flames. Many people were temporarily housed in Ottawa's military drill hall, the Salvation Army barracks and the exhibition grounds. Tents were erected in Hull. Within 48 hours, no one was left without a roof over his head, and there was plenty of food for everyone.

Donations of goods and money poured in from across Canada. "The country most nobly responds," *The Globe* reported two days after the disaster. "People in outside places who wish to help the 15,000 sufferers cannot do better than to get together every piece of cast-off clothing in their houses and send them by express to the City Hall in Ottawa. There is no kind of clothing that will not be useful. Today women could be seen wearing men's coats, while their husbands had on nothing over their shirts."

Almost 40 per cent of the loss was covered by insurance, and reconstruction soon began. Cash donations totalling almost $1 million came in, half from Canada and the rest mostly from Great Britain, British colonies and the United States. Despite the fact that 90 per cent of Hull's population was of French descent, France contributed just $1036. The Ottawa and Hull Relief Fund disbursed payments to more than 3000 people. The fund helped finance 750 new buildings by the end of the year, and it was a major factor in helping the two devastated cities get back on their feet. E. B. Eddy and the other major

Terrorists tried to blow up the Welland Canal

Big explosions have become an ugly feature of life in the late 20th century, but politically motivated acts of mass destruction are not new. One of the wildest terrorists plots in history took place in Canada almost 100 years ago, when a gang of dynamiters tried to blow up a section of the Welland Canal. If these fanatics had succeeded, they would have killed scores of people, smashed many homes and businesses, and crippled the vital transportation link which skirts the unnavigable Niagara River and joins Lake Erie and Lake Ontario.

The story begins in April 1900, when a stout, middle-aged man calling himself Karl Dullman of Washington, D.C., checked into a Niagara Falls hotel. For each of the next several days, Dullman met two men who were staying across the river in a hotel in Niagara Falls, N.Y. This seedy-looking pair, a quick little man named John Nolin and a larger, duller fellow named John Walsh, accompanied Dullman on various horse-and-buggy trips around the area. While they looked like ordinary tourists to casual observers, they were working out the details of a grandiose plot to strike an indirect blow against Britain in the long and bitter fight for Irish independence.

The trio went to several spots in the area, but on two occasions they visited a town called Thorold about 10 miles west of Niagara Falls. It was at Thorold that the Welland Canal climbed the Niagara escarpment via a series of watertight compartments known as locks, each 240 feet long and 40 feet wide. Gates at the head and foot of each lock were opened and closed by chains, enabling ships to enter and remain as the lock was flooded or drained to raise or lower the vessel.

Lock 24 at Thorold was the most vulnerable spot to attack on the 27-mile canal. Lock 24 held back more than a mile of water between itself and Lock 25, the last lock before the canal reached Lake Ontario. The water between Locks 24 and 25 was a minimum of 14 feet deep and as much as 200 feet wide, creating a massive pool of water. If the dynamite had blown the gates, this enormous volume of water would have come roaring down the escarpment, causing a disastrous flash flood.

The deluge would have wiped out the railway station and the homes immediately below the lock and flooded the low-lying flats strewn with mills, factories and homes in the village of Merritton, immediately to the north. The plotters picked the time as carefully as they picked the location for their attack. The terrorists struck on April 21, 1900. The canal had been closed for the winter, but by that time the ice had melted, and it was just a few days before the waterway was scheduled to reopen for the season.

But while they got the location and the timing right, the dynamiters turned out to be inept demolition engineers. That is why they failed.

Nolin and Walsh boarded the train at Niagara Falls about 6 o'clock that

Saturday evening. They got off at Thorold, each carrying a small valise full of dynamite and fuses. They walked a short distance up the railway track, then crossed over to the canal embankment, which they followed up to Lock 24. They ducked behind a storage building, evidently to arrange the fuses. Then one of the men went to the lock's upper gates, while the other went to the lower gates. The twin gates in each location were held in place by steel hinges attached to the concrete abutments of the canal.

The men lit the fuses and used ropes to lower the dynamite eight or 10 feet over the left side of the canal. As the men fled there was a terrific explosion, soon followed by a second blast. The concussion shattered windows in nearby buildings and was heard as far away as Port Dalhousie, eight miles north. The explosions shattered the hinges of both gates, but the gates held and settled to the bottom of the canal, retaining most of the water inside the lock instead of letting it sweep down the escarpment.

Much of the blast was directed outward, away from the gates. If Nolin and Walsh had set off their explosions at the centre of the lock, rather than along the side, they would have forced the gates apart and permitted the water to flow freely. The water pressure would have worked in conjunction with the dynamite, creating a breech in the locks, and the intended disaster would have been unstoppable. But because the dynamite was placed in such a poor location, the gates not only held; they were damaged so little that it was possible to repair them and open the canal on schedule the following Wednesday.

But Nolin and Walsh didn't realize they had failed as they headed back on foot toward Niagara Falls. They had hoped the authorities would be too busy coping with the disaster to immediately concern themselves with apprehending the culprits. But word soon went out by telegraph telling the police what had happened. Several people who had seen Nolin and Walsh provided descriptions of the men.

At about 9:30 p.m., three police officers saw the culprits coming down the road toward Niagara Falls. The officers hid and pounced on Nolin and Walsh, overcoming them and seizing a loaded revolver from the pocket of each man's coat. Nolin, an elf-like man about 35 years old with brown hair and a sandy moustache, claimed to be a machinist from Philadelphia. Walsh, in his late 20s, had a smooth, florid face, and was well built. He claimed to be from Washington, D.C.

It didn't take the authorities long to pick up the third member of the trio, Karl Dullman. Dullman was found in his room in Niagara Falls. He refused to provide any information about himself and denied knowing Nolin and Walsh, despite the fact that dozens of people had seen them travelling around together during the previous week. In fact, the trio had been under light surveillance for the past few days, their cross-border activities having aroused suspicions that they might be smugglers.

Police quickly identified Dullman as the ringleader of the group. He was older than the other two, better dressed, more polished in speech and manner, and cooler in the face of police interrogation.

The Canadian authorities were certain they had the guilty parties, but believed the three men were following directions from powerful forces in the United States or overseas. Several theories were proposed as to who might be behind this dastardly scheme. One suggestion was that the conspirators were sympathetic to the Boers, who at the time were at war with Britain in South Africa.

Another theory was that the men were acting on behalf of unionized grain handlers in nearby Buffalo, N.Y., who were unhappy that ships were bypassing their port by using the Welland Canal to ship grain to Montreal. Rumors even began to circulate that a gang of men from Buffalo were on their way to Niagara Falls to break the trio out of jail. The Canadians were worried enough to call out the militia to guard the jail, but nothing came of the threat.

A third theory, which eventually turned out to be the correct one, was that the men were Irish terrorists. Nolin and Ross had been sent from Dublin to provide the "muscle" for Dullman's scheme to blow up the canal. Dullman, whose real name was Dillon, was a leading member of Clan-na-gael, a group of Americans with ties to the Fenian movement, which wanted to overthrow British rule and establish an Irish state. The Fenians eventually developed into the Irish terrorist group known as Sinn Fein.

This was not the first time the Fenians had tried to strike at Britain through Canada. In 1866, a group led by a former Union army officer crossed the Niagara River near Fort Erie. The Fenians were driven back to the States by Canadian militiamen. It was the last time Americans undertook an armed invasion of Canada. Two more attempts in the early 1870s were aborted by the U.S. government.

The dynamite plotters were tried in Welland, the county seat. *The Globe* reported that Dullman remained aloof from his co-conspirators, perhaps hoping to distance himself from their deeds, perhaps because he was angry because they botched the job. The newspaper said Dullman remained outwardly cool, but there were lines in his face "which are not the lines of age, and although it is in some way a strong face, it is not in any sense prepossessing. He has never been a laboring man, for his hands, contrasted with those of his fellow prisoners, are as soft and white as a woman's. Yesterday, he sat with them folded in front of him, with the easy composure of a man who had dropped into the court room to watch the progress of the trial in which he had nothing more than a passing interest."

The newspaper said that Walsh's appearance was much different, that he "bore out the theory that he was simply the instrument used by Dullman. He did not attempt to follow the intricacies of the evidence, except when his own name was mentioned. He is a young man, many years younger than Dullman, and physically a good specimen of manhood, but his face proclaims him of much lower mental calibre. He sat through the whole day with a vacant stare and parted lips, and to the ordinary spectator he appeared to be what he probably was, a weak-minded catspaw."

The Globe described Nolin as "quick and alert as a terrier, and he helped his counsel, Mr. F. C. McBurney, who is also the legal advisor of Walsh, whenever he had the chance, even to the putting on of another man's hat when he stood up to be identified. He has the face of the Irishman of the comic paper, but he has the intelligence which Walsh lacks, and the appearance of a man who would show great cunning in small matters."

All three were convicted of conspiring to cause an explosion "of a nature likely to endanger life or to cause serious injury to property." The fact that the scheme failed saved them from the gallows. They were sentenced to life in prison. Walsh died of tuberculosis in Kingston penitentiary. The others were released after serving 15 years. The Welland Canal, which narrowly missed becoming the scene of one of the greatest tragedies in Canadian history, still carries ships up and down the Niagara escarpment.

Three dots heard around the world

An inventor named Guglielmo Marconi arrived in St. John's, Newfoundland, in late 1901 to undertake a bold experiment. Marconi was convinced he could transmit telegraph signals through the air, right across the Atlantic Ocean. Many people at the time thought Marconi was a crackpot, but he is now recognized as the inventor of the wireless, one of the first and greatest inventions of the 20th century, the forerunner of radio, television and all the rest of our modern communications equipment.

At the start of this century, as he set up his equipment on Signal Hill overlooking the St. John's harbor, Marconi was breaking new ground. He knew there was a good chance he would fail, and told the curious that he was undertaking routine experiments. That way, he wouldn't have to offer explanations if he failed in his bid to do something which had never been done before.

The 27-year-old scientist had previously demonstrated that he could send messages across relatively short distances. As a teenager in his Italian homeland he had sent signals as far as two miles. After going to England to seek scientific expertise and financial backing, he increased the

Guglielmo Marconi

distance to 18 miles. He got it up to 80 miles in the United States, and by 1901 he had frequently sent wireless messages between ships and shore.

The big question was whether the signals could be sent and received over hundreds and thousands of miles. Marconi had already arranged things on the other side of the ocean. In a village of Poldhu on the east coast of England, he had erected a powerful transmitter and a ring of 20 antennas with masts as high as 200 feet. But could the wireless send a signal from Poldhu to St. John's? Could the wireless provide an alternative to the 14 undersea telegraph cables which already linked the world's two most communications-conscious continents?

At that point, Marconi wasn't even trying to send voices through the air. Like the cable operators, he was sending messages in Morse code, using dots and dashes to spell out words. If he could send such signals through the air across the ocean by radio, he would provide a potentially cheaper and simpler way of linking the continents. But this would only be possible if radio waves could bend. If they were like light waves and moved in straight lines, it wouldn't be possible to send radio messages across great distances.

If radio waves couldn't follow the earth's curvature, they would not reach their distant target. They would skip off into space rather than joining up Poldhu and St. John's. But Marconi was sure that radio waves would bend. He hoped to show that they could make their way around the 150-mile-high arc of the globe which lay between Newfoundland and England.

Marconi had already felt the sting of scepticism from those who said that the technology was more of a gimmick than a useful means of communications. He had run into trouble when more than one transmitter was used at the same time to report the results of yacht races to on-shore receivers. The radio waves had interfered with one another. And while he touted the wireless as a useful tool during wartime, the mobile radio stations he provided to the British in the Boer War didn't work.

The British army asked Marconi's men to mount their equipment on horse-drawn wagons for use in battle. The idea was to provide communication when the enemy cut telegraph lines, or in places where the terrain was too rough to install telegraph poles. But the local climate produced too much atmospheric electricity, interfering with transmissions, and high winds played havoc with the masts, balloons and kites used to support antennas, so the radios in South Africa didn't work.

Sceptics said Marconi was nothing more than a hustler who was trying to make money from an ill-conceived idea. He knew that an impressive demonstration was needed to show that his wireless technology was not just a gimmick. Marconi originally planned to send a signal from Poldhu to Cape Cod, Massachusetts, where he built a station similar to the one in England. The idea was to demonstrate that messages could be sent in both directions between England and the United States. But in November 1901 the Cape Cod station collapsed in a storm.

That left Marconi with two options. He could quit and try again the next year, or he could find another way to prove his point. He chose the latter, and in late November he set sail for St. John's, the closest point to England, which was 1800 miles across the Atlantic. He hoped to use balloons and kites to raise a wire as high as possible, in a bid to receive a signal sent from Poldhu. It would not be as impressive as the two-way dialogue he had hoped to establish between the United States and England, but it would still be an unprecedented achievement. Marconi was eager to keep ahead of his competitors, who were working to achieve a similar result.

He sent a cablegram to Poldhu arranging for wireless signals to be sent each afternoon, starting on Wednesday, Dec. 11. The powerful transmitter, which had an electric force about 100 times stronger than an ordinary station, was to operate from 3 to 6 p.m. local time, which would be from 11:30 a.m. to 2:30 p.m. in Newfoundland.

They were to send the letter "S" in Morse code. It consisted of three dots, three quick strokes of the telegraph key, which Marconi hoped he could pick out against a background of atmospheric interference. But a storm the first day made it difficult to control the 14-foot-diameter balloon Marconi's helper sent up to carry the aerial. Even so, Marconi, sitting in an old building with the wind howling outside, thought he was able to detect three faint dots until the wind ripped the balloon from its moorings.

On the following day, Marconi sent the aerial up with a kite. The high winds made the kite climb and dive wildly, and thus changed its ability to receive signals, but Marconi heard the three-dot pattern at 12:30, 1:10 and 2:20 p.m.

He tried again on Friday and Saturday, hoping for clearer results, but he had no success, so late on Saturday he sent a low-key telegram to a colleague in London. "Signals are being received," he said. "Weather makes continuous tests very difficult. One balloon carried away yesterday."

Knowing from previous experience that any claims he made were greeted with scepticism by his competitors and critics, he planned to obtain stronger evidence before making an announcement of the success of the trans-Atlantic experiment. But on that Saturday afternoon he told inquiring reporters that he had received signals from England, and provided the details when they pressed him. Those reporters used conventional cables to telegraph the news to the wire services, which in turn fed it out to the newspapers.

The big dailies knew a hot story when they saw one on a slow Sunday morning. *The New York Times* of Sunday, Dec. 15, 1901, ran the news from Newfoundland as its top story on Page 1. In the lead paragraph, *The Times* called Marconi's achievement "the most wonderful scientific development of recent times." *The Times* and other newspapers turned young Marconi into a hero. It was an example of what would become a familiar pattern in the 20th century – the bestowing of fame upon an individual by the mass media. Marconi had become a hero.

The papers told how other unscrupulous inventors had tried to get around

Marconi's patent, when in fact they were only imitating him. Reporters interviewed big-wigs from the cable industry, who unconvincingly stated that they did not see Marconi and his wireless as serious competition to their monopolies. The press even suggested that the first trans-Pacific cable, then being laid, might not be needed, if wireless stations could be set up on islands to carry messages across the world's largest ocean.

Thanks to the media coverage of his achievement, offers of support and encouragement poured in. In a significant endorsement, Alexander Graham Bell, the inventor of the telephone, offered Marconi the use of land he owned on Cape Breton to continue his experiments. The Canadian government, which up to that point had shown no interest in the Italian inventor, invited him to Ottawa and gave him money to build a station at Glace Bay, Nova Scotia.

A report in the February 1902 edition of *The Canadian Magazine* said that "Marconi looks more English than Italian, and he speaks English well, with very little trace of foreign accent. He is above the medium height, with the frame of an active man, somewhat slight, but standing up well and not wanting in power. His hair is dark and his young moustache light. He has bright, quick eyes, which have a pleasant way in animated conversation of half closing and twinkling merrily."

In less than a year, the Glace Bay station was able to transmit a message from the governor general, Lord Minto, to King Edward VII in England. Transmission of radio messages by voice rather than Morse code was achieved in 1906. Regular transatlantic service began in 1907. Two years later, Marconi received the Nobel Prize for physics.

He lived to see his invention become the pre-eminent means of instantaneous long-distance communication, and to see the radio receiver become a common household appliance in North America and Europe. When he died in 1937, there was a brief worldwide radio silence to honor the man and his achievements.

Canadians loved their electric trolleys

Electric street railways were a popular means of transportation in Canada's cities at the start of the 20th century. The trolleys, forerunners of today's subway, bus and light rapid transit systems, were cheap, reliable, comfortable and fast.

They caught on with the public as soon as they were introduced in the early 1890s. A decade later, they were operating in most urban centres, including Montreal, Toronto, Ottawa, Hamilton, London, Niagara Falls, St. Catharines, St. John, Winnipeg and Vancouver. By 1900 the annual number of passengers had climbed past the one-hundred-million mark.

They were also a big success with the businessmen who operated them because the profits were very good. In 1899, trolley revenues across Canada totalled $3.8 million, while net earnings were $1.7 million, yielding a profit of almost 45 per cent.

The street railways were not new – only their method of locomotion had changed. In the old days, the power had been supplied by horses. When the cars were converted to electricity, they were faster and more reliable. They also had brighter lights to illuminate the interior and electric heat to keep the passengers warm in the winter.

"The progressive development of the electric street railways in Canada has been nowhere surpassed in the world," bragged *The Canadian Magazine* in an article singing the praises of the new technology.

"Horse power could not keep a street car track clear of snow and ice during winter in most Canadian cities, and no attempt was made to do so. Two sets of street railway equipment were thus required, horse cars and busses for summer, sleighs for winter," the magazine pointed out. "The winter upset all possibility of cleanliness and comfort; to keep people's feet warm, straw was loaded into the bottom of the sleighs, where no possible amount of renewal could keep it clean or decent; there it would lie, unkempt and unsightly, dirty and insanitary, particularly on wet days, contributing dubious odours to the atmosphere of the cars."

The magazine said the electric streetcars were a great leap forward in transportation technology.

"The slow, dirty busses or sleighs, disease-breeding vehicles, confined to the condensed portion of the towns, running at intervals anywhere from 15 minutes to half an hour, were replaced by something infinitely better. People jumped to patronize the improvement, which in turn responded to the patronage, and now are seen magnificently appointed cars following closely one after another to all parts of cities and their suburbs at a speed no one just before the change thought possible."

But winter, a major headache for the old horse-drawn system, still caused a major problem for the new electric lines. It was a challenge to keep the tracks beds and pathways clear of snow. This was accomplished by sending out sweeper cars at the first sign of snow, along with horse-drawn sleighs to haul away the white stuff before it could clog the roadways.

The Canadian Magazine bragged that street railway companies in this country were better at handling snow than their counterparts in northern American states. "Canadian street car companies take no chances with winter storms," the magazine reported. "The companies keep a keen weather eye both on the 'probs' and on the local weather manifestations, and the moment trouble is sniffed, the enemy is tackled. Any symptom of a heavy snowfall, let alone a storm or a blizzard, calls out the electric sweepers."

The price of a ride on the street car was a nickel, but you could buy six tickets for a quarter, and kids rode for half price. Once you got on, you could go anywhere you wanted on the system, thanks to the policy of giving passengers free transfers.

In most cities the electric power to run the street cars came from generating plants fueled by coal. The coal was burned to create steam, which rotated turbines, which produced the electricity. The idea of using hydro-electric power from Niagara Falls had been considered, but at the start of the century Canadian businessmen didn't think this was a practical idea, because a method of economically transmitting power over long distances had not yet been developed.

It wasn't until the big U.S. coal strike of 1902 threatened fuel supplies that Canadians started to look seriously into using the cascading waters of the falls as a source of electric power for communities remote from Niagara. Soon a method of transforming voltages was developed, which allowed electricity to be sent cheaply across great distances. After that, Niagara Falls became Ontario's major source of electricity. It not only powered the trolleys; it made possible the massive industrialization of the province, and thereby increased Ontario's lead as Canada's most progressive and prosperous province.

Chapter 5
How Different They Were

"Oh, what a good preacher is sickness"

Indians today are encouraged to preserve their cultural heritage by holding pow-wows, potlaches and other traditional activities. The federal government eagerly supplies funding for such events, and has officially apologized to the Indian people for trying to stamp out their culture.

But at the start of the century, such activities were strongly discouraged. The government's attempts to ban them, however, were largely unsuccessful, thanks largely to the fact that the Indians continued to do in secret what they could not do openly. They got away with it because they stayed largely to themselves, and because the police were reluctant to get involved and to prosecute them for such "crimes."

Still, the prevailing attitudes of the white population toward such activities were not only negative. From a late-20th-century perspective, it was downright racist. A typical example of popular white sentiments toward Indian customs early in the century can be found in an article which appeared in *The Canadian Magazine*. It was written by Marshall Owen Scott, a member of the Parliamentary Press Gallery.

"The painted red men of the prairies and forests we still have with us," Scott told his readers. "In the Sun Dance, the Potlatch and other pagan practices, the war-whoop is heard, and the tomahawk and scalping-knife flash in the light."

Scott reviewed Indian massacres and other atrocities of previous centuries, and said that thankfully the remnants of "revolting savagery" are fading, and that "civilization is winning its way. The best strains of Indian blood are sending their young to be educated in ever-growing numbers. The most debased of the old pagans of inferior blood are dying out."

He noted that paganism and Christianity exist side-by-side in some Indian villages, but that Christianity was winning. "In the same villages are Sun Dances and the worship of the Most High. Where paganism is supreme there is sloth and foul things unspeakable. Where the prayer of the pale-face is heard, intelligence, thrift and progress appear."

Scott rashly predicted that within a decade, assimilation would be almost complete. "The pagan dances will be numbered to a great extent among the memories of the past, and the Indians in the mass will scarcely be distinguished from the rest of the labouring population in anything but name and the heredity outward stamp on their face."

Scott wasn't alone in his sentiments. A similar view was held by the Roman Catholic Church, which urged the Indians to give up their own rituals and adopt

Catholic rituals. Bishop Dontenwill of Vancouver was delighted when members of the Carrier tribe, shaken by a recent flu epidemic which wiped out 15 per cent of the tribe, burned their traditional masks, rattles and other ceremonial items in July of 1901.

Father Morice, a missionary, had told the Indians that the deaths were divine punishment for refusing to abandon their old ways. "Oh, what a good preacher is sickness," said the good father.

Another magazine article from the beginning of the century offered the following stomach-flipping description of the wolf dance, as performed by the Euclataw Indians of Vancouver Island:

> "The tribe seat themselves in a big circle round a huge fire of pine logs, and wait. First there is heard a series of the most lugubrious howlings and cries from the adjacent underwoods, varied with screams of blood-curdling intensity, solo and in chorus.
>
> "Then there is a fearful outburst of the howlings, and amidst this hideous din 20 or 30 young men, clad from head to foot in wolf skins, with bunches of wolf tails streaming down from the back of their heads, their faces streaked with vari-colored paints, leap madly into the glow of the firelight and immediately proceed to go through the queerest antics, shrieking and caterwauling in the most awful manner.
>
> "Round and round they go, almost into the fire, then almost bursting out of the circle of silent spectators. Madder and madder rises the orgie, faster and faster the leaping wolf-dancers go, louder and louder become their screams, till, at a given signal, they stop, and the silence that follows is almost painful by contrast with the uproar of the preceding moment.
>
> "Then one of the dancers goes up to the chief, taking from under his cloak of skins a wolf cub, which he offers to the chief, who accepts the gift in dead silence. A knife is brought, the struggling cub is placed upon a block of wood, and at one sweep its head is severed from its body.
>
> "All the Indians crowd forward and dip their fingers in the blood, touching their foreheads with the wetted fingers. This is supposed to impart extraordinary courage and endurance."

Still another magazine article predicted that Native rituals and all other vestiges of Indian culture would soon be things of the past. In this oh-so-wrong forecast, Bleasdell Cameron in January 1900 predicted that the Indians of the Northwest Territories would soon be extinct.

He noted a recent drop in population and said it would soon accelerate because

> "the red man is improvident, and ignorant of the laws of health. And he requires room – plenty of room. His instincts, the inheritance handed down to him through many generations of nomadic, savage ancestry crave – demand it. It is his breath of life. The atmosphere of towns is poison in his nostrils; set bounds cramp and fret him as they would a high-spirited horse. He sickens and dies as does a plant denied the sun."

Cameron concluded that "it is a question whether a century hence there will remain in the Plains region of the Northwest a single pure-blood Indian." That prediction can be compared with what has actually happened.

Statistics Canada recently reported that the Native population in Canada amounted to almost 800 000, out a total population of 28.5 million. Stats Canada said the Native population is growing rapidly, particularly among those of childbearing years. Projections indicate that far from being extinct, Natives will make up half the population of Saskatchewan in 50 years. Marshall Owen Scott, who predicted that Canada's Indians would be assimilated early in the 20th century, would have been unpleasantly surprised.

The assimilator's solution to the Indian problem

Time can turn villains into heroes and heroes into villains. Consider Louis Riel, the 19th century rebel and traitor who has been historically rehabilitated in the late 20th century. Until recently, most Canadians thought of Riel as a half-crazed half-breed who led rebellions in the West in the 1870s and 1880s, and got what he deserved – death at the end of a rope for committing treason.

Now, thanks to a politically correct revision of history, Riel is likely to receive a posthumous pardon for his crimes. He is spoken of as a hero and is even being hailed as a Father of Confederation for helping to create the province of Manitoba. The trouble-making Metis, who forced the federal government to call out the militia in the only serious armed rebellion in Canadian history, has been resurrected into a modern-day saint.

But such a dramatic reversal in historical fortune can work the other way, too. Consider William Morris Graham. At the turn of the century, Graham was a highly regarded civil servant who had every reason to believe history would remember him kindly for trying to solve the "Indian problem." He was praised by his superiors for his creative approach toward bringing the Indians into line with the rest of the population. But his efforts to wean the Indians from their traditional ways have come to be seen, from a late 20th-century perspective, as an ill-conceived attempt to destroy the culture of a noble people.

Graham's approach was in keeping with his times. At the start of the 20th century, the importance of cultural diversity in Canada was not widely accepted, and the government certainly didn't hand out money so non-British people could maintain their ethic identities. Respect for foreign values was slim, and it was virtually non-existent for Aboriginal values. Indians were seen more or less as savages. Accordingly, Graham's effort to "civilize" the Indians by turning them into white men was viewed with general approval.

Graham joined the Department of Indian Affairs as a clerk in 1885, the same year Riel was hanged. He advanced steadily in the civil service, first under the Conservative government of Sir John A. Macdonald and his successors, and then, after Wilfrid Laurier's victory in 1896, under the Liberal government. He proved to be an efficient administrator, handling

104 Turn of the Century

Indian boy Thomas Moore before entry into residential school. SPA R-A 8223(1).

Thomas Moore after school entry. SPA R-A 8223(2).

self-sustaining. In a sense, it was Graham's duty to work himself out of a job, by bringing Indians to the point where they became ordinary, self-sufficient members of Canadian society.

But at the turn of the century, the Indians were not a major issue in Canadian politics, and not a lot of effort was put into Indian affairs. After the quelling of the Rebellion of 1885, the Indians posed no further threat to the whites, and had no value in commerce, except in the far North. There were about 100 000 of them at the time, and the thinking the Indians with a good blend of fairness and firmness, and keeping costs to a minimum. This was particularly important under the Liberals, who wanted to spend as little as possible on the Indians, and hoped they would soon be assimilated and thus no longer an expense to the taxpayers.

Meanwhile, the government felt it temporarily had to take control of the lives of the Indians until they "grew up." It treated them like children, regulated their lives, administered their affairs, bombarded them with the Christian religion and expected them to become civilized and ing was that sooner or later they would either die off or be assimilated.

In 1901, at the age of 34, Graham was put in charge of the Indians living in the Qu'Appelle district in the North-West Territories, in what is now southern Saskatchewan. That's where he came up with his scheme to turn Indians into model farmers, and thus into the kind of solid citizens the government wanted them to become.

In those days, many Indian youngsters were taken from their parents and sent to white-run boarding schools. The idea was to break their ties with the past, and turn them into educated young citizens of Canada. These schools were the forerunners of the infamous residential schools in which so much emotional and sexual abuse occurred through much of the century. But even in the schools where there was no such abuse, the children were robbed of their heritage. They were forced to speak English, discouraged from taking part in ancient rituals, and encouraged to abandon their Indian mentality, which was viewed as an unhappy combination of sloth and paganism.

In 1900, according to the annual report of the Department of Indian Affairs, there were about 20 000 Indian youngsters between the ages of 6 and 15. Of those, 3285 were in the nation's 22 industrial schools and 39 boarding schools. Another 6349 were in 226 day schools on reserves.

As Graham saw things, the problem with the schools was that there was no follow-up once the children grew up and graduated. Usually they went back to their former lives and slid back into their old Indian ways. As Graham and other federal bureaucrats saw it, the Indians went "back to the blanket" and lost the benefits of white civilization which had been bestowed upon them in the schools.

Even worse, some of the residential school graduates became misfits. They had become "too white" to fit back into their own society, and they were "too Indian" to join the dominant white culture. They turned out to be a frustrated group of unproductive and troublesome young people. Graham came up with a plan to solve this problem. In 1901, he established a post-graduate program to take some of the brightest alumni from the residential schools and set them up in a model farming operation. The project was situated in a part of the Qu'Appelle reserve known as the File Hills, and so the 19 000-acre experimental farm area became known as the File Hills Colony.

Brass band at File Hills Colony. SPA R-A 19.

The young Indian graduates were married off, given houses and assigned tracts of land to grow wheat and oats. No contact was permitted between the colonists and other Indians who maintained traditional culture, to prevent "retrogression." Ceremonies such as sun dances and pow-wows were prohibited to discourage lapses into tribal ways. The colonists were encouraged to take part in "white" activities. They learned to play baseball, and a brass band was established to give them a suitable "white" outlet for their musical tendencies. The use of Indian languages was forbidden, and the practice of Christianity was encouraged. Sermons in the Roman Catholic and Presbyterian churches on the colony emphasized the importance of such "white" virtues as punctuality, hard work and self-discipline.

Graham and the farm instructors fostered the work ethic to encourage self-sufficiency. Competition between the Indian colonists was encouraged, and there were annual exhibitions and prizes for cattle breeding, growing grain and sewing. Earl Grey, who became governor general of Canada a few years after the colony was established, donated a shield which was awarded each year to the File Hills colonist who produced the best crop.

The colony became such a success that it drew visitors from all parts of Canada and the United States. It was a showpiece of what could be accomplished by Indians if they were put in the right environment. But that, as it turned out, was the fatal flaw in the program. File Hills was a carefully controlled but artificial environment. The system broke down as soon as the restraints were removed. The colony was simply an extension of the white-run residential school system. It didn't teach the Indians to function for themselves, and it robbed them of their culture, leading to major identity and self-esteem problems. In effect, it simply painted a coat of white paint on people whose ancient heritage could not so easily be eradicated.

The File Hills colony was a one-of-a-kind venture, an expensive experiment which was not pursued elsewhere. It was just a drop in the bucket, a haven for only 40 or 50 Indian families in a nation in which the Indians would not die out or be assimilated, but rather would survive and thrive to the point where they are now the fastest-growing segment of the nation's population. Far from being blended in with the mainstream population, the Indians have increased in strength and number and have benefited from the federal government's policy of encouraging all Canadians to retain their heritage.

Who knows what might have happened if efforts similar to the File Hills colony had been undertaken on a massive scale by the government to deal with the "Indian problem"? Would the scheme eventually have "worked," or would the colonies have become just a senior level of the disastrous residential school system? We'll never know, but by and large the efforts of William Morris are seen by contemporary history to have been a misguided attempt at social engineering, a pie-in-the-sky scheme to assimilate a people who turned out to be remarkably resistant to absorption.

Indians had a reputation for good behavior

Criminologists, social workers and aboriginal leaders frequently complain about the large number of Indians imprisoned in Canada today. Aboriginals make up a far greater percentage than their numbers warrant of the people who end up behind bars, particularly in the West. But things weren't always like this. A century ago, Indians were known as peaceful and law-abiding people, and they were rarely sent to jail. The few who got into trouble were usually led astray when someone supplied them with liquor. Doing so was an offence under the law in those days.

"The Indians maintain their reputation for good behavior," A. Bowen Perry, the commissioner of the North-West Mounted Police, said in his annual report for 1900. "There is a steady improvement in their condition, and on some reserves they have large bands of cattle. One Blackfoot Indian has a herd of some 500 head," Perry noted. But alcohol remained a problem. Perry said it was usually sold to the Indians by "half-breeds." In the previous year, 68 people had been charged with supplying liquor to Indians. "The magistrates as a rule deal severely with the culprits, recognizing the demoralizing effect of intoxicants on the Indians."

The NWMP commissioner allayed fears that the Indians were preparing to go on the warpath because many Mounties had left the Territories to fight in the Boer War. "During the early months of the war in South Africa disquieting rumors were abroad that the Indians contemplated rising," Perry said. "These had no foundation whatever. There was sympathy for the Boers among some of our foreign settlements, but of a purely platonic nature."

Those "foreign settlements" were colonies established by Germans, Ukrainians, Doukhobors and others from east and central Europe who had recently immigrated to Canada. Perry said their arrival had widened the duties of the NWMP, not because the newcomers were lawless, but rather because the police were "protecting them from the petty tyranny of some of their own people, and avoiding friction among them and our people, who are often intolerant of their manners and habits, and in fact not inclined favourably toward them."

The Mounties were short of manpower because 178 officers and men had gone overseas to serve with the 2nd Canadian Mounted Rifles, organized and commanded by former NWMP commissioner Lawrence Herchmer, and with the Strathcona Horse Regiment led by Sam Steele, a veteran commissioned NWMP officer. The total strength of the NWMP in those days was only about 750 (compared to about 15 000 RCMP members today). So many Mounties wanted to serve in South Africa, Perry said, that the question was not which ones would go, but rather which ones would have to stay home to make sure the force retained a base of strength. The shortage of men was made up by hiring untrained "special constables" as interpreters, scouts, artisans and the like, and by signing up a large number of recruits, who were eager but lacked the training and experience of the men they replaced.

"The efficient training of a recruit requires 12 months," Perry pointed out. "He must be drilled, set up, taught to ride, learn to shoot with carbine and revolver, acquire a knowledge of his duties and powers as a peace officer, be instructed in simple veterinary knowledge, understand how a horse ought to be shod, and become an efficient prairie man. The latter means a smattering of cooking, being a judge of a horse's work, and able to find his way about, and to look after the comfort of himself and horse."

While most of the new Mounties were successful, a few didn't work out. One recruit got drunk and started a fight with five civilians. "His explanation was that they had jeered at the colour of his coat," Perry explained, "and he felt bound to show what he could do." The recruit was sent to another detachment, but he soon deserted. "The only explanation he ever gave of his desertion was that he was ashamed of himself for having got into trouble." Another recruit had less noble motives for deserting, Perry said. The man was angry because he, along with the rest of the Mounties in his troop, had to carry an extra load on a trip, "and thought proper to show his dissatisfaction by taking another man's pony off the prairie and riding south" across the U.S. border.

So many Mounties were permitted to go to South Africa because things were relatively peaceful in the West. "Considering the varied character of our population, the extent of the territories, and the sparseness of settlement in many districts, there is remarkably little crime," Perry said. He observed that "life and property are as safe as in any part of Canada." His report showed a total of 1351 offences, which ranged from murder (four cases) and wife beating (one case) to being drunk and disorderly (304 cases) and stealing rides from the railway (55 cases).

The most common crime against persons was assault (171 cases). One case was particularly interesting. It happened in the small town of Cardston. "A man had made some filthy remark in connection with the name of a young lady who was visiting there from the United States.... She made the slanderer kneel down at the muzzle of her revolver and make her an ample and public apology." The spunky American woman was disarmed and fined $10.

The theft of livestock was a common offence. Perry reported 54 cases of horse stealing, but pointed out that many cases of alleged theft resulted from the fact that horses grazed year round on the prairies and were frequently not seen by their owners for months. When the owner went looking and couldn't find his horses where he left them, he reported them stolen. But in many cases, the animals had simply been picked up by other settlers. As Perry explained it, a settler would see a horse around his place, probably running with his band. This would go on for a year or more. No one came forward and claimed the horse. The settler took the horse. Then along came the owner. The settler refused to give up the horse, a charge of horse stealing was laid, the settler was arrested and committed for trial, and the judge dismissed the charge.

The commissioner acknowledged that the temptation to steal horses was growing, because the price of horses had recently taken a sharp increase, and livestock thieves were tough to catch. "Horse stealing, cattle stealing and cattle killing are difficult crimes to deal with under western conditions. The animal grazes in the open, the brands are easily obliterated or altered, and when the animal is killed the hide can be destroyed." On top of that, the long, open border with Montana "affords considerable safety to the intelligent and energetic thief."

Perry said that of all the charges laid by the NWMP, 71 per cent resulted in a conviction. The penalties were often severe. A man who seduced a girl under the age of 14 was sentenced to five years in prison and received 10 lashes. A woman who bore an illegitimate child and threw it into a well right after the birth got 23 months in jail. But such crimes were noteworthy because they were infrequent.

The commissioner said NWMP members were getting used to their new uniforms, which replaced helmets, white gloves, cloaks and capes with felt hats, brown gloves and field service jackets. It was the first step in giving Mounties the look that we are familiar with today. Perry said the members of the force were grateful for the addition of jam, dried fruit, oatmeal and canned vegetables to their rations. "Good cooks are only required to give a simple, healthy and appetizing bill of fare." He urged the government to replace the NWMP's obsolete Winchester carbines and Enfield revolvers with modern weapons, and suggested that new saddles be purchased to replace the current ones, which weighted a hefty 45.5 pounds.

In his recent travels through the territories, Perry said,

"I noticed everywhere great increases in settlement, activity in business and a general buoyancy which was not too apparent when I left three years ago (to serve in the Yukon). New towns had sprung up, old towns grown, and settled localities appeared where scarcely a farm house then existed. This expansion caused new demands for police protection. Applications are constantly being received for police protection."

But despite the rapid growth and the shortage of experienced police officers due to the Boer War, Perry concluded, there was "no startling increase in crime, and the state of the country from a police point of view is very satisfactory."

Vicious discrimination against Chinese

Chinese people were the whipping boys of Canadian society at the beginning of the 20th century, especially in British Columbia. They were accused of being liars, gamblers, drug addicts, thieves and tax-evaders. They were social outcasts, and were said to have such filthy personal habits that they were responsible for starting epidemics.

Some 16 000 Chinese lived in British Columbia, as well as 129 000 whites. There was a widespread feeling among the whites that the Chinese didn't belong in this country, and that Ottawa should make sure no more arrived. An editorial in a B.C. newspaper expressed typical sentiments. "The Chinaman is a curse to this country," the Nelson *Miner* declared in

1901. "The government must some day rid the country of that curse. If they do not do it, the people who make and unmake governments will do it for them."

Shades of ethnic cleansing! Today the idea of expelling an entire ethnic group would raise alarm bells among all but the most bigoted citizens. And today the federal government, far from trying to eliminate this ethnic group, is encouraging more Chinese immigrants to come to Canada, especially those with in-demand skills and large bank balances. It's hard to believe that in our grandparents' and great-grandparents' era, people in this country could have been so openly intolerant of the Chinese, and so determined to get rid of them.

But it wasn't just the lunatic fringe that had such racist sentiments. A Royal Commission on Chinese and Japanese immigration appointed by the federal government in 1900 concluded that the Asians were "unfit for full citizenship.... obnoxious to a free community and dangerous to the state."

For years, Ottawa had collected a $50 "head tax" on each Chinese immigrant, in an effort to discourage the entry of Chinese people into Canada. The tax was doubled to $100 in 1900, and jacked up to a whopping $500 in 1903 in response to political pressure, particularly from British Columbia, to keep Chinese people out. A resolution from the British Columbia legislature to the Royal Commission said that "the province is flooded with an undesirable class of people, non-assimilative and most detrimental to the wage-earning classes of the people of the province."

The first Chinese came to Canada in the late 1850s, moving north from California, where they had gone a decade earlier to join the great gold rush. Most of these newcomers worked in B.C.'s Caribou gold fields, but soon they spread throughout the province, working in the fisheries, mines and domestic service. A second wave of Chinese arrived about 25 years later to work on the national railway. They were recruited by the CPR because there was a shortage of labor, and because the Chinese were willing to clear land and build roadbeds for $1 a day, half the rate paid to white laborers. They were unpopular among the white workers because they kept pay low, and because they were so "different."

The British Columbia government passed a law in 1884 to regulate the Chinese population. It said they were "dissimilar in habits and occupation from our people; evade the payment of taxes justly due to the government; are governed by pestilential habits; are useless in instances of emergency; and habitually desecrate grave yards by the removal of bodies therefrom."

The whites said the Chinese could never be assimilated into the mainstream because of their appearance and their habits. In those days, the prevailing sentiment was that it was up to immigrants to learn the language of Canada and fit into the dominant society. The current government policy of encouraging diversity and supporting ethnic cultures lay far in the future. Opium smoking by the Chinese was especially frowned upon. It was seen as a personal vice and a sign of moral degeneration. When Canada's first antidrug laws were adopted in 1908, they were directed primarily against the Chinese.

The whites were also upset by the fact that the Chinese lived in ghettos known as Chinatowns. These places, they said, were dirty and overcrowded. The critics didn't acknowledge that the Chinese lived there because they were too poor to live elsewhere, because they were made to feel unwelcome outside their own communities, and because they were legally forbidden to live in most white areas.

The biggest area of concern was with respect to jobs. The whites complained that the Chinese undercut wages and provided unfair competition for employment. As the Royal Commission of 1900 put it:

> "The one (the white worker) is expected to discharge the ordinary duties of citizenship to himself, his family and his country; rent must be paid, food provided, and the family decently clothed; yet he is put in competition with one (the Chinese worker) who does not assume any of these duties, and who lives under conditions insufferable to a white man. Fifty cents a month or less pays the rent, a few cents a day supplies the food, he has no home, wife or family in this country; he shows no desire to change; he is well content as he is until such time as he can return to China and take his savings with him."

When the Chinese mixed with the whites, it was generally in the area of commerce. They operated laundries, restaurants and other services patronized by whites. The Chinese also worked for whites as domestic servants. An article written in 1900 by Walter C. Nichol, editor of the Vancouver *Province*, reflected the way in which upper-class whites viewed their Chinese employees at the turn of the century. Nichol described a man who was hired by his wife as a house boy.

> "His name was Chow. He was short, loose-jointed, garrulous when with his fellows and jabbering in his native tongue; quiet and uncommunicative around the house. He was 'heap good cook,' he said, and he understood enough English to undertake to sweep, dust, keep the floors polished, light fires, and do the cooking and plain washing for $25 a month."

Nichol made fun of Chow's sly way of avoiding extra work.

> "If we asked him to do anything outside of the duties he had undertaken at the start, his knowledge of the vernacular deserted him. 'Me no sabe' – pronounced 'sabee' with the 'a' long – he would say in that low, plaintive voice of his, and it was quite impossible to make him 'sabe' unless he was promised another dollar a month."

But Nichol managed to find something nice to say about his Chinese servant:

> "The baby would toddle to Chow in all confidence and Chow would smile back and permit the wee one to pull his pigtail, an indignity which, if attempted by a white man, would have provoked a fight. There was something human in Chow after all. My wife had doubted it of all Chinamen before, but when she saw the cordial terms existing between Chow and His Royal Highness, she admitted that Chow

must have some good in him somewhere."

Women pulling plows caused a misunderstanding

When four big shiploads of oppressed foreigners arrived in this country a century ago, they created quite a sensation. The Doukhobors were Russian peasants who had been given refuge in Canada. They had strange ideas, but they also had the potential to be good farmers and welcome additions to the largely empty North-West Territories.

The Doukhobors had been having problems in their homeland for a long time. They were individualists who refused to conform to society. They were also devout pacifists who believed that God lives in each human, and that to kill a person, even in battle, was a grave sin. So they defied Russia's Czar Nicholas when he ordered them to serve in the army. The Doukhobors built a giant bonfire, tossed in the guns that had been issued to them, and calmly awaited the Czar's response.

He retaliated savagely. He confiscated their farms and send troops who stole their food, smashed their homes, imprisoned their men and raped their women. The Doukhobors didn't fight back, and their suffering won the sympathy of Leo Tolstoy, the great Russian novelist. Tolstoy's friend, Prof. James Mavor of the University of Toronto, brought their plight to the attention of the Canadian government, which offered them homes in the West. With financial backing from British Quakers, the Doukhobors arrived in Canada in 1899. About 7500 of them settled in what is now the province of Saskatchewan on 750 000 acres of unbroken land.

The area's Canadian and British settlers didn't know what to make of the newcomers, who were very "different." They spoke a strange language and their religion, while Christian, didn't fit into the usual categories of Protestant and Roman Catholic. They were an offshoot of the Russian Orthodox church, but recognized no authority except the Bible and their own sect's leadership. While there was some infighting among themselves, they generally stuck together because of their mutual need for identity and strength. They called themselves "spirit wrestlers" because they struggled toward spiritual harmony and a life of true Christianity. They worked hard, made good profits and became known for their honesty. One Doukhobor man was said to have travelled 150 miles in bad weather to repay a debt when it fell due.

But sometimes their industriousness was misunderstood. Since they didn't have any farm animals during their first spring in Canada, groups of Doukhobor women hitched themselves to plows to prepare the ground for planting. The men were away, working on railway construction gangs and at other jobs to earn money. When a photo of the women pulling the plow was circulated across Canada, it was taken as an example of the cruelty of Doukhobor men to their women.

A sympathetic report of their rugged and primitive lifestyle was carried in *The Globe* in late 1900. A correspondent who

Doukhobor women pulling plow. SPA R-B 1964(1).

travelled to the Swan River area of the North-West Territories reported that "among the Doukhobors, dentistry seems to be an unknown science, for we met one poor dame taking a 10-mile walk to a neighboring village to have her tooth taken out by a blacksmith. I only hope he had forceps, and did not pry it out with some of his shoeing instruments."

The *Globe* correspondent praised the Russian immigrants for their industriousness and the way in which their women were treated:

> *"It is extraordinary to see the methodical habits of these people. There is no sort of compulsion in the village rules. Everyone works because he feels he ought to work. Here and there you find a 'drone,' but the average is better than one would expect. The women take their share of labor, but when one looks into it, that is not an undue share . . . . We found that perfect equality exists between the sexes. The woman's voice was never loudly raised, but its influence was distinctively felt in the village councils."*

They retained their centuries-old ceremonies, especially their habit of holding gatherings to transmit their history and culture through song and poetry rather than in writing. Large passages of the Book of Life, a collection of hymns and proverbs, were sung or recited around a table set with their traditional and simple foods – bread, salt and water.

But their cultural customs were not the only ones the Doukhobors brought with them to Canada. They brought along their ornery nature as well. They insisted on rejecting government authority in this country, as they had in Russia. They refused to swear allegiance to Queen Victoria, maintaining that to do so would constitute a submission to earthly powers. They believed that they owed allegiance only to God.

They also refused to register their land claims with the government. The Doukhobors lived communally in small villages rather than on homesteads. They refused to register individual land claims within three years after their arrival, as was required under Canada's homesteader legislation. As a result, the Doukhobors lost much of the land they had cultivated. About a quarter-million acres were taken back by the government and sold to other settlers and speculators. But the Doukhobors managed to retain the rest of their land after it was designated as a communal reserve, to get around the homesteader requirement.

Their beliefs sometimes caused them to do strange things. In the fall of 1902, 1700 members of a group called the Sons of God went on a mass pilgrimage toward some vaguely defined Promised Land. Convinced that the enslavement of animals was a sin, they destroyed their clothes and other items made of skins and leather, and turned their farm animals

Peter Verigin. SPA R-B 2194.

loose. Their fellow-Doukhobors tried to persuade them to give up the trek, but they kept at it for two weeks, until the North-West Mounted Police stopped them and transported them back to their homes.

Peter Vaselievich Verigin, the leader of the Doukhobors, arrived from Russia about a month later. Verigin settled the controversial animal issue by proclaiming that horses were "partners" in communal life, and therefore it was permissible to use them. He drove home his point by travelling around in a coach pulled by six fine horses. Verigin purchased a large block of land, had a magnificent house built, and established a village which he named after himself. He wore the finest clothes, and was usually accompanied by a group of young women chanting psalms when he went from place to place. He also kept an 18-year-old brunette woman, who acted as his wife and consort.

Years later, the Doukhobors came to public attention when they adopted a spectacular way to protest when they disagreed with actions of the government. They shed their clothes and went on marches, much to the delight of voyeurs and much to the consternation of the authorities.

French-Canadians were frequently put down

Today an English-Canadian magazine could never get away with suggesting that French-Canadians don't care about the lives of their own children. It could never say that French-Canadians have so many children that they don't care if they lose a few of them to a preventable disease. The publication would be branded as racist, the human rights police would leap into action, and the separatists would have one more reason to seek independence from Canada.

But the lead article in an issue of *Saturday Night* magazine in the summer of 1901 made such a charge, and nobody batted an eyelash, because negative comments about Quebecers were common in English Canada at that time. This was especially true regarding Quebec's lack of support for the Boer War, but this particular article took aim not at the war in South Africa, but rather the one against a disease which was a great killer of children.

The article pointed out that smallpox was still a problem in Canada, despite the fact that vaccination against the disease was widespread. It noted that Quebec had been the last part of Canada to set up a program to vaccinate youngsters, but that in some parts of the province children were still not being immunized. The word "smallpox" used to send chills up people's spines. It was spoken of in the same way that AIDS is talked about today. But while AIDS picks off its victims slowly and one by one, smallpox used to sweep through communities and within weeks leave dozens or even hundreds of victims in its wake.

The smallpox virus was transmitted through fluids discharged from the mouth and nose of an infected person. A rash developed on the victim's face, hands and feet. Within a few days, the rash turned into pus-filled pustules. If these pimple-like sores ran together and formed a scab covering the entire body, death was almost certain. Those who survived were often left with ugly scars or pock marks, but also with protection against future attacks because their blood developed antibodies.

The *Saturday Night* article maintained that French-Canadian parents who failed to have their children immunized were negligent, and possibly murderous. "In Quebec for many years the people refused to be vaccinated or have their children looked after," the article recalled, "and almost every winter there was an epidemic of smallpox. The parents of large families who were also devout Roman Catholics used the text, 'The Lord giveth and the Lord taketh away,' and perhaps they were not unwilling to have some of their numerous progeny removed.

> "At any rate, they had the same comfortable feeling with regard to smallpox as the majority of parents have in connection with measles, whopping cough, scarletina, mumps etc., and were glad when their children were immune from all these things because they had them. If a child or two died, it did not seem to be a heartbreaking matter, inasmuch as they had so many left.
>
> "Some 15 or 16 years ago, Ontario made it impossible for the Quebec authorities to permit this lax administration of sanitary laws, and when Quebec found itself boycotted by the other provinces both as to mail, passenger and freight interchange, it became a link in the chain of compulsory vaccination. Yet it was wonderful how slowly the conviction forced itself upon the French-Canadians that vaccination was not opposed to the will of God nor in the line of preventing disease.
>
> "One splendid feature of French-Canadian character is that they do not try to prevent the birth of children, but in connection with smallpox there was the improper idea that they should not prevent the death of any of them by a disease which is frightfully contagious, disfiguring and nauseous. Now that sanitary officers have got control of this thing in Quebec, the other provinces are able to keep it in check."

Today such language would be considered inflammatory and possibly in breach of the criminal law against promoting race hatred, but at the turn of the century it was common to put down French-Canadians in such blunt terms. Francophones were portrayed as the dregs of the nation, throwbacks to an earlier era, primitive and unintelligent people incapable of fitting into modern society. In many ways, they were viewed by English-Canadians much as black people were seen by racist whites in the United States.

English-Canadian writers regularly claimed that the French in Canada had progressed little since the days when their ancestors arrived in the new world in the 16th and 17th centuries. These writers considered modern British culture to be the best in the world. As they saw it, English-Canadians had to put up with the many second-rate French-Canadians in their midst, but that didn't mean they had to like them, let alone accept them as co-founders of the nation or beg them to stay within Canada.

The most popular patriotic song in English-Canada at the beginning of the century was a slap in the face of French-Canadians. It celebrated their defeat by the British on the Plains of Abraham in the Seven Years' War during the mid-18th century. The song, titled "The Maple Leaf Forever," opens with a tribute to General James Wolfe, whose forces conquered the French at Quebec City. The first verse of the song goes like this: "In days of yore, from Britain's shore/Wolfe the dauntless hero came/And planted firm Britannia's flag/On Canada's fair domain."

The song goes on to praise the British, Scottish and Irish people in Canada. It celebrates Canada's vastness and beauty and, of course, it makes much of the maple leaf, "our emblem dear." It praises the English-Canadian patriots who fought against the Americans in the War of 1812, but makes no mention of French contributions to Canada.

The current idea that Canada was started by two founding races, English and French, would not have been accepted by many bigots in English-Canada at the turn of the century, and the idea that the aboriginal people should also be considered founders of the nation would have been laughed at. A. G. Bradley, a British author who toured Canada extensively during that period, summed up English-Canadian attitudes toward the French in his book titled *Canada in the Twentieth Century*.

Bradley characterized the French-Canadians as "a deeply conservative and self-absorbed people" who were controlled by the Roman Catholic Church. He said the priests had succeeded in keeping their flocks "simple, ignorant, contented and moral." Noting the lack of French support for the Boer War, Bradley said that "one does not expect from so self-centred a people any enthusiasm for our Imperial ventures."

In his travels across Canada, the author found "wholesale prejudice against the French." Bradley found that from coast to coast, English-Canadians frequently expressed anti-French sentiments:

"I have heard it indulged in by scores of people in Canada, and of course it amounts, as it does elsewhere, to a catalogue of the points upon which the French temperament differs from our own, somewhat crudely rubbed in . . . . The French, on their part, have of course inherited like prejudices, but in Canada they are not, I think, quite so pronounced as those of the British."

He noted the almost complete separation of the French and English races in Quebec, and found that Montreal was the only place where they rubbed shoulders in great numbers.

"The French and English of Montreal, though good enough friends and mixing together of necessity in the ordinary course of business, remain almost completely apart in social life," Bradley observed. "It is a rather curious spectacle, this utter lack of social sympathy or fusion among the prosperous classes of a modern and progressive commercial centre."

The feeling that the French of Canada were backwards was not limited to English-Canadians and visitors from Britain. An article in the New York *Times* in late 1901 reflected similar ideas in discussing French-Canadians who had moved to the U.S. to work in New England factories. It described the young francophone women like this:

"From time to time one sees a fresh face, but as a rule the girls have thin figures and sallow skins, and their hair and eyes are lustreless. They are overworked. The French-Canadian women bear more than their share of the burdens of life."

The article said the women got jobs as soon as the law permitted, "while the men and the boys idle about the house or the streets." The women earned from $5 to $10 a week until they got married, when they quit and began to have very large families.

At that point, the *Times* article concluded, the French-Canadian woman was "the prototype of those ancestors who lived out their days on Canadian soil. She causes her family to speak French, that her grandchildren may not grow up ignorant of the tongue of their forefathers, and she teaches them its customs, its religion, becoming a very stronghold of conservatism." Thus, the cycle of French-Canadian backwardness started over again.

Party newspapers loved their politicians

Two days before the federal election of 1900, the Conservative candidate for the riding of Lincoln received a tumultuous welcome at an evening rally in Beamsville, a small Ontario town in the Niagara Peninsula. According to a report in the St. Catharines *Daily Standard*, the Tory hopeful was escorted into town by no fewer than 68 torch-carrying horsemen. The whole community of Beamsville turned out, and there was "nothing but enthusiasm" for Mr. E. A. Lancaster.

The tumultuous welcome for the Conservative candidate got prominent play on the front page of the *Standard* the next day. That wasn't surprising, since every appearance made by Mr. Lancaster during the election campaign received similar treatment. He was big news wherever he went. Readers of the *Standard* couldn't help but get the impression that Lancaster was on his way to a stunning and richly deserved election victory on election day, Nov. 7.

In stark contrast to the enthusiastic account of Mr. Lancaster's rally in Beamsville was a small news item buried inside the same day's paper. That story told of the visit to St. Catharines of a Liberal politician who, under other circumstances and in another newspaper, might have made the front page. He was the Right Honorable Sir Wilfrid Laurier, prime minister of Canada. Yet Laurier was not in Lancaster's league when it came to obtaining news coverage in the St. Catharines *Daily Standard*, which seemed obsessed with providing details of the Conservative candidate's campaign.

There was also something interesting about the way the news events unfolded, or at least the way in which those events were reported by the *Standard*. While Mr. Lancaster was "cheered and cheered again" by the people of Beamsville, the newspaper noted that Laurier got a chilly reception. Laurier's visit was said to have been made in a desperate bid to boost the sagging campaign of the local Liberal candidate, William Gibson. But the prime minister might as well not have bothered, the *Standard* maintained, because Gibson was in a "losing fight" locally, and Laurier himself was going to get clobbered at the national level.

And yet, when the votes were counted a couple of days later, Laurier was not turfed out of office by the voters of Canada. He won a splendid victory, confirmation that he was by far the best and most successful politician of his day in Canada. And as for Mr. Lancaster? While he did indeed win the election in Lincoln riding, as the *Standard* had predicted, the Conservative candidate didn't do well in the town of Beamsville, where Gibson beat him by a four-to-three margin. The Liberal candidate took 94 votes in Beamsville, to Lancaster's 72. So much for the claim that everyone in Beamsville loved him.

How could the *Standard* have been so wrong? How could the editor of the newspaper hold up his head in the community after it became evident that his reporting was so inaccurate? Such questions might well be asked today, but a different set of rules applied when it came to political reporting in Canada at the beginning of the century. In those days, the idea wasn't to be right in calling the outcome of an election. Rather, it was to be on the right side in fighting the election.

The newspapers at the start of the century were, for the most part, political rags. It was a tradition in Canada which went back for many decades, and which continued well into the 20th century. The papers picked a side, depending on the political preferences of their owners, and cranked up the heat every time there was an election.

The owners used their newspapers to further their own political interests. The modern theory that newspapers should serve the whole community had not yet become widely accepted. Editors and reporters working for these old-time papers were required to be open and unrepentant advocates for one side or the other. They weren't flies on the wall, as they are today, looking down on the political landscape from on high, staying out of the contest in an effort to report it accurately and fairly.

Yesterday's newspapermen (they were almost all men) were part of the action, and they had a lot of fun taking part in the game instead of standing on the sidelines. They rejoiced in the vigor of the contest, sharing in the agony of defeat and the thrill of victory. They wrote stories designed not so much to inform the readers as to persuade them, to promote their party's candidates, and to put down the opposition. The news columns performed a function something like advertising and public relations do today.

What the political writers of the era churned out wasn't news; it was propaganda. Readers knew that when they read a story in the newspaper, it was an account prepared by an admitted partisan. Papers didn't try to make subtle and often dubious distinctions between what appeared on the so-called "news pages" and what appeared under various guises, such as editorials, columns, commentaries, viewpoints and the host of other labels used to differentiate between "fact" and "comment."

It was a more honest form of journalism than the sort which is practised today. The newspapers flew their colors for all to see, rather than quietly picking favorites and puffing them up under the pretense that they're simply reporting the news. The old-time journalists were honest about what they were doing, rather than pretending, as reporters do today, to be acting "in the public interest" when they wait for a politician to make a mistake, and then pounce on him for it.

The voters were better served by the partisan papers of a century ago than they are today by the much-larger number of papers, magazines, radio and TV stations and other media outlets. Old-time voters knew that if they read a report of a political event in a newspaper, the report would reflect the party affiliation of the paper. Citizens wishing to be well informed simply read two competing papers, one of them supporting the Liberals and the other the Conservatives.

It was like sitting in court and hearing both the prosecution and defence cases. You could sort out the truth for yourself, rather than having it delivered to you by some all-seeing, all-knowing sage who craftily concealed the axe he had to grind by pretending to report a pseudo-scientific public opinion poll.

Getting both sides was easy in those days, since most communities had two papers which supported one party or the other. In St. Catharines, for instance, the *Standard*'s Conservative leanings were offset by those of a paper called the *Journal*, which was the Liberal mouthpiece. The same situation applied in almost every other town and city, with the papers being owned by local people who went to political meetings as part of their ordinary activities, just as they went to church.

It was a sharp contrast to the situation today, in which most Canadian cities and towns have just one paper, usually owned by a corporation with little interest in politics or anything else in the community except making a profit. The mandate of the typical daily in Canada today is not to generate votes for a political party; it's to generate the greatest-possible profits for the owners.

While the papers of the day made the election of 1900 sound like a real contest, the Liberals had it aced all the way. They had turfed the Conservatives out of office in the election of 1896, and they rolled to a healthy re-election victory four years later. While their newspaper allies helped them to win, the Liberals had a lot of other things going for them.

For starters, they were the party in power, and they used patronage to oil the political wheels. Patronage was so widespread that Laurier appointed one of his relatives to a job as postmaster simply to keep members of his family happy. Government advertising was overwhelmingly placed in papers supporting the party in power, and this made the Liberal papers even keener to keep the Grits in office.

In addition, the economy was booming and people were feeling good about the country. The Liberals generally were providing effective, economical government. The treasury had a surplus. The government was successful in attracting immigrants to Canada, helping to fill up the empty Canadian West and build the national economy. These factors all helped the Liberals in their bid for re-election.

Laurier had a solid base of support in his home province. Quebecers almost always vote for their own, and they did so massively in 1900. Laurier associated himself with the British monarchy and the governor general, which pleased most English-Canadians. He permitted thousands of Canadian volunteers to fight the

Boers in South Africa, gaining popularity with voters outside Quebec. The Liberals also won support from English-Canadians by giving the British a break on import duties for their manufactured goods.

The Grits also had the better leader. Laurier was a sharp politician who was smooth and elegant but had the common touch. His opponent was Sir Charles Tupper, a Maritimer and a holdover from the era of Sir John A. Macdonald and the burned-out Conservative government. Tupper, in a bid to win Quebec votes, was foolish enough to proclaim that Laurier was "too English for me," thereby making Laurier even more acceptable to English-Canadians, and thus ensuring a Liberal victory.

You can get a good idea of how the election campaign went by reading the newspapers of the day, as long as you take care to read papers from both sides. A lot of them are out of business now, but scores of them have been preserved on microfilm. One of the most interesting papers from that time period is the Manitoba *Free Press*, which continues today in the form of the Winnipeg *Free Press*. Today it's your typical non-partisan cash cow, churning out the standard diet of "The Liberals say . . . . The Conservatives say . . . . The NDP says . . . . Reform says . . . . The opinion polls say . . . ." and so forth. But at the turn of the century, the *Free Press* was solidly in the Liberal camp.

In fact, the owner of the paper was Clifford Sifton, the cabinet minister who had done a good job of attracting immigrants to the West, but who was in a stiff battle to hang on to his seat. Sifton represented the Manitoba riding of Brandon, where he faced a Conservative opponent named Hugh John Macdonald, who was the former premier of the province. Coverage of the 1900 election campaign by the *Free Press* is a delight to read, because it was so vigorous in its support of the paper's owner, and so determined to put Macdonald in a bad light.

Typical of *Free Press* coverage is the front-page headline on the day before the election, in which the newspaper announced that there was a "black plot" in Brandon to interfere with the course of democracy. The story said that "it has been ascertained that there is a scheme on foot to spoil Liberal ballots by changing the black pencil in the booth and replacing it with blue pencil, and thus make the ballots marked with blue pencil bad."

Another article revealed that "just how desperate the Conservative cause is felt to be by their central committee here is shown by the desperate methods they are employing to gain votes." The story claims that a top Conservative was threatening railway employees that they would be fired if they voted Liberal. Meanwhile, the paper said, "there was a very large and enthusiastic gathering at Mr. Sifton's central committee rooms here tonight." You get the idea. There was a steady supply of this stuff throughout the election campaign.

When the Liberals won nationally and Sifton won in Brandon, the *Free Press* was wild with enthusiasm. A banner headline proclaimed that "the Laurier government is sustained and Tupper is trounced." Sifton's victory by a then-substantial 600 votes was heralded as the greatest victory in the West. The paper couldn't help but rub it in. The lead editorial solemnly announced that Hugh John Macdonald "is not only among the slain. Politically he is dead. Mr. Sifton's triumph and vindication are complete."

In a final shot a couple of days later, the *Free Press* finally gave a Conservative politician decent coverage. A story on Sir Charles Tupper uncharacteristically quoted him at length, and unedited. But the story was not a blast against the Liberals by the defeated Tory leader. It was an announcement that Tupper was stepping down, having been so badly trounced that he was leaving public life. Tupper was not only defeated nationally; the voters of his own riding had given him the heave-ho. It was the first time in 40 years of politics that Tupper had lost an election, and that was a good enough story for the *Free Press* to make it onto the front page.

By the time the newly elected Parliament met in Ottawa for the first time, the 20th century had arrived and Tupper was long gone. While the Tory newspapers licked their wounds and the Conservative party slowly rebuilt itself, the Liberal press served as a cheerleader for the government and the Liberals continued to ride high. In several speeches he made in the early years of the new century, Laurier proclaimed that if the 19th century was the century of the United States, then the 20th century belonged to Canada.

It was an enthusiastic prediction, and one which turned out to be somewhat optimistic. But one thing was for sure. Politically, at least, the first decade of the 20th century certainly belonged to Laurier. He stayed in office until 1911, when he was finally defeated by the Conservatives.

Needless to say, the Tory press was ecstatic, while the Liberal newspapers saw it as the end of a wonderful era.

Chapter 6
How it Was for Women

Young woman's diary reveals her inner-most thoughts

What was life like for a young Canadian woman at the start of the 20th century? We can get a good idea by reading the diary of Violet Goldsmith, who began writing her innermost thoughts and feelings in what she called her "journal" when she was 19 years old.

Violet's journal reveals her to be a bright and articulate young woman, but you can't help notice how serious-minded and puritanical she is. In many ways she's old-fashioned. Yet in other ways, Violet is like a young woman of our own era, struggling to get an education, embarking upon a career, and eventually finding the "right man" and falling in love.

Let's begin with her attitudes towards sex. Her journal shows that in her late teens and early 20s, she had a standoffish attitude toward men. In one passage she tells how she avoided a romantic entanglement. Violet and several friends were out for an evening stroll.

> "Miss Wilkinson and I were walking together. We met Newton and Hillard, and someone suggested that Miss Wilkinson and Hillard walk together, leaving, I suppose, Newton and me, but no one made a move. Just then Eva Dyer and some others passed and Eva said, `Are you coming back?' I turned and went with her, leaving the crowd laughing. Miss Wilkinson, Newton and Hillard came in after that."

She also tells of a young man who tried another ploy to begin a romance. "I got a very nice letter from Charley Ross today, asking permission to correspond with me, but I must say no," she writes, without further explanation.

In the early 1900s, religion played an important part in Canadian society. Virtually everyone was a member of a church. Violet was a Methodist, a denomination which was especially straight-laced. Violet was even more religious than she otherwise might have been, because her father was a Methodist clergyman. The depth of the young woman's faith can be seen from the following diary entry, made when she was 21: "I am filled with longings for the Spirit-filled life that a few people seem to possess, and I feel sure that I will have it someday, but why not now?"

Violet did not dance; she thought it was sinful. She was also against gambling. Once, at a summer fair, she took a moral stand over what most people today would consider a harmless children's game.

> "Willie and I got into a dispute about a fish pond. He wanted to try it (to win) chocolates, but I held out that it was gambling. Ethyl sided with me, so the others would not go. Willie said some things about religious scruples,

and that he hoped we would keep them up, but I am sure he did not mean it."

She went to Sunday school and church every Sunday morning, and to church again on Sunday evening. She also went to prayer sessions and other religious activities several times a week, as well as to a Methodist young people's group called The League to which she was particularly devoted. But even all those church activities were not enough to satisfy Violet's passionate need to be close to the Lord.

Here's how she described her feelings one day when she was feeling low and searching for her place in the world:

"If I could only say and realize the truth of this: `Oh wondrous bliss, Oh joy sublime; I've Jesus with me all the time.' It seems to me that I do not enjoy the communion that I should in prayer. But even if I thought I should never enjoy more religion than I do now, I am glad I have even that much."

Occasionally Violet attended religious services which were different from her own. In a diary entry made in 1901, she tells of the visit she and some friends made to what she called a "Darkie service." This entry reveals not only her religious attitudes, but also her unconscious racism and religious intolerance – two strong features of early-20th-century Canadian society.

"I expected to see a company of Christians gathered at prayer or a class meeting led by one of themselves," she writes, "but I found that most of them were not Christians and that it is a kind of mission coordinated by a white man. Some Darkies caused a disturbance and the leader broke off his address and gave them the terrors of the Judgment. At the close there was a short testimony meeting: the leader asked those who belong to Jesus to rise. Then he asked those who wanted to belong to Jesus to rise." Two of the young women who accompanied Violet stood up.

"One went forward, but they could make nothing of her, and she bolted out of the room. We stayed a short time praying that the Holy Spirit might follow her and that the others might be willing to surrender their will to God. I pray that good might come of that meeting. The singing was splendid and the room was nice and clean. There was one old Darkie whose face was wrinkled with age. He said that for sixty years or more he had been following Jesus. I thought it was beautiful. I judged that from what the speakers said that the Darkies stayed away from Jesus for fear of the sneers of their companions."

Like most young women of her time, Violet was a tea-totaller. She was on the prohibitionist side in the ongoing debate over the question of whether booze should be outlawed. On a visit to Souris, P.E.I., she observes that "Souris is going to the dogs with liquor. There was a fight between two brothers last evening, and one was pounded so badly that he was left for dead .... Spirituality is dead in Souris. Mrs. Currie (a friend in Souris) says there is not a woman or girl who would pray at a public meeting."

She also tells of the time that some acquaintances, Mr. and Mrs. Holmes, went to Fredericton, and Mr. Holmes came home drunk.

> "The trainmen dumped him on a siding. He was there some time before he knew it. Miss Gilts, the girl Mrs. Holmes left in charge, and I went down and brought him home. Mr. Holmes had a bottle with him and I ran down the hill with it and broke it against the fence. He was cross when they first told him, but he is glad now. He feels very much ashamed of himself this morning."

A couple of years later, when Violet was a university student, she mentions that Carey Nation, the bar-smashing American prohibitionist, spoke on campus. "All the students assembled in the Library and she gave us a splendid address on liquor and tobacco, cigarettes etc. and turned to us girls and lectured us on our influence."

Violet was pretty straight-laced, but she did have some fun. In the early 20th century, that consisted of things like going for rides with a horse and buggy, and taking long walks. She and her friends also held parties, where one of their favorite games was charades. One night the words they had to act out with gestures and signs were really tough ones.

> "Our side went first and we took 'restoration.' They had to give it up. They took 'misunderstood.' We almost had to give it up. At last I thought of it. They teased us about having so many school teachers on our side. When we got home Mabel (her sister) told me she had it in half the time, but would not speak out. Just like her!"

Violet's idea of humor is interesting. She tells about attending a church social, where the witty minister said: "Now I want you all to be very sociable this evening, to come close together and have a good time, and if any of you wish to come closer together than you can this evening, you all know what a minister can do for you."

An incident which took place while she was going to school also struck her as funny:

> "The other day in Dr. Crockett's room he deduced a rule for multiplication of fractions, then asked one of the boys to state the rule. The boy got up, and he could not have been paying attention, for he could not state the rule. He said, 'Multiply – denominators – ' or something, but stated no rule. Dr. Crockett could not hear, and thought he had answered correctly, for he said, 'Very good!' and the boy sat down. The boys behind him clapped him on the back. We all laughed and Dr. Crockett thought it was because the work was so simple."

There was a closeness between students and teachers that you rarely find in colleges and universities today. Here is how Violet describes the retirement of Mr. Mullin, the beloved principal of her normal school (teachers' college):

> "Mr. Branscombe presented Mr. Mullin with a gold-headed cane. As soon as the speech was over, we all stood up and sang 'Farewell Teacher.' Then Mr. Mullin gave a grand reply. Then we sang 'Auld Lang Syne.' Mr. Breech spoke, then Mr. Brittain got up and said, 'Mr. Mullin, ladies and gen-

tlemen of the Normal School, the last day has come . . . .' Then, overcome with emotion, Mr. Breech sat down. Then the male students picked the retiring principal up, chair and all, and carried him around. Someone carried the cane in front of him, and they shouted the school cry. When he was going home they formed two rows and he marched through them. We were all very sad to see him go."

They all went to the train station to bid their beloved principal a final farewell. "When the train left we watched him as long as we could see him . . . . We came back from the station feeling as if we were returning from a funeral."

It was common for a young woman to be trained as a teacher in the early 1900s, but Violet went on to university to get a bachelor's degree, which was quite unusual. Most young people, especially females, didn't go that far in school. What was it like to be a university student in those days? In one way, it was a lot like it is today. Students then, as now, often had money problems. But the amounts seem paltry in comparison to today's high tuition and living costs.

Violet's tuition fees at the University of New Brunswick in Fredericton were $30 a year, or about one one-hundredth of what they are today in current dollars. But $30 was a lot of money in the old days, and there was no student loan program. Violet wouldn't have been able to go if she had not received a scholarship to cover her tuition.

She also needed money for living costs. "Good room and board could be had for $2.00 a day," she points out in her diary, but that too was a lot of money in the early 1900s. Violet tells us she did not want to "borrow money, and graduate in debt," so she did housework and looked after two young children in a professor's home in exchange for food and a place to stay.

Attending YWCA functions and taking part in debates were favorite activities for Violet at university. The topics were quaint. One of them was: "Resolved that the cow is more beneficial to mankind than the horse." In another debate the question was whether "old bachelors are more use to the world than old maids."

That sounds pretty old-fashioned, but many young women today can relate to the agony Violet went through to keep her figure trim. "I was weighed today," she says, "and weigh 122 lbs, a loss of ½ lb. since January. I have started today giving up eating dinner. I do not know how long it will last." She soon found out: "I nearly starved this afternoon, and have decided to eat my dinner after this, after trying the new plan for three days." A few months later she had dropped to 116 pounds, "or according to other scales 117."

What was it like to be an elementary school teacher in those days? No easier than it is today, but the things you had to worry about were different. Serving as a substitute teacher in Carroll's Crossing, N.B., Violet critiqued her first day's performance: "I let the fire go out in the morning, and forgot to put the windows up during physical exercises and recess. Will have any amount of room for improvement if I teach for the next hundred years."

Working in a tough two-room school in the French district outside Bathurst, Nova Scotia, she wrote in her diary that she hasn't made an entry for several months. "Perhaps it is just as well, for those months have been the darkest, dreariest period of my life yet." She found the children tough to control, and finally she was "driven to have one girl expelled. It may have been the best thing I could have done, but I will always feel that I have injured that girl."

Things picked up when Violet headed west. Her father had gone on a "harvest excursion" in 1904, and obtained a homestead 20 miles north of Lumsden on the Regina-Saskatoon rail line. He returned to New Brunswick and took a rail car full of household effects and lumber back to his homestead, where he spent the winter building a house.

Violet and her sister Mabel went west the following summer. Their five-day train trip ended on a Saturday afternoon when they pulled into the station in the booming city of Regina. The next day, they went to church and suffered a slight embarrassment. "After we dropped our pennies on the collection plate, we remembered hearing that there was no money less than a five-cent piece in the west, and we knew that we had given it away that we were from the East."

They soon took the train to Lumsden, where their father met them with the horse and buggy and drove them to his new homestead. "My father had built the house, with some help from the neighbors. It had a peaked roof, which did not leak. The main room served as kitchen and living room. There was an attic bedroom and a lean-to that was big enough for two beds."

Violet got a teaching job in the tiny east Saskatchewan community of Stockholm. Soon after her arrival she noted that the place was populated by "Swedes, Hungarians, Germans, Bohemians and what not," with just two English families. Violet did not approve of the way the people of Stockholm celebrated Dominion Day. "There was a celebration here, a picnic and football games in the afternoon and in the evening an entertainment and dance which lasted till two or three o'clock Sunday morning, a disgrace to a Protestant village."

Classes began the next day, with the 11 children who were present using boards supported by boxes as desks. A couple of days later, one of the children asked to get a drink of water. He went outside "and got his finger in a gopher trap. I hope that will cure him." She spent "nearly all week teaching Thelka Stenberg, 15 years old, subtraction and she does not know it yet. Such are the trials of teaching."

One Thursday in August school was supposed to start late, because the church building was to be used for a wedding at 9 a.m. "Last evening I swept the church and polished the stove and got the children to clean up around the outside of the church and plant poplar trees at the door. This morning I went over early and the children carried house plants and got wild flowers and flags and we fixed up as nicely as we could."

But then things started to go wrong.

"About 9:30 the bridal party arrived, but no clergyman. Mr. McKay appeared about 11 a.m. only to discov-

er that they had no licence. They had to go to Dubuc for it, so it was 3 p.m. when the marriage took place. Of course we had the whole day off from school. The bride thanked me several times for the trouble I had taken, and I know she appreciated my work."

A few days later, Violet reports that she was teaching her students some English. "In one lesson the word 'ballad' occurred, also the word 'damsel.' I explained them as best I could, but one little girl got them mixed up, and when asked to write sentences she wrote, 'The ballad went for the cows.'" On another day, "one of my pupils informed me that alcohol has the power of keeping dead bodies alive."

With October came Thanksgiving, and Violet was in charge of decorating the church.

"We made tiny sheaves of wheat and oats and put them up around the windows. We put up flags and chains of colored paper, and made the place look quite comfortable. Sandra Stenbey drew autumn leaves on the blackboard and they looked beautiful. I printed three verses of the hymn 'Come, ye thankful people, come,' which was the opening hymn. The children went through their flag drill beautifully and everyone was delighted with it. They were encored. I recited 'Simon's Dream' and 'The Change.'"

A few weeks after that Thanksgiving service, a handsome young man walked into the 24-year-old Violet's life and things were never the same again. Here's how it happened:

Violet (Goldsmith) Brown and her husband. SPA R-A 26206.

"The Rev. John Brown came into school and introduced himself to me. On that day I met my fate, though I did not know it. The next Saturday he took me for a drive, and each Saturday since, we went out . . . . On Thursday, Nov. 30, we became engaged. May God bless us, and help me to be a faithful wife. This is very much out of all my plans, but I firmly believe it is God's plan for us both and if so, it must be the very best thing for us. I love him more and more every day."

That's a good place to wrap up Violet's story, since we're interested in the early years of the 20th century. But in case you're curious, the happy couple got married and lived in Saskatchewan until 1906, when they moved to Alberta. They had a family, and after their deaths one of the children donated the old diary to the Saskatchewan Archives in Regina, where you can read it today to get an intimate look at Violet's world a century ago.

Under the law, kids belonged to the father

Twenty-one was the age of majority at the start of the 20th century in Canada. That's when you legally became an adult. Until that time, you were under the control of your father, in theory at least. In practice this applied much more to girls than to boys. When a boy turned 17 or 18, he could pretty well do what he liked, but fathers often asserted their legal authority over their daughters until they turned 21.

The father was legally entitled to decide how his children were educated, what church they belonged to, and how any money they earned would be spent. The law was a throwback to the days when children were deemed to be the possessions of the man who sired them, and it wasn't until much later in the 20th century that the legal rights of children were established. A century ago, the father was so powerful that he could even control the lives of his children from the grave, by appointing a guardian for his children in his will. That guardian, and not the children's mother, had legal control over the children until they turned 21.

Mothers had a lot of moral authority, however. Men were beginning to recognize that marriage was a partnership, not a master-and-servant relationship. But in terms of the law when it came to authority over children, women were "in exactly the same position as a stranger," according to an article written for the National Council of Women in 1900 by Clara Brett Martin, who at the time was Canada's only female lawyer. Martin one of the pioneers of the women's rights movement in Canada; she earned her law degree in 1899 and joined a large law firm in Toronto. Her admission to the bar required changes to the law of Ontario and the regulations of the Law Society.

In her article, Martin said that in the event of a divorce, custody of the children went to the father unless there were very unusual circumstances, such as the imprisonment of the father. If the mother had been guilty of adultery in the divorce action, she was not even entitled to see her children after the divorce.

But Martin noted that in some ways, the law benefitted females by giving them special protection against predatory men. It was a crime, for instance, for a man to have sex with a girl under the age of 16, even if she consented. And a man who lured a girl under 14 into prostitution

A large family. SPA R-A 23775.

could be punished with a maximum sentence of life imprisonment, plus whipping.

Interestingly, a woman in Ontario could get married without her father's consent at the age of 18, but that didn't mean she was free of male authority. Because she was married, she gave up some of the property rights she would enjoy if she were single and had reached the age of 21. Unmarried adult women were pretty much on a par with men when it came to their right to own property, establish a business and generally handle their finances. But married women were under the thumb of their husbands. Again, the law went back to the times when the woman was deemed to be a piece of property. Like a farm animal, the bride was "given away" by her father to her new "owner," her husband.

"Our ancestors insisted upon treating marriage as a suspension of the independent existence of the wife," Martin observed archly. She said that the promise made by the husband at the altar to his bride – "With all my worldly goods I thee endow" – was a hollow one, and until recently things had been very much the other way around. "The notion of unity of husband and wife, meaning thereby the suspension of the wife and the lordship of the husband, seems to have been particularly agreeable to the whole race of English jurists, tickling their grim humor and gratifying their very limited sense of the fitness of things," Martin quipped.

But new, more progressive laws had been passed in the late 1800s giving married women rights to own property in their own names and to bring law suits. Even so, the husband still had physical and sexual control over his wife. The husband could not be charged with assault or kidnapping if he restrained his wife, so long as he did not cause her physical injury. And as far as sex was concerned, he could take it from his wife whenever he wanted, with or without her consent and co-operation. As Martin bluntly explained it, "He can commit a rape upon her and is not liable to an action."

Women could not vote in provincial or federal elections. Women could, however, vote in municipal elections if they owned property in the municipality, but they were not eligible for election to city or town councils. This lack of women's political rights was of great concern to feminists, but they were just beginning to gain strength at the beginning of the century and it was a long time before women won the right to vote at the senior levels of government.

"Canadian women themselves, until lately, have taken very little interest in this movement, and a few years ago were, as a whole, antagonistic to it," according to Henrietta Muir Edwards, who wrote an article on women's political rights for the National Council of Women in the same book that contained Clara Brett Martin's article. The book was prepared for the 1900 World Exhibition in Paris to show women's contributions to Canadian life. The fact that the book was paid for by the federal government is an indication that politicians were becoming aware of the growing women's movement.

Edwards pointed out that as the new century dawned, Canadian women were taking a greater interest in getting the vote. "The higher education of women, their organized efforts to ameliorate the condition of the poor, or benefit the community, their position in the labor market necessitating laws to protect their interests and welfare, have taught our women that on this account it would be well to have a direct influence upon those who govern," Edwards said.

She rejected the idea that women's place was limited to the home, and that women should stay out of politics and limit themselves to trying to influence the way their husbands voted. "Personal influence, of which we hear so much and which, in its place is powerful, is very slow in action," Edwards maintained. "The woman is queen in her home and reigns there, but unfortunately the laws she makes reach no further than her domain. If her laws, written or unwritten, are to be enforced outside, she must come into the political world as well."

It wasn't until many years later that women finally won the vote. The National Council of Women played a key role in the struggle for political rights. In 1916, Manitoba became the first province to permit women to vote in a provincial election. Most other provinces followed suit. Women whose husbands were in the military got the right to vote in the 1917 federal election. In 1918, all female citizens over the age of 21 became eligible to vote in federal elections. But it wasn't until 1940 that Quebec, the last holdout, allowed women to vote in provincial elections.

Children died in alarming numbers

When you visit a hundred-year-old cemetery, you can't help noticing the large number of graves for children. Many of them died the same year they were born, or after just a few years of life. The loss of so many infants and toddlers, felled primarily by diseases which are now largely preventable, was one of the Canada's great national tragedies at the beginning of the 20th century.

The fact that so few Canadian children die today is one of the best indications that we have come a long way in this century when it comes to improving health care. According to the most recent statistics, Canada had 5.6 deaths of children under the age of one for every 1000 births. The infant mortality rate a century ago was 10 times as high.

In the 12 months leading up to the 1901 census, 21 328 children under the age of one year died in Canada. Another 10 019 children between one and four years of age died. That was a huge number of early childhood deaths in a country which had only 5.3 million people.

Young children accounted for 39 per cent of the 81 201 deaths which occurred in Canada that year. The loss of so many children was the main reason the death rate in Canada was so much higher at the beginning of the century. The national death rate, a standard measure of the quality of health care in a country, takes into account the death of people of all ages. The rate was 15.12 deaths per 1000 population at the start of the century. Today, Canada's

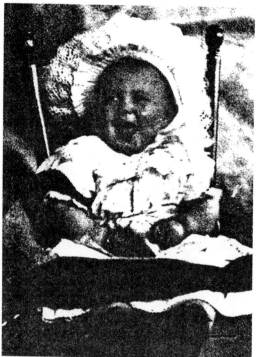

SPA R-A 23775(3).

death rate is just 6.7 deaths per 1000, one of the lowest in the world.

The average lifespan of Canadians has increased by 30 years in this century. While the average life expectancy in Canada at the turn of the century was only about 48, that figure has increased to 78 today. On average, women live about six years longer than men. The 1996 census set a man's life expectancy at birth at 75.7 years, and a woman's at 81.4.

Some of the increase in life expectancy is due to better health care and nutrition today, but a good part of it is due to the fact that the average is not dragged down by so many childhood deaths. Health care for the elderly is also much better now. Today, people over the age of 65 make up about 12 per cent of Canada's population.

Only about four per cent of Canadians were 65 or older in 1901.

The four major killers of young children a century ago were typhoid fever, measles, scarlet fever and diphtheria, which was the worst. There were 3206 deaths due to diphtheria in the census year. There were 1899 deaths due to typhoid, 1101 due to scarlet fever and 1029 due to measles. These diseases have now all been brought under control, but at the turn of the century they were a constant threat to children across Canada, and in some parts of the nation they ran rampant.

Montreal, at the time Canada's largest city, was the worst when it came to childhood deaths. Public health officials compared it to Calcutta, and it gained the unenviable title of being the most dangerous city in the civilized world to be born in. One child in four died before its first birthday in Montreal's slum area. That worked out to 250 deaths per 1000 children under the age of one. In Canada today, the rate of death among children under one year is just six per thousand.

These children died in 1901 for several reasons: The water and milk were impure, and the sewage treatment system was inadequate. Outdoor toilets were the norm. The children's diet was not nutritious, with starches and fats forming most of what they ate. They often remained unvaccinated. The parents didn't follow good sanitation practices. And in those pre-medicare days, their families couldn't afford to take the children to the doctor.

Diphtheria, the number one killer, was caused by highly contagious bacteria. The disease usually established itself in the child's mucous membranes, where the bacteria multiplied and secreted a powerful toxin. This poison damaged the child's heart and central nervous system. A grey-white substance was formed where the bacteria attacked the walls of the nose and throat. This material increased in size and thickness and blocked the victim's air passages. A diphtheria antitoxin was developed in Europe in the 1890s, but it was not widely available in Canada at the start of the 20th century.

Typhoid fever was usually communicated through food or water contaminated by human urine or feces. The typhoid germs thrived in places where the sewage treatment system was inadequate and the drinking water wasn't chlorinated. Typhoid was often passed on by carriers – people who did not come down with the disease themselves, but passed it on to others. Often these people did not realize they were carriers. In a famous case in the United States, a domestic worker was dubbed Typhoid Mary by the press after it was revealed that people often got sick and died after eating food she had prepared.

The symptoms of typhoid were chills followed by a high fever, headache, cough, vomiting and diarrhea. There were no antibiotics in those days to fight the bacteria, and there was no medicare system, so victims were often left untreated. They either got better, or they died.

Scarlet fever was caused by bacteria, which entered the child's body through the nose or mouth. It was transmitted by the coughing and sneezing of infected people, or through contaminated eating utensils. The initial symptoms were headache, sore throat, chills and fever. Red spots appeared in the mouth, followed by a rash which started on the chest and usually spread over the entire body except the face. The fever ran as high as 105 degrees Fahrenheit. Today scarlet fever can be treated with penicillin, but that miracle drug and all the other "magic bullets" we have today had not yet been developed. Aspirin, which was first used in Germany in the 1890s, was a rarity. The only drugs in common use in Canada at the turn of the century were pain killers such as morphine and cocaine.

Measles, the fourth major killing disease of children a hundred years ago, is the only one still with us, but today it is usually a mild form with no lasting effects. Early in the century it was often fatal, because the virus which causes measles produced very high fevers in children.

A form of measles known as rubella or German measles was especially dangerous to pregnant women. Their babies often suffered from abnormalities of the heart and mental retardation. Physicians today frequently recommend abortions to women who have had rubella during the first three months of pregnancy, but in 1901 the dangers of rubella were not well understood, and at any rate abortion was illegal.

A century ago, tuberculosis and pneumonia were the top killers of Canadians of all ages. The 1901 census shows that TB took 9709 lives that year. This amounted to about 12 per cent of all the deaths which occurred that year. Pneumonia and bronchitis took second spot, causing about 10 per cent of the total. In third place were deaths due to intestinal disorders. They killed 9 per cent. Old age was listed as the fourth most-common cause of death. Birth defects held fifth spot. Each was responsible for about 7 per cent of the nation's deaths. The next five causes of death in 1901 were heart disease (6 per cent), stroke (5 per cent), diphtheria (4 per cent), accidents (3 per cent) and cancer (3 per cent.)

Today, heart disease and cancer run neck and neck as Canada's chief causes of death. Each one makes up about 27 per cent of the total. Together they are responsible for more than half the deaths which occur in Canada. Cerebrovascular diseases are in third spot today, with about 7 per cent. Chronic lung diseases are in fourth place with about 4 per cent, followed by accidents, which also take about 4 per cent of the lives. Statistics Canada lists the next five causes of death as pneumonia and influenza (4 per cent), diabetes (2 per cent), suicide, kidney disease and liver disease (all about 1 per cent).

Marriage was meant to last a lifetime

Divorce was almost unheard of in Canada at the beginning of the century. Only 19 of them took place in 1901. According to the national census, there were only 337 divorced men and 324 divorced women across the land. With a population of some 5.3 million, that was a very small number.

Getting a divorce was not only socially frowned upon. In most cases it required an Act of Parliament, in the form of a private bill which started in the Senate, then went to the House of Commons, and then had to be signed by the governor general. The cost of arranging such special legislation was between $800 and $1500, a good deal of money in those days. It meant that only the wealthy could afford a divorce.

Politicians were reluctant to set up divorce courts to make the process cheaper and easier, because they believed that would encourage more people to get a divorce. Today, when we have thousands of divorces each month, and when one out of every three or four marriages ends in failure, it's amazing to see just how unusual divorce was a hundred years ago. And today, when divorces are seemingly obtained with less pain and trouble than it takes to have a root canal, it's amazing to see how hard it was to get a divorce. At the turn of the century, adultery was virtually the only legal reason for ending a marriage, and sexual infidelity had to be proven in great detail. No-fault divorce, so common today, had not yet been invented.

A divorced woman, much more than a divorced man, was looked down upon by society, so much so that some people would not permit a divorcee to come into their homes. This sort of snub was meant to let the divorcee know that she was unwelcome in respectable society, but it also served to protect married women from the threat posed by an unattached woman who might tempt their husbands into illicit sex.

The husband's unfaithfulness was considered less serious than the wife's. A man could obtain a divorce on the grounds of adultery alone, while the wife needed to prove not only adultery on the husband's part, but also extreme cruelty or desertion for two years. The thinking was that while the husband occasionally gave in to his natural desires to have sex outside of marriage, if he returned to the home and got back together with his wife, his transgression was forgivable. But a woman's betrayal of her husband, even once, was unnatural, and thus sufficient grounds to end the marriage.

Women were not powerless, however. Take the case of Annie Pearce Davidson, whose husband Alexander, after 10 years of marriage, started fooling around with a hotel keeper's widow. The couple were bold about it, travelling around together and registering in hotels as man and wife. Annie didn't run to her lawyer and file for divorce. She put up with her husband's infidelity for two years, until Alexander and his girlfriend left town. That might have been the end of it, but three years later Annie discovered that her estranged husband and his lover were living in Rat Portage, a small community in the North-West Territories.

She also found that Alexander and the widow had made a big mistake. They had gone through a marriage ceremony in 1899, thereby committed the crime of bigamy, an offence under the Criminal Code punishable by a jail term. Annie went to the police and laid a complaint. A warrant was issued for the arrest of Alexander and the second Mrs. Davidson. The Manitoba *Free Press* predicted in a detailed story on July 6, 1901, that the arrests would "no doubt cause quite a sensation" in Rat Portage. In its sympathetic portrayal of Annie's humiliation, the paper noted that she "is determined to make an example of her husband and the woman who has been the cause of all her earthly troubles."

The end of a marriage was, in many ways, the end of the world for a woman in 1901. Marriage was thought of as "the pure white life for two." It was meant to be permanent. When a couple promised before their relatives, friends, neighbors and God to remain together "until death us do part," they were expected to keep that pledge. If they had difficulties, they were expected to work them out.

The Protestant churches frowned on divorce, maintaining that divorce was contrary to the Bible's teaching and God's will. Their disapproval was important. Most Canadians regularly attended religious services, and the churches held a strong position of moral authority in the community. Divorce was seen as a threat to society. It was an attack on the family, which was the cornerstone of Canadian society. But the nature of the family itself had changed. The old patriarchal system which prevailed for much of the 19th century had pretty well fallen by the wayside. The husband was no longer the wife's absolute lord and master.

By the early 1900s, the husband and wife were seen as partners, and each had a role to play. The man went out to work and the wife stayed home. He was the breadwinner; she was the homemaker. He was the leader, but she was entitled to status and respect in her role as wife, and even more so if she had also taken on the role of mother. The husband and wife were expected to share affection as well as worldly goods. They were to provide each other with emotional as well as sexual fulfilment, and they were expected to have children.

Living together before marriage was taboo, as was sex before marriage. In the typical wedding ceremony, the bride dressed in white to demonstrate her chastity. She was "given away" by her father, in a throwback to the days when she was "owned" by her father until her marriage, after which she was "owned" by her husband. She promised to "obey" and "serve" her husband. He promised to "comfort" her. But the most important vow was the one in which they mutually promised to "love, honor and keep" each other until death ended the relationship.

Simply walking away from a bad marriage, while it was not as bad as getting a divorce, was discouraged in a variety of ways, legal and social. If the woman left the home, she usually had to leave the children behind with the husband, and she was on her own as far as supporting herself was concerned. If the husband walked out, he was in a fairly good position, as long as he continued to support his wife and children. But if he didn't, the wife could take legal action. In one case reported in the press in 1901, a Montreal woman took her husband to court seeking $10 000 in cash and "maintenance of his wife according to his means and conditions of life."

A wife whose husband didn't leave, but spent all his money on alcohol, could go to a government office, usually described as the Department of Charities, and declare that her husband would not support her. She could then have him arrested. The department would take him to court and obtain an order forcing him to support his wife.

In Quebec, there was one more option for Roman Catholics. They could seek an annulment from a church court. In one case early in the century, a man named Dulpit persuaded the church to invalidate his marriage. Mr. and Mrs. Dulpit were married by a Protestant minister several years earlier. When he wanted out of the marriage, Dulpit claimed the ceremony was invalid because both parties were Catholics at the time of the wedding, and thus could not be validly married by a Protestant clergyman. Mrs. Dulpit, who opposed the annulment, pointed out that the marriage had produced three children, and that the annulment would make the children illegitimate. She also insisted that at the time of the marriage she was not Catholic, and said she planned to take the matter before the civil courts after Rome decided in favor of the husband.

But such cases were unusual. Most couples got married, stayed married, worked out their difficulties, and remained married until their lifelong bond was terminated by the hand of God.

Anti-booze women were on the march

Fred Young was at the top of the list in magistrate's court the day after New Year's in 1901. In Ontario, Hamilton's first official criminal of the new century was charged with the most common of Canadian crimes: being drunk and disorderly.

Young had tied one on to celebrate the New Year, then paid an unwelcome call on his in-laws, the Cliffes, whom he heartily disliked. "Every time he gets drunk he ventilates his spite in no uncertain way, and he did not make any exception because it was New Year's Day," *The Spectator* reported. "About ten o'clock yesterday morning he went to the Cliffe household, James Street North, and proceeded to create rough-house. In a few minutes, he and Papa-in-law Cliffe were struggling in each other's embrace on the sidewalk in front of the house. Just as Inspector McMahon came along, Young got up and landed a left hook on Momma-in-law's neck."

Young promised not to do it again, and the magistrate let him off with a warning. But similar cases occurred across Canada on that first day of court business in the 20th century. In Toronto, where Mary Graham pleaded guilty to being drunk in a public place, the judge asked when she had last appeared before him on the same charge. "Not this year," the regular offender replied. It was a good joke, but the magistrate's sentence was an unamusing 30 days in jail.

Such scenes helped fuel calls for the total prohibition of alcohol in Canada. The temperance crusaders had no trouble finding cases like those of Fred Young and Mary Graham to illustrate the point that drinking was a serious social evil. Each year in Canada, some 11 000 people were convicted of public drunkenness.

Despite the size of the problem, the prohibitionists had little success in imposing their version of morality on Canadian society. In those days, the government was more inclined to let people do as they pleased than it is today. Regulations which we have today, requiring everything from the use of car seatbelts to the reporting of personal income, lay well in the future. There was a much greater sense in the old days that government should play the smallest possible role in people's private lives.

Most national law-makers viewed the question of whether or not to drink as an individual decision. Those who drank to excess were thought of as foolish and weak-willed people who needed to pull themselves up by their own bootstraps and get their lives in order. If they failed, that was a matter for themselves and their families to deal with, with the church and organized charity stepping in where necessary to relieve the harmful impact on the drinker's family.

But the prohibitionists, known as the "drys," believed the government should act, because alcohol caused so much harm to society. They pressured legislators to outlaw the manufacture, importation, sale and consumption of all forms of alcoholic beverages. They said booze was the cause of such social evils as prostitution, gambling, smoking, swearing, indolence, wife-beating and child neglect.

Close the bars and cut off the sale of booze in the stores, they argued, and people like Fred Young and Mary Graham would behave themselves. The possibility that heavy drinkers might keep on drinking, even if it were against the law, was given little weight by the prohibitionists. They insisted that legislated abstinence was the answer, even though laws which already existed to control alcohol, covering such areas as hours of sale and age of purchase, were widely flaunted.

SPA R-A 9944(1)

The prohibitionists were led by the Protestant churches and by two political lobby groups – the Dominion Alliance for the Total Suppression of the Liquor Traffic, and the Women's Christian Temperance Union. The WCTU had 11 000 members in 500 branches across the nation at the start of the century. It was one of the largest and most active women's organizations in Canada. Some of its members were also involved in the women's suffrage movement.

But in 1901, the WCTU was focused on a single objective: to do whatever was necessary to get people to stop drinking. Members of the WCTU encouraged drinkers to "take the pledge" by signing personal contracts which usually began with "I hereby promise, with the help of God, to abstain from the use of all intoxicating liquors." The contracts also included points such as, "Moderate drinking leads to drunkenness, while total abstinence directly from it," and "The Bible pronounces no blessing upon drinking, but many upon total abstinence."

Some men saw the WCTU as a threat, and treated its members with derision. They mocked the women for their puritanical militancy, quipping that WCTU stood for "Women who Constantly Torment Us." But the WCTU had good reason to be concerned. Drinking was an unhealthy part of many Canadians' lives at the start of this century. Government figures showed that in 1900, the per capita consumption of spirits was two-thirds of a gallon a year. On top of that, Canadians annually put away almost four gallons of beer for every man, woman and child in the country.

Working men routinely slaked their thirsts at their neighborhood beer parlor at end of the day. Mining towns, logging camps, ports, railway centres and other places where single men congregated had plenty of rowdy taverns. Members of the upper social classes regularly consumed alcohol, not only on social occasions, but at home with their afternoon and evening meals. It was the thing to do.

But the prohibitionists didn't draw attention to refined drinkers. They cited extreme cases to justify their demand for prohibition. A typical example usually went like this: Joe's 56-hour work week is over. It's pay day, and it's time for Joe to go home to his faithful wife and loving children. But there's a little stop he wants to make along the way. Joe enters the already-crowded tavern, where the company is convivial, the prices are cheap, the women are easy, and the cares of the day can be washed away. Eventually, dead drunk and broke, Joe goes home and takes a few rounds out of his wife and kids before passing out on the floor.

The WCTU found no shortage of horror stories. A survey in a lower-class part of Montreal in the late 1890s found that the local bar was the chief recreational facility in the community, and boozing was the most popular pastime for both men and women. There were 105 licensed saloons and 87 liquor-selling grocery stores in an area with a population of just 38 000. This amounted to one liquor outlet for every 45 families.

The drinking issue came to a head when the WCTU and other prohibitionists persuaded the government to hold a national referendum in 1898. Voters were asked: "Are you in favor of passing an Act prohibiting the importation, manufacture, or sale of spirits, wine, ale, cider and all other alcoholic liquors for use as a beverage?" A majority answered "yes" to this question, but the government was not legally bound by the results of the referendum, and the government chose not to outlaw alcohol at the national level.

The prohibitionists blamed the big-liquor interests, saying that they had used their clout to prevent the government from following the people's will. But the politicians pointed out that only 43 per cent of the electorate had turned out to vote, and that the majority in favor of banning alcohol had been slim (278 000 yes, 265 000 no).

Even more significant, the government said, was the fact that the vote had split along linguistic lines. While English Canada voted substantially in favor of prohibition, Quebec turned it down by a five-to-one margin. In Quebec, booze wasn't seen by most people as a problem, but rather as a part of everyday life. And in Quebec, it was felt that problem drinkers were best dealt with by family members and the parish priest, not by the law.

Finances also encouraged the federal government to let booze remain legal. Prohibition would mean an annual loss of $8 million to the treasury, while the cost of enforcement would have drained an additional $22 million a year from Ottawa's coffers.

Despite Ottawa's refusal to act, the anti-booze activists pressed on. They tried to impose prohibition at the provincial level, and succeeded in Manitoba and Prince Edward Island. They also won "local option" votes in many parts of Nova Scotia and Ontario. The result was that booze was prohibited in some municipalities, while it remained legal in others. There was, of course, a great increase in traffic from the "dry" to the "wet" communities.

You can get a sense of what the prohibitionist movement was like at the start of the century by reading a news account of the WCTU's annual meeting in Ontario. *The Globe*, which had taken a stance against prohibition, reported that the sessions "have been characterized by very deep interest and that businesslike snap which is so noticeable at all meetings of this aggressive body of workers in the cause of temperance."

The newspaper summarized a speech by Rev. Charles Deacon complaining about lax enforcement of liquor laws.

"He deplored particularly the selling of liquor to boys of tender years, saying that few men become drunkards after they reach the age of 21. A large number of drunkards knew the taste of liquor before they were 12 years of age. Little boys 10 years of age had been seen getting drink, and drunk on the streets. He said that in many places bars were open on Saturday nights and Sundays, sometimes until 3 or 4 o'clock in the morning. Then liquor was sold to habitual drunkards. All of these things were directly contrary to the law."

Those who opposed prohibition had much fun at the expense of Carey Nation, a prominent prohibitionist from Kansas who visited Canada in 1901. Mrs. Nation's militant tactics included making surprise raids on bars and smashing the glassware with a hatchet. After she smashed up a couple of bars in Ottawa, there were rumors that Toronto was her next target. *Saturday Night* reported that Mrs. Nation "is variously regarded as a fanatic, a faker, a calculating money-maker, a subject for a lunatic asylum, and a woman who has discovered the one true weapon for the evil of strong drink."

The Globe told its readers that "the leader of the physical force wing of the prohibition party" was the subject of much discussion among Toronto bar owners. "We have a large siphon specially constructed for people who break things," F. H. Thomas of the English Chop House said. "A siphon well charged with soda is a powerful factor in preserving peace, and Mrs. Nation can't object to soda." E. B. Clancy of the Moorish Palace said that if Mrs. Nation "insists on using a hatchet, we'll send her back to the kitchen to work on the steak."

But a spokeswoman for the Ontario branch of the WCTU said Carey Nation should not be taken lightly. "While not many of us would be willing to follow the lead of Mrs. Nation," she said, "we yet find cause for thankfulness that any woman, possessing courage and having the law on her side, could effect more good in a few months than 20 years' work along the quiet lines so many of us are more inclined to follow."

Illegal birth control was commonly practised

Today you can walk into a pharmacy and buy a pack of condoms as easily as you can buy a pack of gum. At the turn of the century, a drug store owner who sold condoms could be sent to jail. According to the Criminal Code in 1901: "Everyone is guilty of an indictable offense and liable to two years' imprisonment who knowingly, without lawful excuse or justification, offers to sell, advertises, publishes an advertisement or has for sale or disposal any medicine, drug or article intended or represented as a means of preventing conception or causing abortion."

But there were all kinds of ways to get around the law. The most common subterfuge was to sell birth control items as "rubber goods" or "women's products." Despite the law, a variety of birth control devices were readily available at the turn of the century. Indeed, the birth rate had been dropping steadily since Confederation. It had fallen about 25 per cent in the 33 years since the country was formed. This was due primarily to the fact that contraception was being widely practised.

The drop in the birth rate was particularly sharp in Ontario. The annual report of the province's Department of Public Health showed that while there had been a steady increase in the number of marriages over the past few years, the number of births had fallen. It was down about four per cent in the year 1900 alone.

This led to newspaper articles and speeches by alarmists decrying the fact that the English-speaking population of Canada was committing "race suicide," while the French-Canadian birth rate remained high. A Montreal newspaper made fun of the hysteria. *Les Debats* sarcastically told Quebec's fertile women that "French-domination will come about through you, and your grateful country will elevate you on its altars." The newspaper predicted that in 25 years, Canada's French population would be as large as its English population.

"Once we reach that point, we will see what a panic there will be among the loyalists of Ontario, so literally terrified by the spectre of French domination that they will begin to emigrate to the United States." The paper warned Ontario that "the French-Canadian supremacy which you so much detest is coming regularly, pitilessly, as the large hand of a clock. At the hour marked it will submerge you beyond return."

James Simpson, an Anglican minister in Charlottetown, P.E.I., preached a sermon early in 1901 saying that women had a duty to bear children. He said those who practised birth control or had abortions were sinners. "Abortion is a crime so inhuman, unchristian and damnable that one would naturally suppose that every woman in Christendom would look upon such a criminal operation with the most utter loathing, detestation and horror," he said.

According to Simpson, terminating a pregnancy was the same as committing murder.

"The very instant conception takes place there is the God-given life, and the sin is the same whether that life is strangled at its very source, or a few weeks, or months, or years afterward .

. . . and while the prevention of conception does not indeed destroy life, it does destroy the potentiality of life, which is moral murder."

While religious and moral leaders were condemning birth control, Canadian men and women were practising it. They knew they had to limit the size of their families to avoid the strain and poverty that resulted when there were too many children to care for.

There were many methods of birth control in those days. The simplest thing was to have sex, but stop before ejaculation, and to ejaculate outside the vagina. This was known by the Latin term "coitus interruptus," but it had a variety of popular names, including "marital masturbation," "the pullback" and "the way." It was effective only if the man exercised a lot of self-control. Some people thought this technique was unhealthy because it weakened the man physically and mentally, and left the woman unfulfilled.

Some couples had sex only when they believed the woman was not ovulating. But this technique, later known as the rhythm method, didn't work well in the early 20th century because the menstrual cycle was not well understood. Sometimes people got it backward and had sex at the worst-possible times. Prolonged nursing of babies was another popular birth control technique, because nursing mothers were less likely to get pregnant.

Condoms were widely used. They were called "shields" and "French safes," and were advertised and sold as "rubber goods." Condoms had an unsavory reputation because they were often used by men to avoid getting venereal disease from prostitutes.

Douches for women were among the most popular birth control devices, and were widely sold as products for "feminine hygiene." They worked well when inserted into the woman soon after she had sex, but delays due to overcrowded living conditions and unheated rooms cut down on effectiveness. One type of douche consisted of a sponge soaked in a sperm-killing solution of vinegar or bicarbonate of soda. Other types included a tube with a rubber bulb on the end, or a fountain-type water bag containing a sperm-killing solution – everything from soapy water and alum to sulfate of zinc.

Another way to prevent conception was to use what was known as a "pessary" or a "womb veil." This was a rubber or membrane barrier inserted into the vagina before sex. The idea was to prevent the sperm from entering the cervix. Such devices were the forerunners of today's diaphragm and cervical cap, and were often prescribed by doctors to correct "uterine retroversions" or for some other legal purpose.

When birth control failed, women used a variety of techniques to abort a pregnancy. One of the most common techniques was simply to undertake strenuous exercise. There were also many home remedies and commercial preparations to induce an abortion in the early stages of pregnancy. One of the most popular was pennyroyal herb mixed with brewer's yeast. Others included sage, snakeweed, gladwin, calamint, honeysuckle, tansy, savin, rue, aloe and marjoram. These were often sold under such names as "woman's friend" and "female pills."

Sometimes women went to doctors and midwives willing to perform illegal abortions. This was risky business because abortionists were usually untrained and unsupervised, and they frequently ran unsanitary, back-alley-type operations. Desperate women who tried to induce abortions themselves with knitting needles, coat hangers and spoon handles often ran into serious trouble from bleeding and infection. But in the legal and moral climate of the day, there was no such thing as a safe and legal abortion at a clinic or in a hospital.

Rules or not, she was the boss

What do you do when a woman insists she's the head of the family? Today you slap her on the back, but things were different back in 1901, when a census taker encountered such a woman and therefore had a problem. The enumerators had been directed to always list the husband first, since the man was assumed to be the head of the household. But this woman would have none of it.

She said it was her house, she ruled and regulated it, and she looked after the people who lived in it, so she was the head of the family. As her husband meekly looked on, the woman scorned the enumerator's arguments that under the law, in religion, and according to the natural order of things, the husband's name must go first on the census form. Eventually the enumerator gave in and the woman got top billing on the census form, but it made no difference in the final statistics. Both the wife and husband appeared in the totals as "married," and their children were categorized as the sons and daughters of the "head of the family," which they certainly were.

That's just one of the stories which emerged during Canada's fourth census. The head-count, taken every 10 years, showed that in 1901 the national population was 5 371 315, which is only about one-sixth of what it is today. There had been a modest increase of 11 per cent since the census of 1891 – a figure which paled in comparison to the whopping climb of 34 per cent which would occur between 1901 and 1911.

The 1901 census was the most complete since the country's founding. An army of 8800 enumerators fanned out across the land, armed with 11 schedules containing 561 questions. They were paid a nickel for each person they counted, and 25 cents for each family form. Enumerators in rural areas got an extra $1.50 a day to hire a horse and buggy.

They collected statistics on everything from people's earnings to their ethnic origins and religious affiliations. There were only seven provinces in those days. Alberta and Saskatchewan, which became provinces in 1905, were lumped together in the Northwest Territories, while Newfoundland was not counted since it was a separate British colony and didn't join Confederation until 1949.

Ontario, the largest province, had 41 per cent of the nation's people. Quebec had 31 per cent. Nova Scotia was third with 9 per cent. New Brunswick had 6 per cent, followed by Manitoba with 5 per cent, British Columbia with 3 per cent and Prince Edward Island with 2 per cent. The remaining 3 per cent lived in the territories, but that's enough dry population statistics. Here's another census anecdote:

In one household, two women claimed to be the wife of the "head of the household." The man refused to say which one was his legal wife, and the enumerator had no legal power to force him to reveal the truth, or to require the women to show their marriage certificates. Nor could the enumerator go to the authorities, because he was sworn to work in secret to protect the privacy of the citizens. So he described them both as the man's wife. In the compilation, one was added to the "married" column and one to the "single" column. From a statistical point of view, it was unnecessary to determine which was which.

The census revealed that Canada was a spinster's paradise. There were only 1 564 011 single females in Canada, compared to 1 748 582 single males. There were 904 091 married females and 928 952 married males. Why were there more married men than married women? Because a lot of immigrant men had left their wives in the old country. A lot of other men had gone to heaven and left their wives in this world. There were 151 181 widows in Canada, and only 73 837 widowers. Divorce was very rare. There were just 337 divorced men and 324 divorced women.

About 62 per cent of the population lived in the country. The rest lived in urban areas, which were defined as cities, towns and incorporated villages with populations of 500 or more. The average work week was 56.7 hours. The average yearly wage for men ranged from $465 in B.C. to $140 in P.E.I. For women it ranged from $335 in the territories to $45 in P.E.I. For children under 16 it ranged from $115 in the territories to $32 in P.E.I.

There were 2 229 600 Roman Catholics, 916 886 Methodists, 842 442 Presbyterians, 680 620 Anglicans and 292 189 Baptists. Less than one per cent of the population failed to specify a religion. The census broke religions down into 47 categories, ranging from Adventists to Zionites. A final, catch-all category called "various sects" included 99 Millennial Dawnites, 19 Gregorians and 31 members of Daniel's Band.

The nation was made up primarily of people from the two founding races. There were 1 260 899 people of English origin, 988 721 of Irish origin, 800 154 of Scottish origin and 13 415 of "other British" stock. Together they made up 57 per cent of the population. There were 1 649 371 of French origin, making up 31 per cent. The remaining 12 per cent were mainly white people from Europe, with those from Germany making up the largest group. In addition, there were 34 481 "halfbreeds" and 93 460 Indians. And speaking of Indians, here's a final census anecdote:

An enumerator who travelled to a remote area forgot to take a flag with him. The Indians told him they had a traditional regard for the customs of the past, when all conferences with whites were held under the Union Jack. They refused to answer the enumerator's question until he showed them the flag. He sent for his flag, and when it arrived they willingly cooperated with the government man, and were thus counted in the national census.

Chapter 7
How Everyday Life Was Lived

Improve your sex life with an electric belt

It's amazing how little has changed this century with respect to the way in which cure-alls are sold to gullible Canadian consumers. While the most outlandish claims have been toned down, today's medicinal hucksters are spouting the same lines and using the same selling techniques their great-grandfathers employed at the turn of the century.

Today's TV commercial shows a vibrant young woman telling us how great she feels this fine morning, thanks to the sleeping pill or laxative she took the night before. An ad which ran in the Toronto *Star* in early January 1901 is remarkably similar. It features a picture of a narrow-waisted young woman admiring herself in the mirror. The ad explains that "so long as fashion makes women wear corsets, they will continue to squeeze their bodies into shapes never intended by Nature – and they will continue to suffer." Then comes the sales pitch.

"The pain and discomfort won't be so bad, and the food will digest easier, however, if you take Hutch. Take two or three at night to move the bowels; take one after each meal to help the food digest and tone the lining of the stomach. This helps the squeezed-up parts to perform their functions, takes out the pain and soreness, and has a wonderful soothing effect." The punch line has a familiar ring: "The woman who wants to get up in the morning feeling fine ought to get some Hutch and take it right away."

There's been a lot of hype in the late 20th century about Viagra, a prescription drug which is supposed to help men improve their sexual performance. But a cure for impotence at the beginning of the century didn't depend on drugs. You didn't even need a prescription for it. The way to restore your lost powers was to wear Dr. McLaughlin's Electric Belt. An ad for this amazing device promises that "weak men can be cured." It features a picture of a woman crowning a muscular man with a laurel wreath, as if he were a Roman emperor.

The text describing the benefits of the electric belt is enticing:

> *"To feel young again; to realize the joyous sparkle of nerve life as it infuses the body with glowing vitality; to feel the magnetic enthusiasm of youthful energy; to be happy, light-hearted and full of joyous impulses; to be free from spells of despondency, from brain-wandering, from the dull, stupid feeling; to have confidence, self-esteem, and the admiration of men and women."*

You had to wear Dr. McLaughlin's Electric Belt for six or eight hours daily, but that wasn't so bad because it was "mostly during sleep. It pours a glowing stream of electric energy into the weak-

146 Turn of the Century

MEN, WOMEN!

**Are You a Nervous, Weak Man?
Are You a Feeble, Sickly Woman?
Have You Pains In Your Back?
Is Your Life One of Misery
Because You Have Lost Health?**

Are you one of those who have wasted the energy of youth, whose spirit is depressed by the lack of vitality, whose strength and ambition are gone, and who feel sick at heart because you see health and strength all about you and yet you have none of it? ARE YOU SUCH A MAN, SUCH A WOMAN?

My Electric Belt is a positive cure for weakness of every kind in men and women. It gives the vitalizing power of electricity direct to all weak parts, developing the full natural vigor and strength, and removing the cause of disease. I want every one who lacks the strength he should possess to use it, and to tell their friends of its surprising effects.

I have the greatest Electric Belt in the world; greatest in curing, greatest in mechanical perfection, and I am a master in the application of it's life-giving power—due to my twenty years of study and experience. I know what it will do and I can guarantee it. If you are weak, man or woman, if you suffer from any nervous trouble, exhaustion, rheumatism, lame back, kidney or stomach trouble, **My Belt Will Cure You.** After you have worn it a few times you will say, as others have said, "I would not part with it for ten times its cost." If you will give me security you can have my Belt and

PAY WHEN CURED.
DR. McLAUGHLIN'S ELECTRIC BELT

unlike anything that has ever been sold before. Not "as good," but better, stronger, more durable, more pleasant to use, than any other electric body appliance on earth. It restores health by pumping a gentle stream of electricity into the weak parts while you sleep. It gives a current which you feel all the time, but it never burns nor blisters, as do the old style Belts. It has a perfect regulator and my special cushion electrodes.

Have you tried and failed to get results from the old-style belts which burn and blister? Or have you used a "30 days' trial belt" which gave no electricity at all? In either case my modern appliance will be a godsend to you. It gives electricity that makes you feel new life in your veins the first time you use it.

My Belt cures all pain and weakness in from 30 to 60 days. Write to-day for my beautifully illustrated 80 page book, full of happy tidings for weak men. Sent closely mailed free.

DR. M. A. McLAUGHLIN, OFFICE HOURS: 9 a.m. to 8.30 p.m. **130 Yonge Street, Toronto, Ont.**

---

ened nerves and organs, filling them with the vigor of youth." The ad assures buyers that this is a quality product. "It does not fall to pieces as the cheaply made belts do, and does not burn nor blister, as old-style belts do." Potential customers are told that these fine electric belts have already cured 50 000 Canadian men "in every town and hamlet in the country." The ad doesn't state the price, but Dr. McLaughlin promises that "you pay only when cured."

Dr. Williams, on the other hand, was up front about his prices. In fact, he was offering a deal. You could buy one box of his "Pink Pills for Pale People" for 50 cents, or six boxes for $2.50. These pills were "the greatest blood-builder and nerve-restorer medical science has yet discovered.... There is no trouble due to poor blood or weak nerves which these pills will not cure." Dr. Williams sold his pills by presenting testimonials. For instance, Mrs. Frank Evans, of 33 Frontenac Street in Montreal, was quoted as saying: "I am now 23 years of age, and since my eleventh year I have suffered far more than my share of agony from the ailments that afflict my sex. At the age of 16 the trouble had grown so bad that I had to undergo an operation."

This did not cure her, nor did three more operations. Then she tried Dr. Williams' Pink Pills. "I have used the pills for several months and have found more relief from them than from the four operations I passed through, and I warmly recommend them to all women suffering from the ailments which afflict so many of my sex." Just what those ailments were is not spelled out, but Mrs. Evans assures us she no longer worries about them. "I had given up all hope when I began the use of the pills, but they have restored me to such health as I have not known for years."

Nerve problems so troubled Miss Margaret Gillis of Whim Road Cross, P.E.I., that "for the past eight years my life has been one of constant misery." Among other things, she would go into spasms and fall unconscious for half an hour. She began taking Dr. Williams' Pink Pills "and in a short while found them helping me. Then another doctor told me he could cure me. I stopped taking the pills, and like the dog in the fable, while grasping at the shadow I lost the substance. I was soon in as wretched condition as ever. The pills were the only thing that had ever helped me and I determined to try them again."

The story, of course, has a happy ending. Miss Gillis tells us that "I continued to take them for nearly nine months, the trouble gradually but surely leaving me, until I am now in almost perfect health and fully released from what I at one time thought would prove a life of constant misery."

Testimonials from patients were so common in turn-of-the-century medical ads that a gimmick was needed to stand out from the crowd. The makers of a product called Ozone trotted out a husband-and-wife team to show that it cured a variety of ailments. The remarkably frank husband, J. B. Banks, said he had been running a successful gift shop and picture-framing business in Toronto for 20 years, but during all those years he had been troubled with eczema in his left leg. "My leg was swollen three times its natural size .... The skin had broken out in places, and matter was oozing from the ulcers. The leg was black and rawish red in parts right up to the hip, and the itching was frightful." Mr. Banks said Ozone did more than alleviate his symptoms. "I believe that Ozone has saved my life."

Not to be outdone, Mrs. Banks described the three agonizing years during which she suffered from bronchial and lung trouble. It was so bad that she had to be propped up in bed so she could breathe. Even though she obtained "the best medical advice in the city," things got worse. She had no fewer than "three hemorrhages of the lungs," and on top of all that, "I suffered exceedingly from female troubles." When she tried a bottle of Ozone it didn't provide much relief, but after the second bottle, "I felt much improved, and when I had taken nine bottles I had quite recovered."

In another ad, Ozone was even said to cure consumption, which was the common name for tuberculosis. The ad showed a picture of a suffering child, with text which said:

> *"It would tear your heart out to see your sturdy little son become a consumptive. Prevent the disease. Give him Powley's Liquified Ozone and make his lungs strong and healthy. We can give you the names and addresses of people who have been cured of chronic consumption by this preparation. They can tell their own story. Please write, for the boy's sake."*

The secret of Powley's was that it "kills the germs which cause the disease." The company said that "there are a thousand and one ailments which spring up, of more or less severity, which can be promptly relieved and ultimately cured by such a preparation." You could buy a small bottle for 50 cents and a large bottle for $1.

If all else failed, you could just buy a bottle of booze which claimed to have medicinal properties. One brand, called Mariani Wine, advertised that it had written endorsements from 8000 Canadian and American physicians. Billing itself as "the ideal French tonic," the manufacturers promised those who drank a bottle "immediate" and "pleasant" relief from their ills.

There were no rules controlling what could be said about the product, but even worse, there were no rules about what could be put into them. Patent medicines were frequently laced with narcotics.

These medicines were sold as pain-killers and cure-alls, and people frequently became addicted to them. Patent medicines were big business, so it was not surprising that the government was reluctant to regulate them. The companies were also major advertisers in the press, so newspapers and magazines of the day were not inclined to raise alarms about the potential health hazards posed by such medicines.

It wasn't until 1906 that opium was outlawed except for medical purposes, and not until 1908 that the federal government passed the Proprietary or Patent Medicine Act. This act prohibited the use of cocaine in over-the-counter medications. It also required the labelling of patent medicines containing heroin and cannabis, so people would know what drugs they were taking into their bodies. A government spokesman said the 1908 law was designed to "safeguard the public interest without, at the same time, committing injustice to the business interests."

But years earlier, at the turn of the century, manufacturers could say whatever they liked about their nostrums, and they could put whatever they liked into them without revealing the ingredients. Here's a typical magazine ad for a product which likely contained narcotics. Under the ominous headline "An Agent of Death," the ad reads as follows:

> *"People often say: `Oh! Constipation doesn't amount to anything. It cures itself if you leave it alone.' But they make a terrible mistake. There is no more fruitful source of death than constipation. And the evils it always brings causes the most agonizing tortures. Constipation paralyzes the*

muscles of the bowels, which are then unable to perform their duties. Foul, decaying waste matter lies in the bowels, instead of being expelled. It causes irritation, inflammation and death. Again, with such matter decaying in the bowels, the liver and kidneys become diseased, the blood is poisoned, heart disease and death result. We see, therefore, how vitally important it is to keep the bowels in proper order.

"Dodd's Dyspepsia Tablets ensure prompt, thorough digestion, and a proper, regular working of the digestive organs. The small brown Tablets reduce the waste matter, soothe and allay all irritation and inflammation, and stimulate the bowels to a regular and perfect working. Perfect health often depends on a small matter. Keep the bowels in good order. There never was, and never will be, a case of constipation, no matter what its cause, no matter how dangerous, in young, in old, that Dodd's Dyspepsia Tablets won't cure."

Another ad claimed that the product it was touting, Japanese Catarrh Cure, did not contain harmful narcotics, but that its competitors' products did. The ad suggested that "you have possibly seen powders, snuffs and tablets you chew advertised to cure catarrh; others advise you to load your stomach with some of their blood purifier. Now if you had an ulcer, a sore, or inflamed surface anywhere else on your body, you would not think of blowing cocaine powders on it, would you?"

The ad warned that

"some of these so-called catarrh remedies contain dangerous narcotics; they relieve at the time, but give rise to a false security; the disease keeps on spreading deeper, until the hearing and lungs are affected. You take more and more of the stuff each time to relieve. Soon you will wake up to the reality of these statements and find you have neglected the proper treatment too long."

Yet even if the patent medicines had been properly labelled, controls were still needed on what could be made available to consumers. A case in Regina in January 1901 illustrates the point. It involved a single woman in her early 30s named Eva Boyd, who was the delicate type. She hated loud noises, frequently felt depressed, and often complained of pain throughout her body. But she found a quick fix for her troubles. Eva injected herself with morphine.

The fact that she was a nurse at the Regina hospital made it easy for Eva to obtain the drug, but even if she hadn't been in the medical profession, it would have been simple and perfectly legal for her to get morphine or any other narcotic she wished to use. They found her one day lying with a shawl over her head. She'd been zonked out like that all day, having gone to bed after working the midnight shift the previous evening. When they went to wake her for supper and discovered Eva in a stupor, they injected her with stimulants, but that didn't help. They even tried hooking her up to a battery in an effort to revive her. But that didn't work either, and she was pronounced dead at 2:30 a.m. the following morning.

An examination of the body revealed old and new puncture wounds. Eva was a junkie. What she did to herself was tragic, but it was not illegal. At the start of the century, there were no laws in this country regulating the use of morphine, cocaine, opium, marijuana or any other drugs. What people chose to put into their bodies for health or recreational purposes was their own concern, with the sole exception of alcohol, which at the time was the only substance widely viewed as a threat to society.

"The criminalization of narcotics is a product of the twentieth century," points out an authority on the subject, Melvyn Green. "The process of legislative revision eventually led to a moral redefinition of narcotic drug use. What was once viewed as a private indulgence came to be regarded almost universally as a public evil."

No social safety net to protect the poor

A deserted wife and mother wrote a letter to the Regina town council in 1901 begging for help. Mrs. Parry Williams wanted assistance in tracking down her deadbeat husband, who disappeared a year and a half earlier. She said she could no longer cope with expenses on her own. The town council reluctantly gave her $8.50 for a train ticket to Winnipeg, so she could put her children in an orphanage.

This was typical of the way government assistance to the needy was handled at the time. Municipalities were reluctant to give handouts to the poor. They were particular leery of supporting deserted wives, on the grounds that providing financial help to such women would encourage men to abandon their families.

Citizens who fell on hard times were not legally entitled to government funds, as they are today. They were expected to turn to family first, their friends second, charities third, and the government only as a last resort. And when relief payments were made, the money came from the local authorities. The provincial or federal governments, although they had more money than the local councils, didn't feel it was their responsibility to provide social benefits to the needy.

It's a far cry from our system today, under which the federal and provincial governments impose heavy taxes and provide tens of billions of dollars each year to help needy Canadians. But that wasn't the government's role at the start of the century. Government played a much smaller part in people's lives in those days, and citizens were much more responsible for their own welfare. There was no unemployment insurance for workers who lost their jobs, no workers' compensation for those who were injured, no medicare to pay doctors and hospital fees, no government pension plans and no old age security cheque automatically deposited in your bank account each month.

The inability to look after oneself financially was seen as evidence of poor character or poor planning. The failure to care for one's self and one's family was seen as a problem of the person's own making, rather than a sign there was something wrong with the system. Those who decry the current cutbacks in our social safety net usually compare the situation today to the way things were back in the more generous 1970s and 1980s. If the comparison were made between today and the early years of this century, Canadians would see that despite the cutbacks, they are living in a relative social paradise.

Those who complain today that food banks have become a permanent feature of Canadian society forget or don't know that there was a time when poor people had to beg for food, rather than just pick it up from a central depot. Today there are calls for government regulation to ensure that what's given out by food banks meets supermarket standards. A century ago, free food of any kind and quality would have been welcomed by poor people.

In the early 1900s, there was a special lack of sympathy for able-bodied people looking for a handout. Those classified by today's welfare system as "single employables" received short shrift if they went looking for a free ride. Instead of getting a cheque to cover their basic needs, they got a sharp suggestion that they smarten up and get a job. But that harsh philosophy ran into the harsh reality of daily life. Poverty was widespread, particularly in the big cities, and many unfortunate Canadians suffered because of the look-out-for-yourself mentality which prevailed.

A study conducted in Montreal near the end of the 19th century documented the sad plight of the poor. Titled *The City Below The Hill*, it drew a sharp contrast

Poor farm family, circa 1900. SPA R-A 7226(2).

between the lives of the poor people of Montreal and those of the wealthy who lived above them on the hill overlooking the St. Lawrence River.

It found that wage levels in the slum area were low, and that living conditions were terrible. The average family income per week was just $10.25, which was barely enough to get by on in 1901. Most of the money went to pay for food and shelter. More than one family member had to work to pay the bills. The study found that one in five workers was a woman, who typically worked in a textile mill, tobacco plant, food-processing plant or store, or as a domestic servant. The average weekly wage for a six-day work week was $8.25 for a man, $4.50 for a woman and $3 for a boy.

The typical full-time employee worked from 8 a.m. to 6 p.m., six days a week, and didn't get paid for his half-hour lunch. Layoffs were frequent, especially in the winter, and when they came the family usually had to survive at a subsistence level. Because their families needed money, kids as young as 10 usually held jobs. Many children who were still in school contributed to the family income by working as part-time messengers, newsboys and delivery boys. Youngsters often quit school and worked in factories, even though the law stated that boys had to be 12 and girls had to be 14 to be employed in such places. Families and employers got around the law easily. All that was needed as proof of age was a statement signed by a parent.

The typical family was made up of a husband, wife and three children who lived in a five-room duplex without hot water. While Montreal by that point had an extensive sewage system, more than half the people living in the study area were still using outdoor toilets. The author of the study, Herbert Ames, was nicknamed "Water Closet Ames" because of his campaign to get rid of what he called "that insanitary abomination . . . that danger to public health and morals . . . the out-of-door-in-the-ground privy."

Ames was part of what came to be known as the Social Gospel Movement. These reformers argued that social problems were generally the result of flaws in society, not inadequacies in the individual. They said it was up to society to help those who had troubles. Ames wanted to encourage businessmen to build adequate housing for the poor, but other Social Gospellers went further. They insisted that the church and charities also had a duty to uplift the downtrodden, and that the state had to play a major role as well, using its taxing power to take money from the well-off and turn it over to the needy.

The Social Gospel movement was just getting started in the early 1900s, but as the century progressed it eventually led to the introduction of income tax, family allowance and many other measures which turned middle- and upper-income Canadian taxpayers into their less-fortunate brothers' keepers. The Halifax *Herald* was far ahead of its time when it foresaw late in the year 1900 that the federal government in Canada would eventually come to play a major role in social welfare in the 20th century.

"It is entirely possible," the *Herald* predicted, "that by the end of the coming century, the national governments may recognize as a duty devolving on them to provide work, wages, and in more general terms, a living for the people at large. It is entirely possible that the 20th century will add much in the way of socialistic government to what the 19th century has so largely begun."

While the *Herald* felt that socialism was already under way, in fact it was barely getting started. Among the few social measures in existence at the time was a government-run "children's aid" to look after neglected and delinquent youngsters in Ontario. Provincial governments across Canada also paid for asylums to house the insane, as well as jails. Poor people worked as long as they could. There was no standard age of retirement, complete with a pension. Old people who lacked money or family to look after them were placed in charitable institutions or county homes which provided spartan accommodation for the indigent.

For the most part, however, Canadians who ran into tough times or hard luck at the turn of the century were helped by the people around them. Typical was a case in which fire struck a family of homesteaders in the North-West Territories. It was 58 degrees below zero at dawn on New Year's Day in 1901 when Mrs. James Flett went out to the stable to attend to her farm animals, leaving her daughters aged two and four in the house. Mrs. Flett, whose husband had died just a few weeks earlier, lived a few miles outside Prince Albert.

Here's how the local paper reported the event: "Happening to look toward the house, she saw the flames bursting out of the windows and running up was just in time to rescue with difficulty the children with only what little clothing they wore at the time, and in just a few short minutes the house and contents had gone up in smoke." Members of the community helped the Fletts create a temporary place to live. "A granary on the homestead is being fitted up and made as comfortable as possible by settlers and townspeople, which will provide a fairly good temporary shelter until a new house is built."

Mrs. Flett's neighbors held fund-raising activities and within a few days came up with $250 for the unfortunate family. It wasn't enough for a new house, but it was a considerable sum, and at least it kept the Fletts from starving until they could find a way to start rebuilding their lives.

Gramophone told funny stories and delivered prayers

Next time an e-mail urges you to buy some junky product, don't complain about the gimmicky sales tactics of the modern era. The hard sell has been around for a long time. Only the delivery device has changed. In the old days, newspapers and magazines carried the message to buy, buy, buy! Your great-grandmother was subjected to the same sales lines used by today's hucksters to unload assorted gadgets and gizmos. The price was great, the quality was superb, but you had to hurry up and order or you might miss out.

Take the newspaper ad for the Genuine Berliner Gramophone, which was offered "on special terms in order to place the gramophone more generally in the homes of the people." The price sounded good: you sent in just $1 and paid another $2 a month for the next eight months. The total came to more than a week's wages for a lot of people. In return for this money, you got a gramophone, the forerunner of the mid-20th-century record player and the ancestor of modern CD player.

This amazing hi-tech device was powered by a spring which you wound up with a crank. A flat, rubber-like disc twirled around on a turntable, with a steel needle running along in the record groove. The sound came out of a large horn. The machine was guaranteed for five years, but how good was the sound? Absolutely terrific, said the ad. It was loud enough to fill the largest church or hall, but adjustable so that the machine would also work well in smaller rooms, where it could be used for "dancing parties." The advantages of the machine were endless.

> "It talks distinctly, telling funny stories, or will deliver a prayer. It sings, or rather reproduces voices of the most notable singers – comic, patriotic, sentimental or sacred songs. It sings hymns like your own church choir. It reproduces every musical instrument – cornet, violin, piano, flute, piccolo, clarionet, banjo, mandolin, etc., etc. It reproduces full bands and orchestras, playing anything from the latest operatic hits to coon songs and cake walks. It is five times as loud as the wax record talking machines, and our records will last 10 times as long as wax ones."

The ad, which ran in a Toronto newspaper, said that when a similar offer was made in Montreal, "the results were simply astounding. Orders came in from every part of Canada and hundreds of unsolicited testimonials have since been received from people in every walk of life – merchants, doctors, teachers, clergymen, lawyers, farmers, clerks, etc., certifying to the delightful qualities of the gramophone, and their satisfaction of their purchase." There was, of course, a need to act quickly. "Orders will be filled in rotation, first come, first served. Therefore, to avoid delay, order at once." But since the ad claimed that over 100 000 of these machines had been sold in the previous year, it was likely that the supply was adequate.

Among the records offered for sale, at an undisclosed price, were "Nearer My God to Thee," "Cake Walk," "I Can't Tell Why I Love You But I Do," "My Old Kentucky Home," "Home Sweet Home," "Put Me Off at Buffalo," "I Stand Up for Jesus," and "Way Down Upon the 'Suwanye' River."

An ad for another amazing product took up a full page in a daily paper in June 1901. It was for the Kin-Hee Quick Coffee Pot and Kin-Hee Mocha and Java Coffee. It cheerfully pointed out that this was "the most important announcement made this century to lovers of a good cup of coffee." That wasn't hard to believe, since the century was less than six months old. What was so good about Kin-Hee coffee and the clunky-looking coffee-maker with the ugly black handle sticking out the side? Well, for one thing you could use pulverized rather than coarsely ground coffee, to get the maximum amount of flavor, and you got a cloth strainer to keep the fine grinds out of your drink.

The ad proclaimed the device to be "the wonder of the century," and perhaps it was, since the same technique is used for home coffee-makers today. But what about speed, you might ask. A pot of coffee could be made in just one minute. Even better, the ad said, you didn't even have to drop an egg into the pot when you used the Kin-Hee Quick Coffee Pot. The coffee sold for 40 cents a pound. That got you a "hermetically sealed" container of the most delicious coffee, which contained "more of the essential oils than any other coffee on the market."

An ad for a washing machine used a technique that's familiar today – a startling statement to catch your attention. This one, produced by the 1900 Washer Company, claimed that the device would do "half your washing free of cost." It said that "you must pay the washer-woman 15 cents an hour. It is hard-earned money at that. If you do your own washing, or have the servant do it, this steaming, back-breaking, hand-chapping, cold-catching, temper-destroying work will cost you more than 15 cents an hour in the end."

Then came the higher mathematics. "It takes eight hours hard labor to do the average family wash. Eight hours, at 15 cents, costs you $1.20 per week for washing. This means $62.40 per year, without reckoning fuel for fires, or wear on clothes. We will save you half of that – or No Pay."

Since you could do the laundry with the machine in four hours instead of eight hours, you would save $31.20 a year, and since the machine would last "at least five years," the total saving would amount to $156, the ad maintained. And how much for the washer? Well, the ad didn't come right out and say, but it did claim that the washer "won't cost you a cent, under our plan, because we let it pay for itself." So the price for this gadget was a then-enormous $156.

That was a fortune to a lot of people, but the wise people at the 1900 Washer Company offered to ship the washer to a potential customer for a one-month free trial. The company hoped that the woman of the house would enjoy spending just four hours a week doing the washing, and that she would be happy to let the wonderful machine's ball bearings and motor springs do "most of the hard work."

After that kind of luxury, they figured, who would ever want to go back to doing the laundry the old-fashioned way? Come to think of it, they were right.

Canadians have been hockey fans for a long time

Canadians were as crazy about hockey a hundred years ago as they are today. They had been enjoying the game since the late 1870s, when it was first played at McGill University in Montreal, and by the start of the 20th century, hockey was well on its way to becoming the national sport.

There were no professional players back then, and the idea that athletes would one day be receiving multi-million-dollar annual salaries would have been greeted with great skepticism. The National Hockey League didn't start until 1917. But long before that, money was beginning to creep into the sport. Turn-of-the-century arena operators charged admission to games, and a few teams quietly started collecting a share of the proceeds in exchange for filling the rink and providing thrills and excitement to the fans.

But in most respects, hockey was played for fun by enthusiastic amateurs. There were men's teams in almost every city and town, and women's hockey was coming into its own. While women were expected to be ladylike in social situations, it was perfectly alright for them to engage in vigorous sporting activity, and hockey provided a splendid opportunity for them to do so.

The rules of hockey were much different back then, but the game was played as roughly and with as much spirit as it is today. Ice hockey was a Canadian version of English field hockey and soccer, played on a shiny surface which this country had no trouble providing in the winter. Each team consisted of seven players, and they all played the whole game. If a player was injured, he left the ice, together with a player from the other team, so the sides remained equal.

The game lasted an hour, and consisted of two 30-minute periods, with a 10-minute break in between. Rinks were smaller. The ice surface had to be at least 112 feet by 58 feet, compared with the usual 200-by-85-foot dimensions of today, but the puck was still a one-inch rubber disk with a three-inch diameter. It even had a fancy name. It was known as the "gutta percha."

There were no blue lines or no centre line in turn-of-the-century hockey. But the idea of having a thin line across the goal mouth was just coming into fashion, because it made it easier for the judge to determine if a goal had been scored. For the same reason, a net was placed behind the pipes to catch the puck if it went into the goal. The dimensions of the goal were six feet by four feet, as they are today, but the goalie didn't wear special equipment. He was dressed like the other players, his only body protection being a pair of light pads covering his shins and knees. There was also a rule that the goalie had to remain standing. The goalie was not allowed to sprawl in front of the goal to block a shot.

There were two players in front of the goalie, corresponding to the defencemen in today's game. One of them was known as the "point." He was usually a burley player who stood directly in front of the goalie and whose main job was to check incoming forwards and control the area right in front of the goal. Positioned in front of the "point" was a player known as the "coverpoint." He was the initial line of defence, and if he was good at his job, he not only checked incoming attackers. He also stole the puck and led an advance against the enemy goal.

There were four forwards, rather than today's three. There were two wingers and a centre, as well as a player known as the rover, who stood behind the centre at face-offs. He was usually the fastest player on the team, and his position was the most fluid. He was expected to attack as well as defend, to back-check, and to fill any position left vacant by a penalty.

The biggest difference between the game today and the version played at the beginning of the century was that there was no forward pass. All players on the attacking team had to remain behind the puck. But lateral passes were allowed, and sometimes you could pass slightly forward, so long as you were even with the puck by the time your team-mate received the pass. Without the forward pass, there was more emphasis on skating and stick-handling, as one team advanced on the other's goal in a sort of all-out charge behind the puck.

A myth has arisen that hockey in the old days was a graceful and gentlemanly sport. But the game was as rough as it is today, and because of the lack of protective equipment, hockey was not a game for sissies. Vigorous body checking was permitted. In fact, people complained as much then as they do today that hockey is spoiled by too much emphasis on fighting and goon-like play, and too little finesse.

Another similarity between the old days and today is the fact that winning the Stanley cup was the ultimate goal of the best hockey players. The cup was awarded each year to the top hockey club in Canada, but in those days it really was just a cup, rather than the giant silver cylinder it has grown into today, to provide space for the names of all the winners over so many years.

The original cup was a bowl which measured 11.25 inches in diameter and was 7.5 inches deep. It was made in England in 1893 at a cost of 10 English pounds. That original cup is what you see today, perched on top of the huge silver barrel which forms the bulk of the glittering 32-pound trophy, which stands almost three feet high.

The cup was created by Lord Stanley of Preston, who was Canada's sixth governor general. Stanley was a great fan of the sport, and two of his sons played on an Ottawa team. He established the cup as a trophy "to be held for year to year by the champion hockey club of the Dominion." He specified that the winners were entitled to keep the cup only temporarily, and had to give it up if they were defeated by a team which challenged them for the prize. Trustees were established to determine which teams were eligible to engage in the annual challenge match.

In 1901 there was little doubt about who should play for the Lord Stanley's cup. The rivalry was a classic east-west struggle between the Montreal Shamrocks and the Winnipeg Victorias, nicknamed the Bisons. The prize was to be awarded to the team that won the best two out of three games. On the evening of Thursday, Jan. 31, 1901, the Victorias were one up in the series, and were trying to take the cup in two straight games. The Montreal team, which faced elimination, had the advantage of home ice. The city's arena, which had about 4000 seats, was packed that night.

The game was hot and heavy right from the start, but a goal by the Winnipeg team's captain, centreman Dan Bain, put the "wearers of the red" ahead late in the first period. The Shamrocks, known as the "wearers of the green," tied the score early in the second period, and the teams went back and forth for almost 30 more minutes until the end of regulation time, when the game remained tied at 1-1.

After a brief rest, the action resumed. Seven minutes into overtime, Bain scored the winner, and the Winnipeg Victorias were the Stanley Cup champs for 1901. Here's how the Manitoba *Free Press*'s report of the great event began: "Hurray for the west! Once more the hockeyists of the effete east have succumbed to the Winnipeg `Bisons,' and the Stanley Cup closed up nicely in a box will be travelling toward the land of the setting sun."

The newspaper gave a play-by-play description of the action, and summarized the pandemonium which broke out in the arena after Bain's winning goal. The cheerleader-style of writing shows how little has changed over the past century with respect to the way Canadian hockey fans respond to victory, and the way Canadian journalists describe the event:

> "The enthusiastic outburst which greeted his performance is beyond the power of pen to describe. Half the people in the rink sat motionless with the word disappointment written all over their countenances; the other half rose as one man and broke into prolonged and frantic cheers . . . . Scores of them poured over the sides of the rink and literally carried the boys into the dressing room, where they were hugged and mauled by their friends."

The newspaper reported that the team would be returning to Winnipeg by train within the next few days, and urged the people of the city to greet the conquering hockey heroes with a suitable display of enthusiasm.

Much was expected of students and teachers

People who graduate from teachers' college today sometimes have trouble finding jobs. That wasn't a problem a century ago, particularly in the North-West Territories. There was a big demand for teachers to work in the new schools which were sprouting up in the booming West. Many of the students were children from central and eastern Europe who came to Canada with their families in response to Ottawa's vigorous immigration campaign. These youngsters presented a challenge to their teachers, who had to familiarize them with Canadian customs and the English language, as well as teach them the required curriculum.

Schools in those days had a detailed program of studies which the students had to master before they could progress to the next level. Students failed if they didn't measure up. They weren't pushed ahead to the next grade, as they are today, no matter how little they had learned. A big cutoff point came at the end of elementary school. What we call Grade 1-8 today was known then as Standards 1-5, and many students ended their schooling at that level. The law required youngsters to go to school from the ages of 7 to 13. Those who wanted to go on to high school had to pass stiff exams, demonstrating competence in reading, spelling, comprehension, writing, grammar, English literature, arithmetic, geography, history and bookkeeping.

You can get an idea of the difficult material elementary students were expected to master by looking at the program of studies for the North-West Territories. The history curriculum was typical. By the time they completed Standard 2, students were expected to be familiar with the lives of Columbus, the Cabots, Jacques Cartier, Champlain, Bishop Laval, Frontenac, La Salle, Montcalm, Wolfe, Sir Guy Carleton,

William Lyon Mackenzie, Papineau, Joseph Howe, Alexander Mackenzie and Sir John A. Macdonald. Teachers for Standard 2 were told not only to go over the life histories of these men, but also to promote "discussion of the chief excellences and defects in their characters to teach moral discrimination and, ultimately, to derive principles of conduct."

The Standard 3 curriculum provided an overview of Canadian history, including the nation's discovery and exploration, the struggle between French and English colonists, the treaty of Paris, the Quebec Act, the Constitutional Act, the War of 1812, the Rebellion of 1837, the Union Act, clergy reserves, various forms of land tenure, the Reciprocity Treaty and the British North America Act. British history was introduced at this level. It included the leading figures of British history from Caractacus to Queen Victoria, with "discussion of their deeds to train moral judgment and incidentally to teach patriotism and civic duty."

Standard 4 included a more detailed study of Canadian history, plus an examination of the various peoples and periods of British history. For instance, the students learned that the Saxons who came to England in the Dark Ages brought with them the germs of many modern features of British life, including the limited monarchy, Parliament, the court system, personal holdings of land, the English language and the Christian religion. The history curriculum for Standard 5, the last level of elementary school, included a comparison of the constitutional struggles in Canada with corresponding ones in England, the operation of Canada's parliamentary, judicial, municipal and school systems, and the duties of citizenship, including voting, holding office, paying taxes and supporting the law.

Covering so much ground with young children was a tall order, but the deputy commissioner of education for the North-West Territories, J. A. Calder, told prospective teachers that even more was expected of them. Writing in the Regina teachers' college yearbook for 1901, Calder advised the students not to take jobs in the West if their heart wasn't in the work, and if they weren't prepared to make sacrifices. "The individual who comes among us for a short time to spy out his land, to improve his health, or to earn sufficient money to meet his expenses at an eastern college is not wanted," Calder told the graduates. He said the West needed teachers with a "missionary spirit." They should also be young, in perfect health, energetic and progressive enough to adapt to conditions in the new western schools.

Conditions were far from ideal. Attendance was often a problem, since many of the children were expected to work on their families' farms. Prairie schools were often set up in municipal halls, churches and other buildings. Even the Regina teachers' college had to improvise. The class of 1901, which started in September and finished just before Christmas, had to meet in Regina's Methodist Church because it was too cold in the regular college building. One of the students, James Bryant, showed the proper spirit in the face of adversity, making light of the fact that he and his colleagues had to study in the church basement. Bryant wrote in the 1901 yearbook that "the hallowed influence of the class room, the dim religious light, and the warm atmosphere in the vicinity of the furnace, reminded us of things to come, and had a softening and refining effect upon our spirits."

According to another student, the curriculum for the four-month teacher-training program was heavy, but the philosophy was clear. It put the emphasis on moral values: "We have studied everything under the sun which would in any way tend to fit us to complete living," he explained, "the earth and the fulness thereof being our field .... To some, perhaps, the number of teeth in a hen, the means of locomotion of the grasshopper, and the digestive system of the fly may seem to be unimportant as a matter of information, but such things, however, are only side lights in the study of nature." But he found there was a broader point behind all the details. The study of nature would hopefully provide insights into the student's own life, which in turn would provide insight into all life. This would lead the student "to look reverently to the author of all life – through nature up to God's nature – the thought that makes life worth living."

Teachers' colleges in those days were known as "normal schools," and the students were referred to as "normalites." The idea was that the teaching methods presented at the normal school would become the norm or standard for all schools within the government's jurisdiction. The Regina Normal School was founded in 1892. The class of 1901 was the largest to date, with 98 students, more than half of them from the East. There were 58 women and 40 men.

Despite the fact that women were in the majority, each of the six working groups was headed by a man. That was the way things were done in those days, but you get a sense that change was in the air when you read the yearbook's predictions for the future of the graduates. Verna Lilian York's classmates predicted that "thou shalt be called the golden-mouthed, like Chrysostom of old, because of thine advocacy of the rights of women to the franchise, to civic office .... to control the sale and consumption of intemperate drinks." Jessie A. McKenzie's fate was that "thou shalt lead in social reforms. Words of wisdom shalt thou speak, as one inspired with the spirit of the prophets. The manners and morals of the Gentiles, fumigated and furbished, shall brighten more and more."

James McKinnon, the class valedictorian, sounded as if he was up to the challenge of teaching in the West. He said he and his classmates would soon be scattered throughout the Territories. "What a splendid tract of country. Hundreds of millions of acres of the best farming land in the world lie in this garden of a continent .... The hum of the advancing multitude can now be heard, yes, the vanguard can now be seen settling among us." He said it was the teachers' work "to raise them up to our levels of society and land" and "to inspire in our pupils a healthy Canadian spirit, a love for our country and a desire to be worthy sons of such a mighty country, Canada."

The nation had a fairly well-developed system of higher education at the turn of the century. It included 15 colleges and 16 universities, the largest of which were the University of Toronto and McGill University in Montreal, which had about 1250 students each. Another 3000 students attended the University of Trinity College and Victoria University, both in Toronto, McMaster in Hamilton, the University of Ottawa, Queen's in Kingston, the University of Manitoba in Winnipeg, Laval in Montreal and Quebec City, and seven small universities in the Maritimes – Acadia, the University of King's College, Dalhousie, the University of New Brunswick, Bishop's, Mt. Allison and St. Francis Xavier.

Discipline was particularly strict at Laval, where the authorities issued the following statement to tell students what was expected:

> "Attention at the lectures, subordination and respect to the officers and professors of the University, within and without the walls of the University and the observance of all its by-laws is required of every student. Improper or obscene language, or anything tending to show the spirit of irreligion or immorality, or of such a nature as to compromise the honour of the University, subjects the guilty party to expulsion. Frequenting gambling or drinking salons, or houses of doubtful reputation, is strictly prohibited. The students cannot form associations among themselves nor make collective demonstrations without permission. Attendance upon all lectures is imperative."

Catalogue was the early equivalent of a shopping mall

When you needed something at the start of the 20th century, you didn't just hop on your horse and trot down to the shopping centre. But it was almost that easy. You took out the Eaton's catalogue and mailed in your order. A few weeks later, your goods arrived at the nearest railway station or post office. It was quick and easy. The catalogue made it possible for people living in rural areas to have access to a wide variety of products.

Leafing through the old Eaton's catalogue today, you get a sense of how our great-grandparents lived. They bought many of the same things we buy today, although there have been many changes in style and fashion. They could get almost everything they needed – clothes, furniture, housewares, sewing machines, medicines, books, guns, jewelry, phonographs, cameras, suitcases, baby carriages, wallpaper and thousands of other items. The catalogue, in effect, was a shopping mall on paper.

The man behind the catalogue was Timothy Eaton, one of the most innovative and successful retailers in Canadian history. Eaton was an Irishman who came to Canada as a young man in 1854. He and his brother operated a store in a small town named St. Mary's in western Ontario. Fifteen years later, Eaton opened his own store at the corner of Queen and Yonge Streets in Toronto. Eaton's store did well. He sold things on a cash-only basis rather than extending credit, and he charged a fixed price rather than bargain-

Two gentlemen in typical Eaton's catalogue merchandise. SPA R-A 17641.

and there were also brief written descriptions to provide details. The cost of each item was stated, and the price in those days was the total price. No PST and GST were added, although you had to pay freight or postal charges. Pricing things at $24.99 or $2.99 to make them seem cheaper was not yet a common sales gimmick, and usually the prices of things in the catalogue were rounded off – $25 for a black sable shoulder scarf, for instance, or a photo album for $3.

But Eaton had other ways to persuade customers to buy. He offered a full refund if people weren't satisfied with what they bought, and he built confidence in his experience and integrity. He bragged that he had "19th century experience" and "20th century ideas." At the bottom of his catalogue pages, he printed messages such as, "Our customers may rely on receiving first-class articles," and "We guarantee to fill mail orders accurately and promptly." He also presented full-blown sales pitches. Here's one from the men's and boys' clothing section of the catalogue:

ing and bartering, the way most other retailers operated at that time.

But the business really took off after he introduced the mail-order catalogue in the mid-1880s. This richly illustrated book, along with Canada's efficient rail and postal services, extended the store's reach to customers throughout the land. Soon Eaton had customers across Canada. To stock his warehouses, he sent buyers to the U.S. and England, and he built a factory in Toronto where many of the things he sold in his catalogue were made.

The catalogue was full of line drawings which illustrated what was available,

"We manufacture our own clothing and personally visit Europe twice yearly, and select our cloths from the English, Scotch and Irish mills, together with our domestic tweeds, gathering together from the different firms the most suitable and satisfactory materials both as to wear and appearance . . . . Satisfy yourself by comparing our clothing with what you usually see. Examine the linings and underlinings, the sewing, the staying and workmanship when finished throughout, and you will readily see how much superior the Eaton

standard of clothing is. That applies to our low-priced goods as well as our high-grade qualities. Buying and making as we do, and having such a tremendous output for our clothing, permit us to offer values that are not easily equalled."

By the turn of the century, the T. Eaton Co. Ltd. was putting out two thick catalogues a year. The spring and summer catalogue for 1901 showed that the company was in tune with the times. It featured a well-dressed couple driving through Toronto's Queen's Park in an automobile. Cars were quite a novelty in those days, and while you couldn't buy one out of the catalogue, you could get the fancy clothes those trendy people were wearing. You could also get work clothes, summer clothes, winter clothes, all kinds of clothes. Items of apparel filled more pages of the catalogue than any other category of merchandise.

By modern standards, women were greatly overdressed, particularly for business and formal occasions. The female figure was swathed in layers of fabric which covered the body from head to toe. The well-dressed matron wore a two-piece suit which had a long-sleeved tunic and a skirt which touched the floor. She wore a flowered hat, and high shoes which were buttoned up onto the ankle. But there was a certain sexiness to her appearance, however, thanks to the tightness of the suit's fit and the narrowness of the waist, which was enhanced with the aid of an undergarment known as a corset. It fit over the bust, waist and abdomen, and was designed to push the breast up and out while reducing the waist to the smallest possible circumference. Corsets were delicate looking on the outside, with satin fabrics and lace, but inside they consisted of steel wires and featherbone ribs which contorted the woman's body into an hourglass shape.

As far as men's clothes were concerned, formal dress was as silly-looking then as it is today. The morning suits and cutaways which were fashionable at the turn of the century resemble outfits that most men today would wear only when getting married or working as butlers. For business and everyday occasions, men wore suits which weren't that different from the ones we see today, except that they buttoned up higher on the chest. Bicycle suits featured trousers which ended just below the knee, with the cuffs tucked into long socks. Hats were a required part of the man's uniform at the start of the century, and came in a wide range of styles. The high-topped silk hat was a mark of rank and distinction, while the fur felt hat was the most common form of male head gear. The standard four-in-hand tie, so much a part of today's business wear, was only one of the neckwear options open to men in the old days. Others included bat-wing bow ties, stylish kerchiefs and comfortable-looking silk and satin puffs.

You could buy hundreds of medicines and drugs from the Eaton's catalogue. You could get everything from acids to zinc compounds. Among the most interesting-sounding items were bee's wax, prepared chalk, castor oil, effervescent phosphate of soda, dandelion extract, dragon's blood gum, horehound, sarsaparilla, jewellers' rouge, Listerine, galls and opium ointment, Chapman's dinner pills, spermaceti, whale-oil soap and rhubarb syrup. You could get a hot water bottle to warm your toes, elastic stockings to support your legs, a 'natural body' brace for "special weaknesses and diseases of women and trusses to help men suffering from ruptures."

In an ominous note, the drug department said that "where the word 'poison' is placed after an item, it is necessary to have physician's prescription accompanying order, which can be repeated if so marked; but where it is a very violent and dangerous poison we require such prescription from physician to accompany each order from you, such as strychnine, morphine, ergot and preparations, arsenic salts (other than Paris green), aconite, red iodide of mercury, cantharides and all poisons in Schedule 1 of Pharmacy Act."

Eaton's sold many books. A Bible with tiny pearl type cost just 25 cents, while a deluxe pulpit Bible with extra-large type, Morocco leather binding, gold edges and colored maps was $8.25. You could get a 13-volume set of the works of William Shakespeare for $3 and a 15-volume set of Charles Dickens' works for $4.75. For just 19 cents apiece, you could pick up such classics as *The Count of Monte Cristo*, Grimms' *Fairy Tales*, *Swiss Family Robinson* and *Wife in Name Only*. For just a penny more, you could buy *Confessions of an Opium Eater* and *Reveries of a Bachelor*.

Horses played a major role in the lives of people at the turn of the century, and Eaton's sold all kinds of things which were needed by the animals and their owners. You could buy buggy harnesses, bridles, ankle boots, horse collars, whisks, body brushes, horse nets, snaffle bits, whips, tethering hobbles, hames, stirrup straps saddles and rain covers.

In the household furnishings department, Eaton's carried everything from wooden wash tubs and butter churns to oil lamps, electric light fixtures, treadle-operated sewing machines, gramophones and carpet sweepers. The catalogue included straight razors and the new Gem safety razors "which renders shaving an easy luxury and totally obviates all danger of cutting the face." The photographic department offered a 4x5 Weno Hawk-eye camera for $8 and a Special Tourist Hawk-eye, complete with movable lens, for $25. You could buy chemicals, photographic paper and other items to process your own pictures at home.

Guns were also sold, with no requirement to produce a certificate, licence or other document to prove you were entitled to own a firearm. You could get a seven-shot revolver for $1.75, a .22-calibre rifle for $3.25, and a double-barrel shotgun for $10.

Ho, ho, ho! Santa slid down the chimney a century ago

The way Canadians celebrate Christmas is one of the things that has changed least over the past 100 years. Just as it is today, Christmas at the turn of the century was a combination of commercialism, religion and family togetherness. About the only new things are Rudolph the red-nosed reindeer and Christmas cards delivered by e-mail.

The newspapers of 1900 were full of ads much like the ones we see today, offering all kinds of items as "special" Christmas gifts, and urging Canadians to spend, spend, spend! Here's a typical ad, run by the Eaton's store in Toronto in *The Globe* three days before Christmas:

> "Now comes the Rush! Bigger crowds at the store than ever before. And such pleasant, good-natured crowds, too, who are being served by us better and with greater satisfaction than ever before. We have an abundance of gifts – things that can be chosen in a hurry."

While the tone is familiar, the products and prices certainly date this entreaty to show how much you care by pulling out your wallet. You could buy a stuffed animal for 25 cents, a Bible for 50 cents, French kid gloves for a dollar, a Bissell carpet sweeper for $1.50, and a lady's seal jacket for $195, which was more than a typical factory laborer earned in two months.

Across the street at the store operated by Robert Simpson, the doors stayed open on Christmas Eve until 10 p.m., which is even later than stores now remain open on that special night. Commercialism didn't take a rest even on Christmas Day. In *The Globe* for Dec. 25, 1900, Eaton's ran a big picture of Santa Claus going down the chimney with the following text:

> "What a jolly old fellow Santa Claus really is, and what gladness and joy he has brought to thousands of happy hearts this morning. Has he not done magnificent for you this season? But this store had to help this grand old gift-king. Had we not helped as we did, some of you might have been disappointed this morning."

Santa was old stuff, even back then. He had been popularized decades earlier in United States by Clement Moore in his poem *The Night Before Christmas*, and by illustrator Thomas Nast in his popular magazine covers.

Boxing Day sales were a feature of Christmas at the turn of the century, as they are today. Here's how Eaton's sought to lure customers to its downtown Toronto store on Dec. 26, 1900: "It will require something extra good to bring you out shopping on Wednesday, right after Christmas, but we have made careful plans to have you at this store." The ad

Christmas shopping. <u>Saturday Night</u>, *December 1900.*

promised to sell "dollar pictures for 50 cents," and "Genuine Starr Hockey Skates" for 85 cents. You could also get canned tomatoes for a nickel, and girls' school boots for 50 cents.

Howell Brothers, a store in Windsor, ran an ad in the local newspaper suggesting that money received for Christmas should be spent as fast as possible. "Those who have received their Christmas gifts in the form of ready cash should convert it into some more suitable present, so that it may be retained as a remembrance through the coming years . . . . our stock is still in as good shape as ever for the holiday shoppers."

That's not to say that Christmas at the turn of the century was completely commercialized, any more than it is today. Churches were packed on Christmas Eve and Christmas Day, and trains were jammed with people going to visit relatives and friends. The mails were clogged with cards conveying season's greetings. And as *The Globe* pointed out, "Christmas Day was for the most part celebrated in the homes of the people, in accordance with the good old traditional British custom."

On Christmas Day in Toronto, the streets were quiet except for a brief parade of troops returning from the Boer War. Celebrations honoring them were postponed until after the holiday. *The Globe* reported that there were fewer drunks on the streets than in previous years, but all was not harmony and bliss. Then, as now, newspapers found a tragedy on Christmas Day to sadden the readers' hearts. The 1900 version of the traditional Yuletide sob story went like this:

"William Lenden, a 15-year-old lad living with his parents at 18 Woolsley Street, was quarrelling with his father, Henry J. Lenden, a Grand Trunk Railway employee, nearly all day yesterday. Finally the boy became very violent and attacked his father with a large bread knife, inflicting on him two severe wounds, one over the left eye and the other on the nose." The father went to the hospital and the son went to jail.

Another echo of today is the way in which people opened their hearts to the poor during the Christmas season. In 1900, the Irish Protestant Benevolent Society in Toronto helped 131 families by placing orders with butchers and grocers, rather than providing meals directly. This "avoided hurting the feelings of those who have not become want-hardened." The St. George's Society followed tradition and gave out food directly. It provided 6500 pounds of meat, 1400 loaves of bread and large quantities of tea, sugar, biscuits and candies to needy people.

While the number of charitable cases was down because of the prosperity of the times, a spokesman for the St. George Society pointed out that "the poor we'll have always with us. You know, that's Scripture." *The Globe* noted that "even in the homes of the poorest of people there is plenty of good cheer and good fellowship. Never has there been a Christmas when the various charitable organizations received fewer calls for aid than they have this year."

But Christmas commercialism was never far from the surface. Equating the quality of Christmas with the spending of money, *The Globe* was pleased to note that in 1900, "the great body of people . . . are better able to buy good presents to gladden the hearts of their friends than in any previous year."

Did you hear the one about the man who dropped 50 feet?

What made people laugh at the beginning of the 20th century? Here are a few jokes from those days:

Book seller at door: "I would like to show you this beautiful work. It tells about the habits of strange animals."

Severe lady: "I don't need it; I have been married four times."

Benevolent old man, giving money to a bum: "Now I hope you won't spend this dime for horrible liquor."

Bum: "No, sir; I'll ask for the best he's got."

One crocodile to another, as naked black people bathe in the Nile: "What will you have, dearest?"

The other crocodile: "A little dark meat, without dressing, please."

1st man: "Yesterday, I saw a man drop 50 feet from the window to the sidewalk."

2nd man: "Killed quick, I guess."

1st man: "Not, not even hurt."

2nd man: "Why not?"

1st man: "They were pigs' feet."

Fancy man: "Hurry up, my dear! We'll be late for the theatre."

Woman in front of mirror: "Why, I've been hurrying for the past hour and a half."

Husband: "Confound this razor! It is horribly dull."

Wife: "That's strange. It wasn't a bit dull this morning when I sharpened my pencil with it."

Woman: "Were you ever in a railroad disaster?"

Man: "Yes. I once kissed the wrong girl in a tunnel."

Jack: "What are you giving up for Lent?"

His fiancée: "Kisses."

Jack: "Well, this seems like a suitable place. Suppose you give up a few."

Willie Rich: "My father's home was built on an architect's plan."

Sammie Poor: "Ah, that's nothing. My dad's home was built on the instalment plan."

Attorney: "You won't be convicted. The jury will disagree."

Client: "Are you sure of that?"

Attorney: "I know it. Two of the members are man and wife."

City editor: "You speak here of the ballet dancer's feet 'twinkling.' Did they resemble the stars in any way?"

Green reporter: "Oh, no, sir; the star's feet were much larger."

1st rat: "What are you eating that bag of fertilizer for?"

2nd rat: "I'm cultivating my voice."

1st woman swimmer: "Do you think my bathing suit would cause complaint at the seashore?"

2nd woman swimmer: "There is no room for complaint."

Willie boy: "What I need is a blue hat to match my eyes."

Miss Snubbins: "Why don't you get a soft hat, too?"

Maid: "My fiancé is in a business where he's sure to rise, ma'am."

Mrs. Elite: "What is that, Mary?"

Maid: "He's a lineman, ma'am."

Johnny was spelling his way through a marriage notice in the morning paper. "At high noon," he read, "the clergyman took his stand beneath the floral bell, and to the music of the wedding march, the contradicting parties moved down the ___."

"Not 'contradicting,' Johnnny," interrupted his older sister. " 'Contracting.'"

"Well," stoutly contended Johnny, "they'll be contradicting parties after a while."

"You are the thirteenth tramp that has asked me for something to eat today," said the woman, viciously.

"Don't let that worry you, ma'am," replied the tramp. "I'm not superstitious."

A Scotch divine took one of his parishioners to task for his non-attendance at kirk. The man replied: "I dinna like lang sermons."

The parson, with some wrath, replied: "John, ye'll dee, and go to a place where ye'll not have the privilege of hearing long or short sermons."

"That may be," said John, "but it winna be for lack of parsons."

The wife, scornfully: "Why don't you stay away from home when you're drunk?"

Husband: "'Cause I'm drunk."

A woman recently had a visitor who stayed on and on. Finally he turned his attention to one of her dogs. "Can he do tricks?" the man asked.

"Yes," she said. "If you whistle twice to him he'll fetch your hat."

The steed presented to a trusty friend

Will give thee joy and pleasure without end,

But please, remember what the ancients say:

"Ope not his mouth his molars to survey."

Our baby seems to have a natural taste for the piano. He gnawed half the polish off one leg.

The honeymoon was over and they were comfortably settled in their snug little house. The husband returned home from business and was grieved to find his wife crying.

"Oh, George," she sobbed, "I made a beautiful pie, all by myself, and Fido went and ate the whole thing."

"Never mind, my dear," said George. "We can easily afford another dog."

Life is full of trials, and the lawyers are glad for it.

Horses played a big role in the old days

Horses were a fundamental feature of Canadian life a century ago – so much so that they lent their name to their times. It was with good reason that the period is referred to as "the horse and buggy era," which was in full flower at the start of the 20th century. The era gradually declined as the century advanced, but it didn't come to a close until after the end of the Second World War. So there are plenty of people around today who have personal experience with this memorable way of life in turn-of-the-century Canada.

Ken Dilts is one of those people. A genial man in his late 70s who lives in the Niagara Peninsula, Mr. Dilts grew up on a farm and spent many years around all kinds of horses. He says that when we think of all the differences between the way things are today and the way they were a hundred years ago, perhaps the most pronounced change is the way in which the horse has given way to the machine.

"A century ago," says Mr. Dilts, "the horse was king. Much of what people did and how they lived revolved around their relationship with the horse. Now the horse has been reduced, for the most part, to a mere pet and a source of amusement. People ride horses for sport and exercise. They go to the track to bet on horses. Other than that, the once-essential horse has pretty much had its day."

With hindsight, Mr. Dilts points out, we can see that the decline of the horse was inevitable, but if you had told farm people in 1901 that these hard-working animals would be used primarily for "hobby riding" by the end of the century, you would have encountered a great deal of cynicism. "How would we plough the fields? How would we get our crops to market?" the farmers of early-20th-century Canada would have asked. "Who would do all the heavy work around here?"

If you had told city people of that time that someday there would no longer be scores of horses pulling loads through the streets, and no streams of horse urine and piles of manure sending out distinctive aromas into the city air, they would have questioned your judgment. "How would the coal be delivered to our homes?" they would have asked skeptically. "How would we get to all the places where the trains and the street cars don't run?"

Eleven kids on a horse. SPA Williams Collection.

You couldn't blame them for being skeptical, says Mr. Dilts. The horse was firmly ensconced in Canadian society at the beginning of the 20th century. People with motor cars were a rarity in 1901, and nobody had ever seen a motorized truck or tractor, because they hadn't been invented yet. Those early cars were expensive, experimental and the subject of jokes, because they were so silly looking and so unreliable. Cartoonists of the day delighted in showing a car broken down at the side of the road, with people in smart-looking horse-drawn carriages passing by laughing and shouting, "Get a horse!"

Equine-powered transportation was so firmly entrenched at the start of the century that when the McLaughlin Carriage Company's big factory in Oshawa, Ont., burned down, the owners didn't give the slightest thought to seizing the opportunity to convert to automobile production. When they rebuilt in the spring of 1900, they went right back to their old line of horse-drawn products. Thanks to the strong economy, the carriage and sleigh business was booming. It wasn't until seven or eight years later that the company started making a few Buick cars as a sideline, and it was quite a few years after that before the McLaughlin's finally stopped making buggies altogether and became part of the General Motors automotive empire.

When Ransom Olds, the developer of the Oldsmobile automobile, began promoting his new car early in the new century, he had a big selling job to do. Olds wooed customers by playing up the advantages of mechanization over the traditional means of transport. He made a good case, for the truth was that despite its pervasiveness and genuine usefulness, the horse did indeed have several disadvantages. In contrasting the horse to his new gas-powered vehicle, Olds pointed out that the auto "never kicks or bites, never tires out on long runs, and during hot weather you can ride fast enough to make a breeze without sweating the horse. It does not require care in the stable, and only eats while it is on the road."

Olds might have added another line to his sales pitch, claiming that the car was potentially safer than the horse. Buggy accidents were frequent, and often fatal. Spirited horses were hard to control, and buggies didn't offer passengers much protection when they hit a tree or went into a ditch. An American writer named Jack O'Conner put it well when he described the way in which a horse might react to an unexpected noise or sight. "The horse is a large, powerful stupid beast given to strange fantasies and sudden panics. An unfamiliar noise, a piece of newspaper blowing in the wind, a fluttering garment – almost anything can throw a horse into a panic," O'Conner pointed out.

Experts say that the dominant instinct of horses is fear. Wild horses were always subject to sudden attack by meat-eating predators, and their fear and rapid flight instincts are what saved them as a species. Horses survived by running from any unfamiliar sight, sound or smell which might have been a tip-off that danger was near. They didn't wait around to determine if their fears were justified. They just took off. The experts also say that horses have long memories, and that an unpleasant experience which a horse had as a foal might be retained and trigger a reaction years later when some seemingly trivial event occurred. Thus, the horse might rear and bolt for no apparent reason.

But while horses could sometimes be dangerous and unpredictable, there was for the most part a good working relationship between man and beast, and a good deal of affection between them and their owners. People clearly liked their horses in those days, and horses grew to know and perhaps even to love their owners, or at least to become comfortable with them, and to do as they were told.

It is sometimes said that the dog is man's best friend, but in those days, it was the horse that was man's best friend, because the horse did so much for the man, and asked so little in return. It was, however, more of a master-slave relationship than a friendship or partnership, and there is some question as to whether horses had the intelligence to form more than an instinctive bond with their owners. Cases of horses showing affection for their owners were often cited anecdotally, but how much of that love actually existed in the horse's mind, and how much in the owner's, was open to dispute.

People used to say that horses couldn't be very smart; otherwise they would never permit people to ride on their backs and make them pull heavy ploughs and buggies. But wits responded that horses must be intelligent, because they managed to get plenty to eat and a warm place to sleep, and besides, they were smart enough never to place bets on people. More seriously, some people argued that the proud bearing and smart look of horses was evidence of animal intelligence and perhaps even nobility. Fanciful people even compared the horse's willing and dutiful service to man to that of man with respect to God.

Ken Dilts says the horses he knew in his youth may not have been too bright, but they were capable of learning, if you knew how to teach them. Generally, it was a matter of being patient and consistent, and letting the horse know what was expected. Often this meant putting a young horse with an older one, so that the young horse would copy the behavior of the older beast. And as a rule, steady and gentle instruction and correction was the order of the day. But occasionally, however, it was necessary to be harsh. Once, after a horse kicked him, Mr. Dilts whipped the horse with a leather strap several times. The horse got the message, and never kicked him or anyone else again.

But that was an exceptional case. Mr. Dilts has many fond memories of the way in which he interacted with the animals. He recalls running between the legs of horses when he and his playmates were children, and never having any fear that the horse would hurt him or the other kids. He says that runaways and other cases of horse misbehavior were rare, and that the horse was not only usually well-behaved, but far and away the most useful animal on the farm.

In fact, says Mr. Dilts, "the horse was a crucial part of society, but he was just taken for granted. Horses were everywhere, and people accepted them as part of their surroundings, just as we do today with cars and trucks. But at the turn of the century, the horse was really the king. He was essential for short-haul transportation in the urban areas and for a whole variety of things in the country. He worked along with the farmer all day to plough the fields, pull the wagon and do all the heavy work. The horse was in effect an extension of the farmer, giving him the muscle-power he needed to perform his tasks, and the horse also took him into town and to church."

You could get a lot out of a horse if you knew how to treat it, Mr. Dilts points out. The horse responded best to a calm and gentle approach which had been drummed into his head through repetition. For example, there were only a handful of verbal commands that you used to tell a horse what to do. When you wanted it to go left, you said "ha," when you wanted it to go right, you said "gee," when you wanted it to move you said "giddy up," and when you wanted it to stop you said "whoa." Synonyms wouldn't do, because the horse didn't know what the words meant. It was just responding to a sound which had been "programmed" into its memory.

It was important to stay calm, so that the horse stayed clam. An excited horse was apt to be unpredictable, but even if it did what it was supposed to do, it would only last for a couple of hours before it tired out. A relaxed horse, on the other hand, could keep going all day. The farmer and the horse who combined to get the job done at a slow and steady pace made the best team. Generally, they worked a nine- or a 10-hour day, with both horse and man taking time for breakfast and lunch before calling it quits for supper. Typically, a work horse would eat three meals a day, usually consisting of a pile of hay, a gallon of oats and a good drink of water.

When taking a trip to church or town, "the wise farmer never set rigid deadlines or cut his time into half-hour or quarter-hour segments," recalls Mr. Dilts. "He took a laid-back approach and he got there when he and his horse got there. Society as a whole was a lot slower and more relaxed in those days, in large measure due to the fact that an unhurried approach worked best with the horse."

While to many people today, a horse is just a horse, Canadians at the turn of the century knew that there were many different types, and that there were considerable differences between them. The names of the various types were just as familiar to the people of those days as are the names and characteristics of the various kinds of cars to people today. Just as you're unlikely to confuse a BMW with a Cadillac, it was easy for people to tell the difference, for instance, between a hackney and a shire horse. While they were both English in origin and quite tall, the hackney was lighter, quicker, smarter-looking and used mainly for pulling a carriage, while the shire was an ungainly, heavy horse with a plodding manner which was used for ploughing and pulling wagons.

Other horses which were common in Canada in those days included the Belgian, the Clydesdale and the Percheron. They were all work horses, and they all traced their origin back through the centuries to Europe in the days when horses were bred for size and strength to carry knights in armor. These big beasts, which weighed around a ton, were known as draught horses, and like all horses, their height was of great interest to people. Height was measured in units known as "hands." Traditionally, this was the height of a man's clenched and upright hand, between his top and bottom knuckles. The horse's height was measured as so many hands from the ground to the high point of the back, which was known as the withers. Typically, a Percheron might stand 16 hands tall. The distance became standardized at four inches, so the Percheron might be 64 inches tall, which was a good, tall horse.

Another common horse in Canada at the time was the Morgan, which was an all-purpose animal. If a farmer could afford only one horse, his best choice was a Morgan, which could pull a plough through the field and a buggy along a muddy road, and which was noted for its general strength and endurance. There were also, of course, thoroughbred horses in those days, used then as now mainly for racing. But while today only a limited number of well-to-do people are members of the horsy set, in those days virtually everyone with money owned at least one thoroughbred. Having an expensive thoroughbred horse was as much a mark of status then as having an expensive foreign car is today.

Rhodes Grant, who wrote extensively about the history of his home town of Martintown in Eastern Ontario at the turn of the century, fondly recalled that there was also "the French-Canadian horse, a rather small black horse with a kinky mane and tail and they were as tough as iron. Many people liked to have horses with some French-Canadian blood in them, for that reason." He noted that there were also some broncos around, brought in from the West, as well as the occasional Arabs and Shetland ponies for the children.

In his book titled *Horse and Buggy Days in Martintown*, Mr. Grant said that the people of the community, which is near Cornwall, Ont., did not see their first automobile until 1904 and their first truck until 1916. So at the turn of the century "horses were the only means of transportation, outside of shank's mare, of course, and the railways and boats." The term "riding shank's mare" meant that you were walking. But more commonly, if you were going any distance, you were being carried or pulled by a horse. This was so common that it became part of the background to Canadian society, and when you look in most history books, there is little or no mention of horses, any more than there is any mention of fresh air and sunshine, because they were so much taken for granted.

"Everyone drove horses or rode horses and handled horses and they talked about horses the same as people talk about cars and tractors today," recalled Mr. Grant. "We could not have lived without them; they were indispensable. We learned how to harness them and hitch then up and handle them. We learned not to trot them up hill or worse down hill. We learned, most of us the hard way, not to give a horse water when it was overheated – a sure way to founder him. We learned to look at their teeth so we could tell how old they were. We learned to subconsciously watch their ears at all times, for a horse twitches his ears when he is thinking of doing something nasty."

Mr. Grant said that horse-trading was as complicated and full of potential pitfalls as buying a used car is today. Then, as now, the buyer was wise to be wary. A crooked horse trader would lie about the condition and age of a horse, and might go so far as to alter the teeth of an animal to make it appear younger. For instance, he might file down ridges in the teeth to make them look younger, or restore the tell-tale indentations in the foreteeth of an older horse to make them look like the teeth of a six- or seven-year-old animal. According to Mr. Grant, only the very sharp and the very old knew all there was to know about horses:

"By the time a man was eighty he was almost ready to go out and trade horses with the gypsies. A gypsy could take an old broken-down nag and in an hour or two turn him into a fiery mettlesome steed. Then, after some unwary farmer had bought him, he would slump down into a wreck again. It was said that dynamite was the secret. Dissolve a stick of dynamite and pour the nitro glycerine down the horse's throat. Guaranteed to make an old horse young for an hour or two."

Fortunately, most people didn't go to such lengths to sell horses or to reinvigorate them. While some old horses were sent to the glue factory or the dog food plant, it was common for a farmer to let an old horse retire and live out his days at leisure as a reward for faithful service. But eventually, as the century progressed, the breeding of horses was gradually curtailed as the need for new animals declined, and the old horses died off, the victims of modern mechanization.

There was irony in the fact that the industrial revolution, which eventually produced the automobiles and trucks and tractors which did the horses out of their jobs, was made possible by horses. They were available to haul the raw materials from the trains to the factories, to carry the manufactured goods from the stores to the people's homes, and to pull the improved ploughs, reapers and other agricultural implements which increased the productivity of the modern farm.

When the horse and buggy era finally ended in the 20th century, it was the end of an ancient alliance which went back for thousands of years, to the days when wild horses were first captured and trained by man. Historians have pointed out that without the horse, man would not have been able to extend his range and dominance across the planet, and to have reached our current state of high mechanization. Thanks to the mobility and muscle power once supplied by the horse, we have been able to reach the point of no longer needing the horse to enjoy our lifestyle.

But in a fitting conclusion to the 20th century, recent years have seen the production of a spate of books, movies, and magazine articles, extolling the wonders and virtues of horses. We find all kinds of information about the best way to whisper to horses, the best way to keep their hooves clean, the best way to tell what they are thinking and so forth. Canadians about to enter the new millennium are gobbling this stuff up faster than a hungry horse can consume a bag full of oats.

It makes you wonder if, a hundred years from now, people will look fondly back upon the days of the early 21st century, when people actually moved from place to place in machines known as cars and trucks, and when it was still possible to go out to a ranch, lay out a wad of cash big enough to choke a horse, climb on the back of one of the beasts and go for a ride down Memory Lane.